Acclaim for *PLEASE, MISTER POSTMAN*

'Like Johnson's previous memoirs, this latest instalment
carries a first-class stamp'
Caroline Jowett, *DAILY EXPRESS*

'A charming book'
GUARDIAN

'Witty, self-deprecating, sometimes uproariously
funny and sometimes unbearably sad. It shines like
a candle in the naughty world of inauthentic
politicians and public alienation'
David Marquand, *NEW STATESMAN*

'Johnson's new book delivers'
Patrick Kidd, *THE TIMES*

'Immensely readable'
SCOTLAND ON SUNDAY

'Superb . . . One of those rare books . . . that
everyone will enjoy'
DAILY EXPRESS

'A beautifully evoked account'
Sinclair McKay, *DAILY TELEGRAPH*

'A truly superb and beautifully written memoir'
THE GOOD BOOK

'The best political testament I have ever read'
Peter Wilby, *NEW STATESMAN*

'This boy can write . . . there's nothing second-rate
about his writing. He is a natural'
SPECTATOR

'A wonderful elegy for a life that has only just passed into
history . . . Beautifully written, affecting and sad'
John Rentoul, *INDEPENDENT ON SUNDAY*

'A fascinating piece of social history'
Daisy Goodwin, *SUNDAY TIMES*

'Johnson's writing style is easy, relaxed, self-deprecating.
His recall and eye for detail are impressive'
Chris Mullin, *OBSERVER*

'Full of delights'
Francis Wheen, *MAIL ON SUNDAY*

'Beautifully written . . . and vividly observed'
DAILY MAIL

To Aud, Fred

Please, Mister Postman

Alan Johnson

Best Wishes,

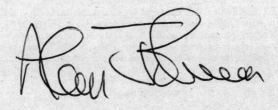

CORGI BOOKS

TRANSWORLD PUBLISHERS
61–63 Uxbridge Road, London W5 5SA
www.transworldbooks.co.uk

Transworld is part of the Penguin Random House group of companies
whose addresses can be found at global.penguinrandomhouse.com

Penguin
Random House
UK

First published in Great Britain in 2014 by Bantam Press
an imprint of Transworld Publishers
Corgi edition published in 2015

A CIP catalogue record for this book
is available from the British Library.

ISBN
9780552170659

Typeset in Minion by Falcon Oast Graphic Art Ltd.
Printed and bound by Clays Ltd, St Ives plc

Penguin Random House is committed to a sustainable
future for our business, our readers and our planet. This book is made
from Forest Stewardship Council® certified paper.

MIX
Paper from
responsible sources
FSC® C018179

5 7 9 10 8 6

In memory of Mike Whitaker

Chapter 1

IT'S CHRISTMAS EVE 1967. A Saturday. Four o'clock in the afternoon. I'm waiting for Mike.

Mrs Kenny's large flat in Hamlet Gardens, Hammersmith, is empty except for me, cocooned in the room I rent at the elbow of the L-shaped passage.

I am seventeen years old, a shelf-stacker at Anthony Jackson's supermarket on the Upper Richmond Road in East Sheen – a temporary measure, I tell myself, to fill the interval between school and rock stardom. Ahead lies 1968, plump with promise. I am convinced that for the band I'm with, the In-Betweens, this will be the year we hit the big time.

What actually lay ahead in 1968 was the end of my nascent music career, marriage, fatherhood, a new job as a postman and a return to my home turf – London W10.

Anthony Jackson's had closed that lunchtime. Johnny Farugia, its larger-than-life Maltese manager, had taken his devoted staff (Kath, Sandra and me) to the pub opposite for a Christmas drink.

The store was more of a self-service corner shop than a fully fledged supermarket, but its single cash register had been ringing almost permanently throughout the Christmas period. We'd worked hard and our boss wanted to show his appreciation. I explained that I had to be home by 3.30pm because Mike, my brother-in-law, was picking me up in his Rover 110 to drive me to Watford, where I was to spend Christmas with him, my sister Linda and my four-month-old niece.

Johnny Farugia fussed over us in the pub, insisting on buying all the drinks. After clinking our glasses in a Christmas toast he distributed our presents.

'Hard work – is all I asking,' he announced in the English that remained eccentric after fifteen years in the country he adored. ('You fuckin' Brits, you dun deserve dis country. Always you moan. You dun appreciate wad you got.')

I knew what my present was as soon as I saw the shape of the package. Johnny was well aware that I idolized the Beatles. He'd heard me wax lyrical about *Sergeant Pepper's Lonely Hearts Club Band*, the album that had astounded and delighted the world on its release in June, becoming the soundtrack to the summer of love. And we'd stood together in the warehouse at the back of the store, like mourners at a funeral, as 'A Day in the Life', the final song on the album, wafted its beauty from the big, blue portable radio. During the year the pirate stations that had been our only source of continuous pop had been outlawed by an Act of Parliament and Radio 1 had been launched by the BBC to replace them. In a final act of defiance, Radio London had gone off the air to the strains of this track, which had been banned by the BBC on the grounds that it glorified the drug LSD. Dear old Auntie apparently had no such reservations about another number from the album, 'Lucy in the Sky with Diamonds', which they happily and unsuspectingly played.

The highlight of the three-channel television schedules that Christmas was to be the Beatles' *Magical Mystery Tour* film on Boxing Day, the soundtrack for which had been released as a six-track EP (extended play) disc.

My magical mystery Christmas present had cost Johnny Farugia 19s 6d. I knew that because the Fab Four had insisted that the record must be sold for under a quid. The band always showed huge consideration for their fans, rarely lifting singles (or even 'B' sides) from their albums, printing the lyrics on their LP sleeves (commonplace now but unheard of prior to *Sergeant Pepper*) and demanding that the prices of their masterpieces be kept as low as possible.

Now, a few hours after that Christmas drink, I sat in the fusty, damask comfort of my room, waiting for Mike.

Mike Whitaker. Dear Mike. He'd been a hero to me from the moment we met and my brother-in-law since he'd married Linda in September 1966.

Mike had come into our lives just as my mother's heart condition worsened and entered its final phase. It was he who quietly and solidly supported Linda and me through our mother's last illness and her death; he who had paid for the rose bush and the little plaque marking the spot in Kensal Green cemetery where her ashes were scattered:

Lilian May Johnson
Born: 11th May 1921
Died: 4th March 1964
Rest in Peace

There were, and remain, three great passions in my life – music, books and football – and Mike shared the first two. Like me he was largely autodidactic, having left school at fifteen to work for Henry's Radios, an electrical store in Praed Street off the Edgware Road, where he was now the manager, earning extra money from private work he did on the side.

He devoured historical biographies and science fiction, particularly the books of Ray Bradbury, introducing me to *The Illustrated Man* and *Something Wicked This Way Comes*. He loved Aubrey Beardsley's drawings and posters and the records of Bob Dylan, discovered by Mike before hardly anyone else in England had heard of him.

Mike longed to look like his cinematic hero James Dean. His kind, open face certainly had the required cleft chin and dimples. But with his sky-blue eyes and corn-blond hair – angelic looks that, as far as I was concerned, matched his personality – he always reminded me of the actor David McCallum who starred in *The Man From U.N.C.L.E.* TV series.

Kind, thoughtful, intelligent – and late. I'd been back in my room by 2.30pm but an hour later he still hadn't arrived. In those pre-mobile phone days, if somebody got delayed or failed to turn up there was nothing to do but wait. With the widowed Mrs Kenny and her grown-up son (who lived with her but was seldom seen) spending Christmas in Ireland, I had the run of the place. Nevertheless I stuck to my room as usual. I'd moved into these digs at sixteen and my landlady and I had the perfect understanding. I would put my £2-a-week rent on the kitchen table for her every Friday and she left me to my own devices to do what I wanted, when I wanted and with whom I wanted in my room.

Right now, with Mike more than two hours late, what I wanted to do was strum my much-loved Spanish guitar, bought for me by my mother ten years before after a modest win on the pools. As the winter light faded the table lamps illuminated the furniture – bed, wardrobe, plush armchair – that belonged to a previous age. I was reluctant to put another shilling in the meter which fed the two-bar electric heater, as the flat seemed somehow to generate its own warmth.

I still remember the song I wrote in the gathering dusk as I waited for Mike that Christmas Eve afternoon. It was based on a real experience I'd had a few weeks earlier. I'd been going somewhere on the tube ('Home again, the people crushed and crammed inside the train,') at the height of the rush hour ('squeezed a seat, staring at my feet to hide the strain') when a dazzling girl got on. I hadn't been able to take my eyes off her ('My eyes were raised, I gazed amazed as she walked in the door. In midi-mac, her auburn hair just flowed across her back'). I watched her light a cigarette ('Reached in her bag, and found a fag amongst her bric-a-brac') but then, a few stops on, she melted into the jostling crowd of passengers ('As the doors flew back, like a hunting pack, swarms of people left the train. Lost from sight, she wasn't there when I looked back again.')

The song was long finished by the time Mike eventually rang my doorbell just after 7pm. I wasn't angry. I could never be angry with Mike. In any case the hours had not been wasted. The delay had allowed me to write a half-decent new song that I was pleased with.

Mike's smile was infectious and, as always, he immediately offered one of his untipped Senior Service cigarettes.

'Sorry I'm late,' he said as we walked down the stairs to his car. 'I went for a drink after work.'

As we approached the Rover I could see that there was somebody sitting in the front passenger seat.

'Oh, this is Harry,' said Mike, by way of introduction to an elderly Irish gentleman who exuded a tipsy bonhomie. 'He's coming home with us for Christmas.'

I learned that Harry had been a fixture in the pubs on the Edgware Road for years. Hearing him bemoan the fact that he'd be spending Christmas on his own, Mike insisted on taking him to Watford to spend Christmas Day with him and Linda. And me.

This was not untypical of my brother-in-law. He'd already rung Linda from the pub to warn her. Her response had been that there was plenty of food and that Harry (who she'd never met before) would be welcome, which was not untypical of my sister. I remembered the childhood Christmases Linda had rescued for me when our mother had been in hospital and we'd found ourselves alone. Now she was rescuing Harry's.

First, though, we had to get to Watford. I can't remember how much motorway, if any, actually existed south of Watford then. The stretch of the M1, Britain's first inter-city motorway, carrying traffic from the north to the outskirts of London, was still under construction at the time. Whatever the case, Mike stuck to the ordinary roads. It was just as well.

As I sat on the stitched leather of the plush rear seat it began to dawn on me, to my increasing horror, that Mike was very, very drunk. I was already aware that Harry had over-imbibed but that didn't matter so much – he wasn't behind the steering wheel. All the same, it would have been helpful if he'd uttered the odd word of caution to encourage Mike to modify his reckless driving. As it was, alcohol had made him equally oblivious of danger.

Through the city our progress was disciplined by traffic lights and zebra crossings, but once we were out of London we careered round bends, skirted ditches and accelerated at every opportunity on the dark, wet roads of Hertfordshire. While I cowered, terrified, in the back, Harry was chatting away as if perched at the bar of the Coach and Horses telling yarns. Every five or ten minutes Harry would ceremoniously produce a small bottle of whisky from the pocket of his raincoat, take a good slug and offer it round. Thankfully, Mike declined, as did I.

There was no legal requirement then for seat belts even to be fitted, let alone for drivers or their passengers actually to wear them. (Drink-driving, on the other hand, was definitely illegal, though the blood alcohol limit for driving had been in force for only a couple of years and social attitudes were slow to catch up. The breathalyser had been brought in just two months earlier, amid protests about infringements of civil liberties.) I remonstrated with Mike as best I could as I was thrown from side to side in the back of this unguided missile, which could have been fuelled by the fumes emanating from the front seats. In response to my exhortations to slow down, Mike told me soothingly to stop worrying. We needed to step on it as he'd be in big trouble with Linda if we didn't get home soon.

When the car finally pulled up in the suburban peace of St James' Road, Watford, the relief was overwhelming. I felt like James Stewart in the final scene of *It's a Wonderful Life*: exhilarated by the knowledge that I was now more certain to live beyond the age of seventeen and to experience all that life still had in store for me.

~

The future I had mapped out in my mind had taken a different course before 1968 had even dawned when, at a pre-New Year party at Mike and Linda's, I met Judith Elizabeth Cox. Within a few months I had asked her to be my wife. Judy was a single mother. Her daughter Natalie, born in 1966, would complete the picture of domestic bliss that we'd begun to paint in our imaginations. Judy and Natalie lived with Judy's grandmother in Camelford Road back in Notting Hill, just off Ladbroke Grove, amid the streets where Linda and I had spent our childhood. Our plan was to put our names down for a council house as soon as we were married. Until that materialized we would make Camelford Road our first marital home.

I took advantage of my weekly half-day off to catch the train up to Watford and break the news to Linda. Anthony Jackson's, in common with every other shop on the Upper Richmond Road, closed at lunchtime on Wednesdays. Half-day closing was still a British institution. It gave shop workers a welcome break and was cheerfully tolerated by an inconvenienced public, who had never known things any other way.

I often stayed overnight in Watford in the spare room that had been earmarked for my permanent residency when Linda married Mike and left the council flat we'd shared on the Wilberforce estate in Battersea. We'd argued then about my insistence on remaining in London instead of moving with Linda out to what I regarded as the northern countryside.

Initially I had stayed with kindly Mr and Mrs Cox (no relation to Judy), the parents of my primary-school best friend, whose home had been a sanctuary for me as a child. When the Coxes were rehoused I had moved on to my room at Mrs Kenny's.

That had been a mild disagreement compared with her reaction to the news that Judy and I had entered the quaint institution known as engagement and were planning to be married in July.

Linda was horrified. My whole future would be ruined, she told me. It wasn't that she had anything against Judy – indeed they were good friends, having met at Brixton College where they had both trained to be nursery nurses. She'd also known Beppe, Natalie's Italian father, who'd been engaged to Judy for three years before fleeing back to his homeland when he found out she was pregnant. What would I do if Beppe wanted access to the child? she wanted to know. How would I cope with being a teenage father? Did I realize how unusual it was for a husband to be four years younger than his wife?

Linda was impassioned but unconvincing. She herself had married a month or so after her nineteenth birthday and Mike was four years older than she was. Just as Linda had found happiness with him, so I would with Judy. The age difference wasn't a problem between Linda and Mike. Why should it be a problem between Judy and me?

I remember deploying all of these arguments in my smart-arse way as Linda stomped around the kitchen of her neat semi, desperately trying to find the line of argument that would prevent a breach of what she saw as her duty of care.

There was something about my sister that I only came to appreciate much later. I didn't realize quite how intensely she missed our mother. For me, under the shelter of Linda's wing, recovering from Lily's death had been easier. It was Linda who had shared that big double bed with our mother after our father left and listened every night as she talked about her life, her regrets, her sorrows, her fears, her hopes for our future.

Linda had taken responsibility for eradicating the fears and fulfilling the hopes. She worked to clear the debts in an effort to ensure that when Lily was allowed home from hospital she'd have an easier life – one that didn't involve scrubbing and cleaning for other people. She strove for a future in which our mother would find joy and solace in the grandchildren Linda so desperately wanted her to live to see.

But Lily had died. And part of Linda died with her.

Bereft of Lily's physical presence, Linda clung to the belief that her mother was still with her in spirit. At her own wedding reception, where she felt Lily's absence acutely, she had taken me to one side and told me she was convinced our mother was there in the room with us. She looked for signs in everything, visiting fortune-tellers, reading horoscopes, consulting mediums. One of her more eccentric pursuits was scanning the number plates of passing cars in search of my mother's initials, LMJ. Whether travelling on a bus, sitting in the passenger seat of Mike's car or walking to the shops, she'd feel compelled to search for that exact combination.

The house Mike had bought in Watford was only a few doors away from his parents' home but if Linda had harboured any hopes that her sense of loss might be eased by forging a bond with her mother-in-law she was to be sadly disappointed. She found no echo of Lily's maternal love in Irene Whitaker. Far from viewing Linda as a surrogate daughter, Irene had always seemed resentful of the intrusion into the close relationship she had with her son and matters did not improve after their marriage.

There was no trace of Mike's placid temperament in Irene. She was already estranged from her own daughter, after cutting her off because she didn't like her lifestyle. Linda was thrilled to find out she was pregnant three months after her wedding. She was married, the pregnancy was planned and, expecting her delight to be shared by the grandmother-to-be, she went to tell her the news.

'You stupid cow,' spluttered Irene. 'How could you get pregnant so soon? Haven't you heard of birth control? You should have waited at least three years before even thinking of having children.'

Thus this joyful event – one that had actually involved the willing participation of her son – was condemned by Irene as some kind of terrible error of judgement on Linda's part. The relationship never recovered.

Irene's nature had without doubt been shaped by the terrible trauma she had suffered as a small child. Her mother had committed suicide after discovering that Irene's father was having an affair. She had been found with her throat and both wrists slit and four-year-old Irene sitting quietly beside her.

With Mike's parents living so close my sister had little escape from the hostile atmosphere created by Irene and not much fraternal support from me, the brother who continually defied her wishes.

Linda was well aware of what Lily had wanted for me – that I should qualify as a draughtsman and lead a happy life free of squalor and debt – and she saw it as her job to support me towards that goal. To date I hadn't exactly been co-operative. I'd left school at fifteen when Linda urged me to stay on. I'd refused to move to Watford with her and Mike. Now I was adding to her sense of having failed Lily, and of having failed me, by announcing that, at the tender age of eighteen, I would be marrying a woman with a child and moving back to the mean streets where we'd grown up, with no prospects of becoming a draughtsman or indeed of entering any other qualified profession.

But there was nothing she could do to overcome my resolve. Perhaps she tried to get Mike to speak to me 'man to man', I don't know. If she did, the mission would have foundered on his natural geniality and reluctance to engage in any kind of confrontation.

My mind was made up. I would be married in the summer of 1968.

Chapter 2

As Judy and I planned our future, my musical career suffered a crushing blow. On the verge of what the In-Betweens were confident would be our breakthrough, all of our musical equipment (including my precious Höfner Verithin guitar) was stolen from the room above the Pied Bull pub in Islington where we stored it between gigs.

I couldn't afford to buy a new guitar. I'd only just finished paying off the thirty-month hire-purchase instalments on an amplifier that had been stolen (uninsured, needless to say) when my first band, the Area, had been the victims of another robbery. It was clear that domestic bliss would be unsustainable on my wages at Anthony Jackson's with or without the money the band had shared from gigs we performed. I was going to have to get a better-paid and more secure job.

It was Sham, the bass guitarist in the In-Betweens, who pointed me in the direction of the Post Office. He was a post-man higher grade, or PHG (a rank identified by the gold crowns fixed to the lapels of the uniform jacket), at the Northern District Office, the main sorting office for north London. PHGs were the ones who stayed indoors to sort letters and carry out minor clerical duties. The pay wasn't great, he told me, but as a result the Post Office found it hard to attract staff, which meant there were always loads of vacancies and plenty of opportunities for overtime.

Actually there was another reason why I felt it might be time to leave Anthony Jackson's. The chain was being subsumed into Tesco, the company I had quit on a point of principle just over a year earlier. (I accept there was some ambiguity over the exact terms of my departure, with me claiming I'd resigned and Tesco claiming I'd been sacked.) Johnny Farugia was keen for me to stay. He even got the district manager to talk to me about promotion opportunities. But the more I thought about becoming a postman, the keener I was to don that smart navy blue serge uniform.

And so, in June 1968, I became a postman in Barnes, London SW13.

The music was going to have to take a back seat for a time. Sham, a tall, genial black guy, wanted me to form another band with him. For him, music was a creative outlet and a form of relaxation he could dovetail successfully with his steady job and stable family life. For me at that point, juggling a new musical venture with a new job and the need to work all the overtime I could get, while establishing a family life with Judy, just didn't seem feasible. I would, I decided, continue to write songs and return to performing at an as yet unspecified time in the future.

∼

Barnes was the stately home of Royal Mail delivery offices. A large brick palace on Barnes Green with a picturesque duck pond on its threshold, it was big enough to accommodate three times the number of staff that actually worked there. Despite its grandeur, it was one of the smaller postmen's delivery offices (PDOs) in London. There were just thirty of us rattling round its elegant interior.

I'd already received my training on outward sorting (letters collected for delivery to other areas) during my two weeks at the London Postal Training School near King's Cross station. Now I was to have three days' training in the office on inward sorting (letters coming into Barnes to be sorted to one of the twenty-four delivery rounds, or 'walks').

The entire mail system for what was then still the General Post Office was operated by hand. The only machine was a stamp-canceller, which postmarked all the outward letters. The part of it that recorded the date was subject to tight security. All kinds of scams could be facilitated through unauthorized access to a GPO date stamp, such as counterfeit proof of postage for pools claims and so on.

Two postmen worked permanent nights, starting at our 'parent' office at Wandsworth, SW18, where, along with night workers from other offices, they'd sort the incoming mail for PDOs across south-west London. At around 3am, once a sufficient load had accumulated for Barnes, they'd be driven there in a mail van and begin to inward sort the Barnes mail on site.

There were two starting times for the delivery staff, 5.30am and 6am. On arrival they would finish off the inward sorting before collecting the mail for their own walk, taking it to the delivery bench for 'prepping' (arranging it in order) and then tying it into hand-sized bundles numbered in the sequence in which they were to be delivered.

Deliveries were timed to finish at 9.30am – a strict service standard. So important was it that the majority of customers received their first post before leaving the house for work that the inward sorting would, if necessary, be cut off before it had all been processed to ensure that postmen could complete their walks by 9.30. What remained would be taken on the less important and much lighter second delivery later in the morning.

The men – and in Barnes, it was all men – were due back at the sorting office by about 9.45. There they would do their redirections (a free service at that time for customers who'd moved house) and deal with any 'dead' letters (mail returned marked 'unknown at this address', for example) before heading upstairs to the canteen for breakfast.

One postman, Reg, was in charge of running the canteen. He was approaching retirement and had a lung disease which meant he wasn't fit enough to do deliveries. He'd make tea for the men early in the morning while deliveries were being prepped and then cook eggs, sausage, bacon and beans for them when they got back. Breakfast cost a shilling, and an extra penny for each slice of toast.

At 10.30am we'd be back down from breakfast to dispatch the outward letters, posted in Barnes and collected from every pillarbox by our two postmen/drivers. The letters would be tipped on to the 'facing table' where they all had to be turned the same way up, with 'shorts' separated from 'longs', ready for the stamp-cancelling machine. Packets would be passed to a man with a hand stamp and cancelled individually.

We'd do a cursory breakdown of this outward mail, but most of it went to Wandsworth to be sorted more precisely. Next we'd prepare the second delivery, which consisted mainly of circulars and pools coupons.

Such were the mechanics of the job; the familiar rhythm of a great public institution serving the needs of the 10,000 or so residents of the charming riverside district of London SW13. It was a process that would have barely changed in the hundred-odd years since Rowland Hill's reforms and the Penny Black had made postal services available to the masses. We postmen were uniformed civil servants proud to be performing a public service essential to the country's social fabric.

~

While Linda had found out she was expecting her first child three months after her wedding, I learned I was to be a father three months before mine. I was still only seventeen.

Judy and I absorbed the news with mixed emotions. While we were both delighted that, with our wedding date fixed and my application for a 'steady job' with the Post Office submitted, the framework for our family was in place, there were anxieties, too.

I had looked upon Natalie as my own daughter from the outset and was determined that she should see me as her dad. She had never met her biological father and there had been no communication whatsoever from Italy and thus no indication of whether he had any intention of ever fulfilling any of his paternal responsibilities. Now she would very quickly acquire a sibling and, while I was thrilled at the prospect of fathering a child, I acknowledged that parenthood wasn't likely to come naturally to me. But I'd persevere and I had the example of my own father to guide me in what not to do – a kind of reverse role model.

For Judy, there were other considerations. She had already endured the stigma of being an unmarried mother, attitudes having changed little in working-class communities through the so-called 'swinging sixties', and was concerned about suffering further damage to her reputation. She didn't want our marriage to be labelled a shotgun wedding. So we agreed to keep the pregnancy a secret for as long as we could in the hope that we could get past the wedding before it became apparent. Only Linda and Judy's nan were to be told. When they were, the news added to Linda's disappointment and increased the hostility Nan was already displaying towards me.

Nan's name was Mary Syer, but she was never called anything other than Nan by us. In the dark clothes she had worn ever since the death of her husband in the mid-1950s, and with her grey hair pulled tight into a bun like an over-sized Brillo pad, she cut a forbidding figure. I can't say, looking back, that I blame her for disapproving of me.

Judy's mother had died in childbirth, along with the baby, when Judy was barely a year old. Her father had promptly run off with a woman with whom he was having an affair. When her maternal grandparents discovered what had happened, they took Judy in and brought her up as their own. Her brothers spent their entire childhoods in Dr Barnardo's.

Nan understandably took pride in the way her grand-daughter had flourished in her care. Having passed her Eleven-Plus, Judy had gone on to one of the most prestigious schools in west London, Burlington Grammar School for Girls, leaving with six O-Levels. She then attended a teaching college before switching to train as a nursery nurse.

Nan had already had to cope with the granddaughter of whom she was so proud becoming an unmarried mother. Imagine how she must have felt when Judy dropped the bombshell that she was to be married to a seventeen-year-old shelf-stacker with no money and zero prospects. In the circumstances Nan displayed huge generosity in allowing me to move into her home after the wedding.

Our little soap opera was being played out against the backdrop of social and political revolution. That spring, students were rioting in the USA and across Europe. In London 10,000 people, mostly students, demonstrated in Trafalgar Square against US involvement in the Vietnam War. Trouble flared after protesters who had marched from Trafalgar Square to the US Embassy in Grosvenor Square clashed with police. There were many injuries to demonstrators and police, and 200 were arrested. In France a couple of months later, student protests rapidly escalated into widespread strikes and protests that paralysed the country for a fortnight. The French government's heavy-handed response and use of the notorious CRS riot police only inflamed the situation. At one point tanks were deployed on the streets of Paris.

At home, the activist Tariq Ali was leading a student movement to abolish money and abandon capitalism. Everywhere, it seemed, students were threatening to overthrow the established order – tuning in, turning on and dropping out.

For Judy and me and millions like us, these events might just as well have been taking place in a parallel universe for all the difference they made to us. Had we been university students, I'd have been about to begin a degree course while Judy would have just completed hers. Perhaps we'd have been more caught up in the groundswell of support for political and social change. As it was we were preoccupied with narrower concerns more directly and immediately relevant to our everyday lives. I was interested in what was happening in the world, and I read *The Times*, my newspaper of choice, assiduously most days – but none of it felt as if it had anything much to do with us.

Apart from being impressed, watching the trouble in France on the evening news, by the way French male students dressed, their cashmere jumpers draped carelessly across their shoulders as they manned the barricades, and trying to imitate the look as Judy, Natalie and I promenaded around Hyde Park on Sunday afternoons, I was emotionally uninvolved. We were merely interested spectators of events that were taking place in the name of our generation. I was about to become a married man with two children. I didn't want to abolish money – I needed to earn the bloody stuff.

~

Linda came to terms with the fact that I was to be married to her friend and contemporary and was there to support us when we married at Hammersmith register office. In fact it was she who took the photographs. Nan suppressed her disapproval to attend. My closest friend, schoolmate, former bandmate and workmate at Tesco, Andrew Wiltshire, was best man. There was no honeymoon. At the Post Office, annual leave was allocated according to seniority and, as a recent recruit, I was required to take my two weeks' summer holiday in May. It seemed you had to put in about twenty years' service to get a break in July. Still, we couldn't have afforded a honeymoon anyway.

The Syers had rented the top two floors of 2 Camelford Road since just before the war. By the time I moved in the ground floor and basement had been empty for years. Unlike the condemned homes of my childhood in nearby Southam Street and Walmer Road, it wasn't a slum. It was more like the cosy rooms at Lancaster Road, where I'd lived with the Coxes. There was a small kitchen, two bedrooms and a spacious living room with a sofa and two armchairs, one of which was Nan's, identified by its antimacassar, worn arms and a little footstool positioned in front of the electric fire.

There was no central heating, of course, but the coldest thing about the house was Nan's obvious disdain for me. While we rarely spoke, she succeeded in making her hostility clear, leaving the living room when I came in to watch the telly or, on one occasion, turning out the light in the kitchen where I was reading the paper to avoid obliging her to leave the living room. As I sat in the dark, my eyes still trained on the previously visible newspaper, she muttered about the need to save electricity. When she had to speak to me, muttering was her preferred form of communication. But she was fine with Judy and Natalie and I became used to the undeclared cold war between us.

I cycled from Notting Hill to work in Barnes every day on Judy's trendy small-wheeled Moulton bike. Barnes was, and remains, a highly desirable location. Hugh Cudlipp, the chairman of Mirror Group Newspapers and subsequently of the International Publishing Corporation, had a large, modern house on Church Road. The walks trudged by us postmen every morning were populated by film stars such as Lynn Redgrave and Sylvia Syms, along with actors who were not yet as well known, among them Timothy West and his wife Prunella Scales, and Frank Thornton, still to become known to millions as Captain Peacock in the sitcom *Are You Being Served?* Luminaries from other spheres of public life, including the former Welsh rugby star and broadcaster Cliff Morgan and assorted government ministers, artists and writers, were also dotted around the patch.

I had a wider knowledge of the area than most of my colleagues. While every Barnes postman had to know which streets were on which delivery to deal with the inward sorting, few had the experience I gained on the ground, because by the time I left Barnes I had done all of the walks. Choice of duties, like choice of annual leave, was assigned on the basis of seniority. (The Post Office was dominated by ex-servicemen and this was reflected in its culture. We didn't come to work, we came 'on duty'; we didn't go on holiday, we went 'on leave'; and we didn't sign for jobs but for 'duties'.) As the junior man I had the 'duty' nobody else wanted. I was one of two 'reserves' covering the deliveries of men who were sick or on annual leave, which meant I eventually got to do every delivery in the office.

I knew which ones were easy – the walks where I could be back in the office by 9am and spend a leisurely hour and a half having breakfast and playing snooker on the half-size table in the canteen – and the ones that were a struggle to finish on time. I was soon warned off getting back to the office too early by an old hand who pointed out that if I was ever seen to finish a walk unduly quickly, more streets might end up being added to it, to the disadvantage of the regular postman, who was invariably much older than me and not so fast on his feet. It was a fair point. The majority of my colleagues seemed to be at least thirty years older than me.

In order to ensure that deliveries were being carried out in their proper sequence and to spot the early finishers there was a patrol officer. Mr Turner was a supervisor whose only task was to drive round the streets every morning in a Royal Mail Morris Minor van checking up on the delivery men. He covered Mortlake, the separate office delivering to London SW14, as well as Barnes, but that didn't make his work exactly onerous or worthy of his much higher salary. When I delivered at the eastern end of Castlenau I'd join the regular postmen in crossing the Thames to a Hammersmith café for a cup of tea and a read of the papers. London W6 was beyond the bounds of Mr Turner's empire and provided sanctuary from his officious gaze.

Most of the men at Barnes had fought in the war and had experiences they rarely mentioned, but which gave them a quiet wisdom. The steady routine of our office may have bordered on the mundane, but there was nothing mundane about the men I worked beside.

Frank Dainton had served as a Guardsman. Tall and straight-backed, he always wore the uniform waistcoat (rarely adopted by other postmen), no matter how hot the weather. He'd previously worked as one of the Queen's postmen when in SW1, the office that handled all the mail for Buckingham Palace. One of Frank's duties had been to attend Parliament at the end of each daily session to collect a scroll upon which a House of Commons clerk had recorded, in copperplate handwriting on thick parchment (perhaps with a quill pen), the highlights of that day's sitting. Frank would wait outside the small post office in Central Lobby, often until the small hours or even, when there was an all-night sitting, the following morning. Once proceedings had concluded and the clerk had completed his task, Frank would be summoned from the green leather seats where he'd been dozing to collect the scroll, which had to be taken immediately to the palace to be handed to one of Her Majesty's equerries.

This presentation of the day's events by a loyal subject was the traditional way for the monarch to be kept informed of parliamentary activities. And there was no more loyal subject in the land than Frank Dainton, a fierce defender of the royal family in the surprisingly frequent discussions about their relevance in a fast-changing world.

'Nobby' Clark had been on the beaches of Dunkirk. As was the case with all the ex-servicemen at Barnes, this information had to be prised out of him. None of them boasted about their experiences.

For some reason lost in the mists of time, it was an unwritten rule that all men named Clark were known as Nobby, so I never knew his real Christian name. His great hero was the singer Al Bowlly, who had been killed in action during the war but not before providing Nobby with a repertoire of songs with which he'd serenade us each day, somehow managing to sing lustily while gripping a lit pipe between his teeth.

Another pipe-smoker was Ted Philpott, a studious character with longish, swept-back hair and a curved-stem pipe, the type that Sherlock Holmes smoked. He looked like a university don but his degree subject was snooker. Every breakfast break would find him at the half-size snooker table, jacket off, thick blue braces on display, ready to take on all-comers. The custom was that the winner remained at the table until he was beaten. I can't remember which regiment Ted had served in but they must have played a hell of a lot of snooker – he rarely left the table. One quiet morning Ted taught me the basics of the game and its less popular cousin, billiards. Occasionally thereafter I'd be given the chance to join the rest of the office in being beaten by him.

Les Griffiths had served in the Fleet Air Arm. Permanently suntanned in the days before sun lamps, he loved being a post-man and was as happy in his work as anyone I've ever known.

The lives of Nobby, Frank, Ted, Les and all the other postmen of a certain age, and the lives of their parents, had been defined by war in Europe. It was unremarkable in their generation to have been exposed to its horrors and so their experiences went unremarked, except sometimes among themselves – among fellow soldiers. Even those too young to have fought in the war had completed national service, sometimes having seen action abroad in Korea or Aden. I listened intently, fascinated by their stories, hoping that the chain of events that had led to a world war every twenty years or so had now been broken.

Snooker was part of a daily routine that rarely altered. As we mucked in with the inward sorting first thing in the morning, there would be a mild altercation about something whereupon Peter Simonelli, who saw himself as the sardonic observer of sorting-office life, would mutter to those around him: 'And another happy day begins at Barnes PDO.'

As we prepped our second delivery mid-morning, whenever the loud ring of the office phone started up – all phones rang loudly then – Freddie Binks, a rakish thirty-something, would shout, 'If it's for me, don't answer it.' Every bloody time. The same joke, repeated day after day. Then Nobby Clark would burst into a chorus of 'Goodnight Sweetheart' as Les Griffiths pleaded with him in mock disgust to spare us from the torture.

Freddie Binks was the office Lothario, always claiming to have been seduced by housewives on his walk. Balding with a stooped physique, he was no Cary Grant and his boasts didn't seem feasible to me, particularly as I remained unseduced during my year at Barnes (and indeed throughout my entire thirteen years delivering the Queen's mail).

There was one address in Glebe Road where, Andy Trevelyan, the regular postman, told us, the lady of the house would stand at the window and bare her substantial chest every morning for his personal entertainment.

We London postmen carried the mail for our delivery in a sack slung across our backs and tied at the chest. This delivery sack was an important part of our equipment (I was advised by Frank Dainton to look out for a sack with 'Republic of Ireland' printed across the top because these were made of softer material. Once taken home and boiled a few times, they would become even softer and would be bleached pure white).

Out on the walk the postman would have one bundle of letters in his hand and, at predetermined points, he would untie the sack, perhaps resting it on a wall of convenient height, to take out the next bundle.

On this particular delivery, Andy would arrive at the wall opposite the house of erotica at 7.55 precisely each morning, just as Mrs Breast-Barer was on the doorstep in her housecoat seeing her husband off to work. While Andy was performing the ritual of extracting the next bundle of mail, taking longer than necessary, Mrs B-B would go upstairs and, at eight o'clock exactly, would appear at the upstairs window, brushing her long hair, impressive breasts on full display. She never looked at Andy, instead gazing dreamily into the distance as if he wasn't there. The show lasted for a minute or two before concluding with the drawing of the curtains.

Having heard this story I couldn't wait to get the opportunity to do Andy's walk, willing him to take some of his leave or perhaps break a limb when I was available to cover. Eventually, one wet morning, my chance came. Andy had a day off and I was given the walk. I set off on my circuit of the quiet streets at the back of Barnes Green, carefully timing my approach to the only address I was interested in. I stopped at the wall opposite the house at 7.55, hands shaking with nervous excitement. Sure enough, the husband emerged from the front door, unfurling an umbrella. Mrs B-B gave him an affectionate peck on the cheek as they stood on the doorstep together.

My head disappeared into the top of my Irish sack as I tried to make myself invisible. The front door closed and a heart-thumping few minutes later there she was, at the window, displaying her breasts in exactly the way Andy had described. She was old enough to be my mother but beautiful in her maturity as she gazed into the distance, brushing her thick, auburn hair without giving the slightest indication that she knew I was there staring up at her.

After a minute or two she put down the hairbrush and pulled the curtains. The show was over. There was something in those sad eyes that made me reluctant ever to see it again.

Two other characters at Barnes were, I suppose, the most important people in the office. Our supervisor (whose rank was assistant inspector) was coincidentally named Mr Barnes. The men disliked him intensely. Humourless and officious, he was seen as being entirely surplus to requirements in an office that virtually ran itself. Worst of all, on the rare occasion when there was a problem to be resolved on the sorting-office floor, just the situation in which a supervisor was needed, Mr Barnes would shut himself in his office hoping it would go away. If an early connection failed, leading to a significant quantity of mail for delivery arriving just before we were due to go out, or if there was a problem with an influx of pools coupons (which were voluminous and bulky), Mr Barnes simply vanished. In a small office of thirty men where everyone pulled together, this dereliction of duty was met with scorn and derision, particularly by the ex-servicemen.

The man we relied upon to sort things out was the other important person I must mention: our local representative of the Union of Post Office Workers (UPW), Billy Fairs.

I'd been approached to join the union on my first day in the office by Reg, the office cook, who was also the branch treasurer. As well as explaining the importance of joining, he suggested I take out a policy with the UPW Insurance Society that would mature when I reached the retirement age of sixty and supplement my civil-service pension. Although I found it impossible to focus on retirement while still in my teens, I duly signed up for everything Reg put in front of me, which included something called the Civil Service Sanatorium. While the contributions made a dent in my wages of £10 per week, it seemed a prudent thing to do.

Within a week or so I'd received my UPW membership card.

My knowledge of current affairs, if embryonic, was sufficient for me to understand the role of trade unions and my experience at Tesco was enough to convince me of their necessity.

Billy Fairs was the first union representative with whom I'd ever come into contact and he was a fine standard-bearer for trade-unionism: good-natured and unassuming, but with a sharp brain and a strong sense of public duty. He and Les Griffiths were the two staunchest union men in the office, sharing the thankless role of union rep. At the time I joined Billy was taking his turn.

Billy was the other 'reserve' at Barnes. Whereas I had my job foisted on me as the rookie, Billy was a reserve because he chose to be. Partly this was to minimize any disruption caused by him having to attend meetings but another reason, he told me, was that it was the best way for him to gain a proper understanding of all the jobs his members had to do.

In one of the rare weeks when Billy and I had no walks to cover we would be detailed to deliver telephone directories. This involved filling an ancient Royal Mail handcart, a crimson-painted, basket-weave contraption on wooden wheels, with these fat, heavy phone books and placing them on the doorsteps of the telephone subscribers of Barnes.

Not every house had a telephone but most did and some were divided into flats requiring a whole library of directories. We worked with a pack of printed cards telling us where each subscriber lived. It was a hard slog and Billy did the lion's share, insisting on pushing the barrow and checking the cards as well as helping me to carry the directories to the door.

There was no cutting corners with Billy. Every duty he covered was meticulously performed. It was a characteristic of almost every union rep with whom I came into contact. They did the job properly, arguing that those who didn't were letting down their colleagues as well as the public.

The clearest example of corner-cutting was 'shabbing' the second delivery. I know not where the term came from but to 'shab' was to hold back items from the second delivery until the first delivery the next day. Shabbing in its mildest form was keeping back a pools coupon that was the only item going to the top floor of a block of flats when the postman was bound to be returning with much more mail the following morning. In the most severe manifestation of the practice, the entire second delivery would be held back to be reintroduced into the system the next day, the motive being to get home earlier.

While supervisors would turn a blind eye to shabbing, Billy was uncompromising in his insistence that our deliveries should be completed literally to the letter.

Although I can't remember ever considering the matter in these terms, if I had been asked back then to choose between a future in management or with the union – if I had, in effect, been asked to be Mr Barnes or Billy Fairs – the union definitely presented the more inspiring, if less remunerative, career path.

Chapter 3

THERE WAS A further injection of young blood at Barnes when my best friend and best man Andrew Wiltshire joined me there. Andrew was a restless spirit. He'd already had three jobs since leaving school at fifteeen to pursue pop stardom alongside me as the drummer in the Area. The last had been as a butcher, which he had soon come to detest. We had worked together during my ill-fated career with Tesco and now he too fancied trying his hand at being a Barnes postman.

Andrew had been going steady with Ann Cheetham since our days with the Area. I'd been at primary school with Ann before her family moved out to Aylesbury and she was a niece of Mrs Cox's. They were now engaged and Ann had taken over the tenancy of my room at Mrs Kenny's in Hamlet Gardens when I'd married.

Andrew cycled to work every day from his parents' house near White City on an old sit-up-and-beg bike his dad had given him. More often than not, riding Judy's cutting-edge Moulton, I'd meet him on Hammersmith Bridge in the insulated hush of the early morning. We'd pull our bikes off the road, light a cigarette and lean on the balustrade watching the Thames flow beneath us. It wasn't exactly Wordsworth on Westminster Bridge, but for us it had its own profundity.

I would moan to Andrew about life in Camelford Road and he'd tell me of his plans to marry Ann, buy a house and settle in a job that paid good money, one where he could wear a suit and drive a company car.

As the birth of our baby approached I worked all the over-time I could, sometimes in Wandsworth, where all the mail from postal districts SW13 to SW20 was processed every evening. Even there the only automation was the moving chain that brought up the mail sacks from the vans unloading below and tipped them on to the facing table, which was large enough to accommodate the forty or so men gathered around it.

Having faced the letters we'd move en masse to the sorting frames for outward primary sorting (it was the postmen higher grade, with their crowned lapels, who did the secondary, more specialized sorting, breaking down, let's say Scotland, into its various counties and major cities). On the primary sorting we'd incentivize our endeavours and liven up the humdrum work a bit by contributing sixpence (2½p in today's money) each to a sorting competition. Each group of five would have a kitty of half a crown (12½p) that would go to the first man to get a letter in every one of the forty-eight boxes on the sorting frame.

I suppose it's inevitable that somebody at some point must have thrown the letters into any old box just to win the prize, but if it happened at all it wouldn't have been very often. We postmen were extraordinarily conscientious about ensuring that mail went to its proper destination.

In the little time I had back at Camelford Road in the evenings I would often walk Nan's dog, Suzie, primarily to get out of the house, but also to try to ingratiate myself with the dog's mistress.

Camelford Road ran from St Marks Road, via Ladbroke Crescent, into Ladbroke Grove, so walking Suzie allowed me to revisit some of my old haunts. Many of them were already gone. Buildings that had been condemned before the war, and subsequently exploited by slum landlords who crammed them full of as many people as possible for extortionate rents, were finally being demolished to make way for the A40 extension.

Ruston Close (formerly Rillington Place), where Johnny Carter, the milkman who gave me my first proper weekend job, used to sit in the milk float and make me collect the money owed by the tenants of the infamous number 10, was still standing, though most of its houses were boarded up by this time. It had been given a stay of execution to allow shooting of the film *10 Rillington Place*, starring Richard Attenborough as the serial killer John Christie, whose chilling murders there in the 1940s and early 1950s were responsible for the notoriety of the address. As soon as filming was completed, it would be gone, and the locale redeveloped in a way that obscured the very site of one of the most notorious houses in criminal history.

Suzie and I would amble down Cambridge Gardens, up Oxford Gardens and back along St Marks Road, avoiding Ladbroke Grove. The atmosphere on the streets, where an undercurrent of intimidation had always been perceptible to some extent, had become much worse in the four years I'd been away. The population of Notting Hill seemed to be divided between those who welcomed the sight of a police officer and those who feared it. Those in the latter category were pre-dominantly black, particularly teenage boys who were regularly subjected to all kinds of provocation by a police force that reflected the worst prejudices of local people – the kind of prejudices I'd witnessed as a child and which had been cynically harnessed by Oswald Mosley in the 1959 general election campaign.

The streets of Notting Hill had become even more dangerous than I'd remembered them. All of this – Nan's hostility, the escalating tension in the area, the turmoil caused by the destruction of entire streets to build the new road and flyover – rapidly eroded my lifelong resistance to moving out of London.

As we'd planned, Judy and I had put our names on the waiting list for a council house as soon as we were married. It was a very long list but Camelford Road, too, was due for demolition and we'd been told that this would place an obligation on the council to rehouse us.

I mentioned this to Andrew in our dawn discussions on Hammersmith Bridge. He suggested I should try to secure a place on the idyllic council estate in leafy Barnes: beautiful gabled cottages behind wooden latched gates with tidy front gardens. Given their desirability and the long queue of families who'd applied to live there, we both knew this was a pipe dream. Wherever we were sent, it was highly unlikely to be London SW13.

~

Christmas 1968. My first experience of 'Christmas Pressure' at the Post Office: the period from early December when the normal working rhythms and processes would be changed to cope with the tidal wave of festive greetings that would be washed up on our sorting-office shore. Entire battalions of casuals, mostly students, were recruited throughout the country. You could hardly cross a sorting-office floor anywhere in Britain without tripping over a sociology undergraduate from Sheffield University or an Oxbridge scholar waiting to be shown how to tie a bundle of letters.

At most offices, the students delivered the mail while the permanent staff stayed in the office, sorting and preparing.

All the regulars were put on twelve-hour shifts but, as the reserves, Billy Fairs and I picked up nights. Over Christmas all the Barnes mail had to be sorted at our office rather than at Wandsworth. Our two regular night sorters were supplemented by ten others, roughly reflecting the increase in the volume of mail.

Every afternoon Judy would wake me at about 4.30pm, whereupon I'd eat whatever she and Nan were going to be having for dinner as my breakfast. Then I'd watch *Jackanory* with Natalie and lounge about reading for an hour or so. I'd rejoined Ladbroke Grove Library, where our mother had first signed up Linda and me as toddlers, and had become obsessed with books on modern history – subjects such as the police strikes of 1918-19, the General Strike of 1926 and the Suez Crisis, which had impinged on my consciousness as a child but which I'd never understood.

I'd cycle to Barnes to start work at 8pm. After a couple of hours' sorting most of us would retreat to the Sun, the ancient pub facing Barnes Green, to down a couple of pints before it closed at half-past ten. Then we'd sort through the night, breaking off periodically to prep the walks ready for when the casuals started at around 7.30am (normal service standards were suspended over Christmas).

I loved Christmas Pressure. For a start it was a chance to earn more money. That first year, Judy had stopped work, with the baby imminent, and money was tight. I volunteered for an extra two hours' overtime every morning cleaning the office toilet, so I was working a fourteen-hour shift in total.

Christmas was also unusual in that it brought an influx of people of my own age. Apart from Andrew, there was only one other man under thirty on the regular staff – Brian Green, a fellow Queens Park Rangers and Beatles devotee. 'Hey Jude' had been released as a single in the summer, and the seminal LP *The White Album* a month before Christmas. I'd valued having someone at work with whom I could share my utter astonishment that music as wonderful as this could be produced by four working-class kids from Liverpool. With the exception of Andrew, none of my other workmates was interested.

Our older colleagues were constantly wondering what we were doing in the Post Office when there were so many better-paid jobs around. We were on about £10 a week, including London weighting (the additional allowance that acknowledged the higher cost of living in the capital), but structured on the 'incremental scales' that were typical of the civil service. This meant that your pay would rise in increments every year until the maximum was reached at a certain age (twenty-four for postmen; much older for clerical staff and telephonists). So, ludicrously, somebody joining as a postman aged twenty-five or older went straight on to maximum pay, earning much more than younger colleagues who might have been been doing the job for six or seven years. It was age discrimination, pure and simple, and I was seized by the sheer injustice of it.

Brian Green, two years older than me, was equally outraged. He was also about four stone heavier (I was as skinny as I'd always been, weighing around ten and a half stone), which made me a bit nippier when we went for a kick-around at a local park after finishing work some lunchtimes. Like me, Brian revered Rodney Marsh and we'd spend hours trying to replicate the exotic skills of our hero with a plastic football before I mounted the Moulton to cycle home. Rangers had made it to Division 1 that season for the first time in the club's history, though with Rodney injured we would be heading straight back down again after an abject showing in the top flight.

Brian joined Billy Fairs and me on the Christmas night shift, which finished on Christmas Eve. A year earlier to the day I'd been stacking shelves at Anthony Jackson's and living alone in a rented room, dreaming of rock stardom. In just twelve months I had been transformed into a married postman with one child and another due any minute.

The banter in the office that morning centred on Norman Reid, who had one of the best walks in Barnes – Queen's Ride, where the richest, most distinguished residents lived. I'd covered his walk for a fortnight when he was on leave and considered it to be the easiest I'd ever done. Norman used the abundance of spare time he had after finishing his delivery to good effect. He would marshal the rubbish bins for collection and reunite them with their owners when the dustmen left them abandoned on the pavement; he'd run errands, collecting prescriptions or fetching groceries for the wealthy elderly folk who formed the majority of his customers.

As a result, Norman always, I was told, received a small fortune in 'Christmas boxes', tips from grateful customers, and would be subjected to a tirade of (mostly) good-humoured ribbing from his fellow postmen. Small and wiry with a natural wit, Norman would defend his obsequiousness vigorously.

This Christmas Eve Norman had become a national figure. One of his customers was the famous *Daily Mirror* writer and agony aunt Marjorie Proops. She had devoted an entire page in the paper's Christmas edition to the man she named as the finest postman in Britain: Norman Reid. Poor Norman had to run the gauntlet of a barrage of insults – though they carried, it has to be said, a note of pride at the reflected glory he had brought to Barnes PDO.

I laughed all the way through my final two hours of toilet-cleaning on overtime, put the *Daily Mirror* into the pannier of the bike and cycled home through the foggy Christmas Eve dawn.

I found the house at Camelford Road quiet and deserted. A note was propped against a sauce bottle on the kitchen table. It was from Nan, and as might be expected, contained no niceties – just a simple message in large letters: 'Judy in labour. Taken her to St Charles hospital with Natalie.'

I sat down to wait it out. I didn't have much of a clue what I was supposed to do but I had a pretty good idea that I wouldn't be welcome at the hospital. Even if I'd been at home when Judy had gone into labour there would have been no question of me being with my wife at the birth of our child. Attitudes might have been starting to change, but for the most part these were still the days when the father was expected to stay well out of the way, preferably in a pub buying his mates beer and cigars. I wasn't in the pub but I was certainly well out of the way, waiting at Camelford Road for news as Judy gave birth to our daughter Emma Jane Johnson on Christmas Eve 1968 about a mile down the road.

Although I was tired out from the long hours of Christmas Pressure, Emma's birth reinvigorated me with an energy fired by the intense joy of fatherhood and the pride I took in having created this beautiful blonde child.

~

The 1960s were entering their final year. Andrew and I leaned over the railings of Hammersmith Bridge as if watching that eventful decade floating away beneath us.

There was much for us to talk about as we savoured the acrid taste of the day's first cigarette in those precious ten minutes before our working day began.

Andrew and Ann were to be married in April: a proper church wedding in Ann's adopted home town of Aylesbury. I'd expected to be his best man, as he had been mine, but now he broke the news to me that his parents were insisting his brother John should fulfil that role. I was miffed. Why did he have to do what his parents said? It was his wedding, his life, his decision. But I kept my counsel, as usual, greeting this development with a casual shrug and a drag on my fag.

My silent protest certainly didn't extend to a boycott of the wedding. I would be on parade that spring in a light blue woollen suit I'd saved for (the second suit I'd owned – the first was of black and white Donegal tweed). I always left the third button of the three-button jacket undone to allow me to plunge my hands into the straight-front pockets of the trousers, drawing the jacket back into two flaps to reveal the intricate lining. Matters of dress protocol were important to me. My only other jacket had been a blue collarless one in the 'Beatles' style, purchased with money I'd saved from my milk and paraffin rounds when I was thirteen. I didn't wear it for long because as soon as the Beatles saw how ubiquitous their trademark jackets had become they stopped wearing them, which meant that we devotees had to drop them as well.

Did Andrew and I ever discuss politics in those Hammersmith Bridge conversations? I don't think that we did, but we both had a growing sense that we were perfectly entitled to be heard in any discussions between the men around us at Barnes, including their frequent heated political debates, even though we knew we wouldn't have been considered worthy participants if we had interjected. I recall Brian Green once having the temerity to offer an opinion one morning in the canteen, where an argument was raging over some event in the news. The reaction was swift, with Frank Dainton retorting rather pompously that this 'was not a conversation for juveniles'.

Granted, back then 'juvenile' was just a synonym for 'young', whereas nowadays it tends to be used more pejoratively to suggest a lack of maturity. Football clubs advertised reduced entry fees for 'juveniles'; teenage miscreants were 'juvenile delinquents'. Today he probably would have said 'kids' – but today he'd have been less likely to voice such a sentiment at all.

Strange as it may sound, although I bought *The Times* regularly I never read it in front of anyone at work. I would keep it stashed in the sack or the pannier of my bike and take it home to peruse later. To have sat reading it in the canteen would have looked pretentious, as if I were showing off; it would have suggested I felt somehow superior to colleagues who mostly read the *Mirror* or the *Express* (apart from Ted Philpott who, when he wasn't thrashing someone at snooker, quietly puffed on his pipe behind a copy of the *Daily Telegraph*).

It seemed natural for Ted to be reading a 'quality' paper, whereas in my case it would have been incongruous. So I hid mine as if it were a pornographic magazine. In truth there was much in *The Times* I found incomprehensible, such as many of the leader columns and articles opposite them which seemed to be written in a code I didn't know but which I was intent on deciphering.

I supplemented my daily dose of current affairs with magazines such as *Punch* and *Newsweek*. Not that I paid for them. The population of Barnes were great subscribers to magazines, which would be sent out to them in the post protected only by a brown paper sleeve with the name and address of the recipient slipped over each folded copy. I would slip them out and have a read as I sat on my delivery frame with a cup of tea before heading off to start the walk.

I loved the look and feel of these magazines as well as the content, which I found so interesting that when I saw an advertisement for a free news magazine, delivered at no charge to your home each month, I applied for it straight away. When the first copy plopped through the letterbox at 2 Camelford Road, it quickly became apparent, to my dismay, that it was no more than religious propaganda masquerading as some competitor to *Time* magazine. The title of the magazine escapes me but it was a printed version of the kind of fiery sermons by the American evangelist Garner Ted Armstrong that had been broadcast before the pop shows on Radio Luxembourg when I was a kid. I know it would have disappointed my mother but I'd already decided I was an atheist. Even if I hadn't, this dogma-soaked version of the news might well have made me one.

As Andrew and I stood chatting in the early dawn of 1969 we were about to become part of a news story ourselves. The Post Office was preparing to go on strike.

One morning that January, when I returned to the office after the first delivery, Reg was waiting to usher us all upstairs for a union meeting. In my seven months as a member of the UPW I'd never been to such a gathering, nor had I heard of any being called to which I could have gone. Billy Fairs and Reg Allen distributed the union's monthly magazine, the *Post*, but I can't claim to have paid nearly as much attention to that as I did to my newspaper and my customers' current-affairs periodicals.

It was a wet day and, after removing our waterproofs in the drying room on the ground floor, we were keen to be up in the canteen getting a hot breakfast inside us. Instead we were being directed to a room on the third floor where, according to Reg, officials of the union's London District Council (LDC) were waiting to speak to us.

In we trooped, cold and bedraggled. There were no chairs, so we remained on our feet as Billy Fairs introduced the main speaker, Dickie Lawlor, the secretary of the LDC, a man with a powerful presence and a strong voice. He told us we were going to be called out on a one-day strike on 30 January.

Among the ranks of Post Office workers was a group of 3,000 highly skilled operatives known as overseas telegraph officers, or OTOs, who handled the long-distance transmission of electronically derived textual messages, otherwise known as telegrams. Revolutionary in the nineteenth century, this was still a significant, albeit declining, form of communication in the late sixties.

Dickie Lawlor told us how disgracefully these 'brothers' had been treated. The civil-service grades to which their pay was linked had received a 5 per cent increase the previous June but a demand for a similar rise for OTOs had been met with an insistence by the Post Office that they accept productivity 'strings', which were not attached to the settlement for other grades. The OTOs had voted to go on strike but their action had failed to convince management to drop the 'strings'.

Ours was an amalgamated union and although this issue didn't affect postal workers, we must show solidarity with a minority grade. That was what trade unionism was about: standing together in support of each other and not allowing those with the least muscle to be picked off.

The UPW executive council had decided that all grades in the nineteen largest cities and towns in Britain would be called out on strike in support of the OTOs. It would be the first national strike in the union's almost fifty-year history.

Dickie Lawlor spoke eloquently enough. He and his two colleagues from the LDC were visiting every London sorting office over the next few days so were pressed for time. Were there any questions? Would there be any strike pay? somebody asked. No, came the firm answer. It was neither affordable nor desirable in a short strike of this nature. A few men, including Billy Fairs, reinforced Dickie's message. OTOs would be expected to support us if we were in dispute, so now we must support them.

Just as the meeting was about to finish, Ted Philpott raised his hand. He wanted to know why we hadn't been balloted. Surely the union's rules stipulated that we be consulted in this way as the OTOs had been? Dickie replied that the rules didn't require a ballot. They vested the power to make that decision in the executive council, which consisted mainly of lay members like us, elected annually. If we wanted to change the union's rules to make a ballot obligatory there was a conference every year where such things were decided. 'This is your union,' he told us. 'You make the rules.' He pointed out that a ballot would take weeks to organize and that it would weaken the union's ability to protect its members if such a measure were insisted upon in all circumstances.

Ted put his pipe back in his mouth and reflected on this response as we all trooped down to the canteen for a truncated breakfast break. There was a bit of muttering about the high wages the OTOs were paid compared with ours and the fact that we'd had nothing approaching a 5 per cent rise the previous year, but in general these ex-soldiers had decided that there was a battle to be won, they'd received their orders and they understood what was expected of them.

Chapter 4

WHILE I WAS still tiptoeing around Nan at Camelford Road, Linda had managed to put some distance between herself and her difficult mother-in-law by persuading Mike to move to Tring. Linda was pregnant with their second child and more space was needed.

That January we went over to visit Linda and Mike in their new three-bedroomed house. Mike picked up Judy, myself, Natalie and baby Emma from Camelford Road in his Rover and conveyed us all to Tring considerably more slowly and safely than he'd driven me to Watford at Christmas just over a year earlier.

We loved the house – detached with a long back garden and overlooked by the verdant hills of Hertfordshire. Natalie and her cousin Renay (Linda had chosen the name after hearing the Area playing 'Walk Away Renée' in its original pre-Four Tops version, amending the spelling in a bid to ensure it wasn't mispronounced) fussed over baby Emma, who was already beginning to sprout what would become a mass of blonde curls.

Mike and I left the two women and three little girls shortly after our arrival. He wanted to show me his new local, the Anchor on Tring High Street. The landlord already seemed to know him well and had begun to pull his pint even before he'd settled himself into his usual spot at the corner of the bar.

I was more of an observer than a talker but I'd always relished talking to Mike. Sometimes I was conscious of talking at him as I attempted to impress him with bits of information and lines of argument I'd gleaned from my surreptitious reading of my customers' magazines and odd snatches of the few *Times* leaders I had managed to understand. Eternally patient, Mike would absorb my half-formed teenage gibberish before setting out his own considered view of whatever subject it was I raised.

He was a working-class Tory whose politics had been forged by the history books he'd read. He had emphatically condemned Enoch Powell's infamous 'Rivers of Blood' speech the previous year, in which the Conservative MP had denounced Commonwealth immigration, when most of the adult voices I heard at the time had been speaking up for Powell. But he couldn't see how there could be equality without repression. The monarch was a natural head of state, in his view; a presidency was a contrived construct that would serve only to undermine a parliamentary democracy. He felt that our Labour prime minister, Harold Wilson, was taking the country backwards whereas Ted Heath, the leader of the opposition, whom he greatly admired, would, if elected, take us forward into Europe, where our destiny lay. I was never confident enough at that stage to test my own political view against Mike's softly spoken wisdom.

And so we chatted on, a box of a hundred Senior Service

untipped lying open on the bar in front of him, on offer to me and anyone else in the pub. (One – or maybe more than one – of the many grateful private customers for whom Mike fixed electrical appliances kept him constantly supplied.) I told him about the strike and he said that unions had grown too powerful and needed to have their wings clipped. If Wilson couldn't do it, Heath would.

I disagreed. Mike might not need the protection of a union, I argued as I reached for yet another of his fags, but millions of workers had no skills with which to bargain. For us, collective action was the only way to fight exploitation. Mike smiled, his blue eyes twinkling. 'Hark at you,' he said. 'Well on the way to becoming a bolshie shop steward.'

The strike duly took place on 30 January 1969. As far as I'm aware, there was no picket line outside Barnes PDO. If there was, I wasn't on it. For me the strike meant a welcome five-day week instead of the six days I was used to working.

Losing a day's pay was a blow to the family finances, of course, but I used this unexpected day at leisure to good effect by preparing one of my poems for publication. I still had the copy of the *Writers' and Artists' Yearbook* that my English teacher, Mr Carlen, had encouraged me to buy during my final year at school. It was four years out of date by now, but I thought most of the publishers' addresses listed there were unlikely to have changed. I'd sent detective stories I had written, together with the occasional poem, to various obscure magazines and was rather proud of the rejection slips that came back. It seemed to me that every author I'd read about had been through the pain of rejection before achieving literary acclaim, so I saw it as a rung on the ladder to success.

I hadn't had a great deal of time to write very much more since leaving school, apart from the songs I always felt would offer a faster route to fame and fortune. Then my eye had been caught by an advertisement inviting submissions for a volume of poetry, *Spring Poets '69*, to be published in May. It was a vanity publication: writers would have to pay for the privilege of seeing their work in print rather than being paid for it. Still, the vision of my elegantly formulated and deeply significant lines appearing in full in a proper, professionally produced hardback volume, with my name alongside them, was too exciting an opportunity to miss.

I think the cost was around £5 per poem – more than half a week's wages for me. I had saved enough to submit a single offering, a poem entitled 'Youth', and spent the day of the strike tapping away at an old typewriter Judy had acquired in her teens as a Christmas present. The next day, when postal services resumed, I sent it off, along with my postal order for £5, to the Regency Press in New Oxford Street. I'd just made the deadline for submissions.

We returned after the strike to a backlog of mail strewn across the sorting-office floor in sacks that had remained unopened for a couple of days. Mr Barnes strolled around with his hands behind his back, looking officious. An agreement had been reached with Billy Fairs as to how we would deal with the arrears. There would be one delivery in the morning followed by a second, with a similar volume of mail, in the afternoon, to be completed by about 5pm. This suited us fine. The overtime would compensate for the day's pay we had lost.

The same day, the postmaster general, John Stonehouse, announced that he was prepared to negotiate. Billy called us together on 1 February to tell us that, following six hours of discussion with the UPW, the Post Office had agreed to award the 5 per cent increase our OTO colleagues had demanded, unencumbered by productivity 'strings' and backdated to the previous August. A further increase of 2 per cent, dependent on improved productivity, would be awarded from 1 April. That day's *Times* described this as a 'complete capitulation' by the government.

Our noble sacrifice in support of a minority grade had led to a satisfactory settlement but Billy Fairs was not one for flowery rhetoric. His victory speech consisted merely of a muted 'well done, lads' before we resumed delivery of the Queen's mail and picked up the threads of the familiar routine of Barnes PDO. Everything was back to normal – except in one small but significant respect. Nobody would speak to Ted Philpott. Ted Philpott had come into work on 30 January. Ted Philpott had broken the strike.

I don't know how this fact became known. Billy hadn't announced it in his little speech. Nobody mentioned Ted's name; the information seemed somehow to be conveyed on the ether. Suddenly, nobody was saying 'good morning' to Ted and the usual pleasantries went unexchanged. In the parlance of the age, he had been sent to Coventry. Nobody was aggressive towards him or argued with him about the strike. It was worse, much worse than that. Ted Philpott was simply ignored.

In the canteen he would rise from the breakfast table hopefully, snooker cue in hand, but nobody would play against him. After a while he'd retreat behind his *Daily Telegraph*, puffing his pipe, alone in a roomful of men.

I was at Barnes for only five more months, and in all that time nobody spoke to Ted Philpott. For all I know his isolation lasted until his retirement. I was as guilty as my workmates of inflicting this terrible punishment. I colluded in trying to break a man's spirit and it's something I've been ashamed of ever since.

~

On a Saturday lunchtime in May, I was sitting in The Sun opposite Barnes Green. I'd finished my delivery and was enjoying a pint before cycling home. I was keeping an ear out in case the pay phone fixed to the wall of the pub should ring. Judy had the number and I'd asked her to call me if the parcel she'd gone to collect from our local sorting office (she'd been out when our postman had attempted to deliver it) proved to be the one I'd been waiting for.

The phone rang and I leaped up to answer it. Sure enough, it was Judy, calling from the phone box on the corner of St Marks Road. In her hand was a parcel from the Regency Press. She wouldn't open it, she promised, until I arrived home.

The only person I'd told about the publication of my poem was Andrew, who sat nursing a pint next to me. I poured the beer I had left into his glass and rushed away in a state of excited anticipation.

Back at Camelford Road, there it was unwrapped, in my hands. *Spring Poets '69*, subtitled 'An anthology of contemporary verse'. The hardback book carried a sale price of 45s (50s by post). According to the back cover, it was available in the USA and Canada for $8. I wasn't naïve enough to imagine that this book would be bought anywhere but I turned it reverently in my hands, admiring its neat design and skilful binding.

It contained 504 poems. At £5 a shot, the publishers had collected a whopping £2,520 from us vain and gullible poets. This sum would easily have covered the printing costs and provided the publishers with a handsome profit. There was no need for them to bother attempting actually to sell it to anyone. They couldn't lose: no wonder the cover advertised a further collection, *Twentieth Century Poets*, that would be available later in the year.

The poems featured in *Spring Poets '69* were awful, mine included. Most of the contributors had paid for several pieces of work to be published. Indeed, a certain Isabella Oswald Finlayson had fourteen poems in the book – £60 worth.

On page 205 I found my solitary contribution:

Youth

In frantic years we grow
To be people of the world
In frantic years that are supposed to teach us.
And we never really know
Why we're supposed to know
As a thousand clammy hands stretch out to reach us
And as we sail the balmy years
On our cushioned little cloud
We have no mind or thought of what's ahead
Each pimply worry dies in the freedom of our cries
And crumples on the shelter of our bed
It takes a lot to learn

An awful lot to learn
That all the time you ran your future followed
The beard is on your face
You've slammed the book and lost your place
And the bitter pill of life is slowly swallowed.

I concede that it's not exactly T.S. Eliot. However, in my defence, I reckon it's positively Shakespearean compared with some of the other poems contained in this (to quote the blurb on the cover) 'fine anthology'.

Take, for instance, 'Kippers' by Sheila Smurthwaite. Here's an extract.

Everything's a pity. Everything's sad.
Like a wet kipper slapped against a wall that's sad.
I am a kipper. I feel the same as the kipper must've felt.
   Hooked, caught,
pulled in, smoked, cured, dried, packed, opened, cooked.
Then thrown against a wall.
A waste. A pity. Sad.
But gone now.
Funny smell!

Funny smell or not, nothing could dampen the thrill of possessing a proper hardback book with my own poem in it. I already had the disc recorded by my first band, The Area ('A Hard Life', with one of my compositions, 'I Have Seen', on the 'B' side). By the age of eighteen, I was both a recording artist and a published poet. The small detail that it was a demo disc and a vanity publication was, to me, immaterial. I was convinced that these achievements were just the foundations of an artistic career to which I would return when circumstances allowed.

My immediate ambitions were rather less lofty. I'd applied to be a Post Office driver. Andrew had already passed his driving test, thanks to lessons his parents had bought him for his eighteenth birthday. At Barnes he had soon progressed from delivering letters to driving vans. I found out that the Post Office had its own driving instructors and that they would actually pay me to learn to drive, putting me through a special civil-service driving test at the end of the course. It was too good an opportunity to miss. My application was successful and one day in the spring of 1969 Mr Barnes informed me that I was to report to Croydon sorting office, from which the driving school operated, the following Monday.

Along with another postman, from Raynes Park, I was taken out in an adapted Morris 1000 van. It had dual controls and a rear seat in the body of the van where the non-driving pupil could sit between spells behind the wheel.

Our tutor was a man of military bearing. He wore a suit (we were in uniform) and said little that wasn't strictly related to his task of teaching us to drive during two intensive weeks of training. One of the first things he told us was that all Post Office vans had unsynchronized manual transmission gears. This meant nothing to me as I had absolutely no driving experience whatsoever, but I nodded my head as if it did. I soon discovered what it signified. We had to learn to 'double declutch' – to put the gearstick into neutral and then pump the clutch again to change up. To change down you had to return the transmission to neutral before performing a delicate little manoeuvre, giving the accelerator a spurt at the same time as slipping into the lower gear.

My colleague from Raynes Park was older than me and had unsuccessfully completed several driving school courses using saloon cars with synchronized gears, in which this technique wasn't needed. My lack of experience worked to my advantage when it came to double declutching and I found it easier than he did. By the end of the first week's training I was happily motoring round the country lanes of Surrey like Mr Toad, double declutching my way to a driving licence – until fate intervened.

Our instructor informed us that he was taking the following Monday off, which meant we would have to report to our delivery offices that day and resume our driving course on the Tuesday. I chose that Monday morning to oversleep. I was still in my probationary year as a postman and my ability to get to work on time was an essential measure of my suitability for the job. I'd already been late a couple of times. We were allowed five minutes' grace, but any longer and Mr Barnes would put a red cross next to the name of any offender on the attendance sheet, officially recording him as late. This was a task Mr Barnes performed with enthusiasm. While he'd spend most of the morning bunkered in his office, first thing he would hover over the attendance sheet like an eagle waiting to swoop on its prey.

My start time at Barnes was 5.30am. Waking with a jolt twenty minutes after the alarm had gone off, I realized to my despair that it was pouring with rain, which meant losing valuable time struggling into my Post Office-issue oilskins. I cycled to work as fast as I could and arrived just as Mr Barnes was uncapping the nib of his big red pen. I was within the final seconds of my five-minute grace period.

I made my way to the sorting frames and just as Peter Simonelli began to say: 'And another happy day begins at Barnes PDO,' I fainted. Clean away. Fell to the floor like a sack of spuds.

This has happened to me on a couple of other occasions, once before and once since: I have simply overheated and gone spark out.

When I came round Mr Barnes announced that I'd need to go for a medical and in the meantime I couldn't continue on the driving course which, in the circumstances, was fair enough, I suppose. The medical was to take place at Armour House in the City of London. But as things turned out I never had it. Before it could be arranged, I was off to pastures new.

We had received a letter from the council telling us that our house was being compulsorily purchased to be demolished. Camelford Road, like Southam Street, Walmer Road and Lancaster Road before it, would be falling under the wrecking ball. Nan would have a choice of relocations, but as Judy and I had been on the housing list for less than a year we would be given one offer, take it or leave it. If it wasn't acceptable we'd have to find our own accommodation. The only reason the council had even this tenuous obligation to us was their compulsory purchase of our home.

Nan quickly settled on a move to sheltered accommodation on the Cuckoo Estate in Hanwell, a cosy flat where pets were allowed and where she would retain her independence at the same time as becoming part of a new community. As for us, there was absolutely no prospect of being able to raise a deposit to buy a house, let alone meet mortgage repayments. We had no choice but to accept whatever we were offered. We just hoped it would prove to be the opportunity we'd been waiting for: a fresh start in a family home of our own.

Chapter 5

'Excuse me. Do you know how to get to the Britwell estate?'

It was a sunny June day in 1969 and Judy and I were outside the station in Slough, Buckinghamshire, thirty miles west of London. We had just arrived on the 9.30 train from Paddington. In my hand was a letter from the London County Council offering us a council house in Long Furlong Drive on the Britwell estate, Slough. We'd come to explore this 'offer', fervently hoping that the rustic-sounding road would live up to our expectations.

The two Thames Valley policemen to whom my question was addressed were chatting beside their pale blue Ford Anglia. They looked at each other knowingly.

'Do we know how to get to the Britwell?' one of them said. 'We should do, we have to go there often enough.'

The other one asked Judy why we were going there. Judy told him. 'Well, I wouldn't live on the Britwell for all the tea in China,' was his helpful advice. We caught the bus as directed, travelling in silence, thinking about what the policemen had said. Camelford Road was hardly Sunnybrook Farm. On

Saturday nights we could hear the commotion outside the notorious KPH, the Kensington Palace Hotel, just down the road, as chucking-out time unleashed hundreds of inebriated men from the pubs of Notting Hill on to the streets at the same time. Violence was a constant undertone in our part of west London. Surely the Britwell estate couldn't be worse than where we were living now?

The bus turned off the Bath Road at the Three Tuns and proceeded so far down Farnham Road that we were almost on the manicured lawns of Farnham Royal before it suddenly veered left. This was the Britwell. Rows of pretty houses panned out behind latched wooden gates and narrow paths. Another turn and we were on Long Furlong Drive, which was indeed very long. I gazed at the bucolic scenery out of the left-hand window. A mound of greenery separated the residential area from the confines of the grim Slough Trading Estate, where the Mars factory, one of the town's largest employers, scented the air around the Britwell with a perpetual aroma of warm chocolate.

Judy nudged me to draw my attention to the view from the opposite window: a community centre flanked by football pitches. On a long brick wall at the back was painted, in huge letters, 'Keep Britwell White'.

The bus took us on to the council offices in Wentworth Avenue, a turning off Long Furlong Drive remarkable only for featuring the one building on this huge estate, constructed in the previous decade, that could be even loosely described as a tower block. The rest of it consisted of houses and low-rise flats set in acres of open green space with lots of trees – a legacy of the orchard Britwell had once been.

The letter we had brought from the LCC was addressed to Judy. Householders had to be over twenty-one, the so-called age of majority. I had just turned nineteen. Judy was now twenty-three, so the council house would need to be in her name. We collected the keys from the council offices and walked round to the house we had come to view. It was set back in the corner of two rows of terraced houses grouped around a green – at the end of its row, which made it semi-detached. A two-bedroomed house with gardens front and back. The windows were boarded up to deter vandals and the grass was unkempt and overgrown. Inside there was a long downstairs room running the width of the house, a snug kitchen, two bedrooms and a loft.

My mother had spent her entire adult life on the council waiting list, bringing up her children in barely habitable, multi-occupied slums. Her dream had been to have her own front door to a house like this. She had died, aged forty-two, still waiting. The offer of a council house came two weeks after her funeral. Now here we were, Judy and me, at the beginning of our married lives, with the chance to move straight into this solid, modern, well-appointed house. It was a chance we grasped with delight. We had no hesitation in accepting the one lifeline we had been given by the council. We would make the Britwell estate our home.

∽

My plan was to try to transfer with the Post Office. When I rang Slough sorting office to inquire about vacancies, the guy I spoke to almost burst out laughing. They had more vacancies, apparently, than almost any other office in London and the south-east. When would I care to start?

Jobs were plentiful in Slough owing to the town's thriving economy, which dated back to the 1920s, when the enormous trading estate was built on the site of a First World War vehicle depot. It was not only the first business park in Europe but, at almost 500 acres, remains the biggest to this day.

It was the impact on the town of this inter-war munitions dump that prompted John Betjeman's infamous 1937 poem:

> Come, friendly bombs, and fall on Slough!
> It isn't fit for humans now,
> There isn't grass to graze a cow,
> Swarm over, Death!

Although Betjeman's intention was to lament industrialization and the blighting of England's landscape in general, rather than Slough in particular, the mud has stuck, much to the continuing disgust of the townspeople. If Judy or I had read this before accepting the house on the Britwell, we might have thought twice about it. By the time we did read the poem I was able to appreciate it while disagreeing strongly with its specific reference to the town we were happy to call home. Having been born into a street that literally wasn't 'fit for humans', I knew the difference between a place that was and one that wasn't.

It may have been the staff shortage at the Post Office that led to my successful 'establishment' at the end of my twelve-month probationary period at Barnes, in spite of my less than un-blemished lateness record and before the medical was arranged. If so it was lucky for me, as a postman had to be 'established' to apply for a transfer. Billy Fairs sorted everything out for me. He told me I would retain my London weighting on a mark-time basis – in other words, until the provincial pay caught up with my wages.

It was with sadness that I left that beautifully appointed sorting office for the last time, cycling off past the pond on Barnes Green and down Church Street towards Castlenau. This prosperous peninsula on the curve of the Thames had been a wonderful place to learn to be a postman. I had said my farewells to Billy and Frank Dainton, Freddie Binks, Les Griffiths, Peter Simonelli, Brian Green and all the other post-men at Barnes. Apart from Andrew, I never saw any of them again.

~

On 5 July 1969, the Rolling Stones gave a free concert in Hyde Park and I left Notting Hill for the last time. We'd probably have gone to the concert ourselves if we hadn't had something more important to do. While the flower children were listening to Mick Jagger's recitation of Shelley in homage to Brian Jones, who'd died a couple of days earlier, we were loading our possessions into a small removals van to be driven thirty miles west to Slough. Judy had saved up some money with which we had bought a second-hand sofa, a blue Formica-topped kitchen table and some chairs. We took with us the big old iron bed that had belonged to Judy's grandparents and the cots and cradles of our two little girls.

On a gloriously hot summer's day, the four of us squeezed on to the bench seat next to the removal man, winding down the windows to breathe in the warm air. The van drove along the Great West Road, past the art-deco glory of the Hoover Building, out beyond what we still called London airport and towards the rolling Chiltern Hills of Buckinghamshire. The A4 cut straight through Slough High Street, lorries and vans dispersing shoppers who hurried across the main road, seeking sanctuary on the pavement as the traffic roared past.

When we arrived at our new home the van bumped up over the kerb of Long Furlong Drive on to the little green around which ten houses nestled. The neighbours who had cars used the green as a convenient parking place so our removal man did the same, churning up the brown dust that was all that was left of the grass.

The council had assured us that the house would be ready but we found it still boarded up, with huge sheets of plywood bolted into the brick on either side of the windows to discourage vandals. It was already midday. One of our new neighbours told us that the council offices in Wentworth Avenue, five minutes' walk away, would be open for another hour.

On my way to notify the council of our arrival I remembered the reaction of those two policemen who'd directed us here on our first visit to Slough. Walking the unfamiliar streets of Britwell, I tried to assess the level of danger; to sense, as I had as a kid in North Kensington, the trouble spots, the streets it was wiser to avoid. Nothing registered on my Richter scale. It felt like a peaceful village on a summer's afternoon. Children played in the pleasant streets, men washed cars, women tended their front gardens or walked back from the Wentworth Avenue shops struggling with bags of groceries. The Britwell seemed to me to be more Arcadian than anarchic.

The council workmen came at about four o'clock to let in the light. The dismantling of the boards felt like a fitting relaunch of our lives; the sun flooding in a grand opening for our little house. As the long summer's day began to fade, with Natalie and Emma asleep in their own room for the first time, Judy and I stood at the back door surveying the first garden either of us had ever had. We both felt disorientated but elated, too. Perhaps the policemen who'd warned us off the Britwell had been locals dismayed by the influx of London council tenants on to their patch. Whatever their reasons, they had been wrong. This was a Saturday night and yet there was silence except for the sound of television programmes filtering through the open windows of the houses that backed on to ours. We listened, like two anthropologists, to the comforting sounds of domesticity.

~

Slough might have been only thirty miles from London but to me it was another world. And the post office there was so different from what I was used to that it was like having a new job altogether. The small delivery office at Barnes bore no resemblance whatsoever to Slough. Even the bigger site at Wandsworth, with its dark mahogany fixtures and fittings, seemed like a Victorian preservation project compared with Slough's modern, cream-painted metal and occasional bursts of plastic. Slough was an all-singing, all-dancing Post Office hub. It had a telephone exchange, attached to the sorting office in Wellington Street, and a separate parcels office on the trading estate.

There were around 200 delivery frames at the 'inward' end of the vast sorting-office floor. The 'outward' section at the other end was dominated by what looked like an oversized concrete mixer, or a prop from *Dr Who*. It was called a Seg Alf – segregator and letter-facer, to give it its full title. The mail collected from Slough's pillarboxes and businesses would be tipped in at one end and churned in a giant drum, which separated the packets from the letters that emerged in their thousands, as if by magic, through slats in the side.

At Wandsworth the men would work together on every aspect of the dispatch, like a swarm of bees moving from task to task. The only automation was the moving chain that brought the mail sacks up from the vans unloading below.

In the Slough office staff worked separately. Some fed the Seg Alf monster, others sorted or tied bags. Bundles were secured with red rubber bands. In London, in a revolutionary attempt at modernization, the supervisors had encouraged us to use these elastic bands rather than the big rolls of waxed string impaled on metal spikes beneath each sorting frame.

The men were having none of this. Nobody – but nobody – used those rubber bands during my days in London, even though it would have made the job quicker and easier. We struck our small blow against de-skilling by tying every bundle with the slip knot we'd been taught to use during our two weeks at the London Postal Training School.

Infuriatingly, whereas in London I'd been taught to sort letters 'stamp first', with the top right-hand corner of the letter going to the back of the frame, in Slough the stamp had to face outwards. Only London did 'stamp first' sorting, I was told. The rest of the country – and for all I knew, the entire world – sorted 'stamp last'. Even the terminology was different. In London the first delivery was known as the GP or general post; the second delivery was 'the tens' or 'the Irish' (it went out at 10am, once the post from Ireland had arrived). Slough used the more prosaic and straightforward 'night mail' and 'day mail'. The malpractice of 'shabbing' in London became 'baking' in Slough.

In my natty light brown cotton summer uniform jacket with its half-belt, double vents and red piping around the collar and sleeves, I cut a lonely figure. In Slough the summer jacket was a dull grey affair with no adornments. After a few weeks of parading my London fashion statement, I was driven by the urge to conform to the uniform stores to kit myself out in shapeless grey. It is the purpose of a uniform, I suppose, to stifle individuality.

The most serious difference between London and 'the provinces' was in the way mail was delivered. On my first proper day after a short period being shown the ropes, I was allocated a delivery on the Britwell estate, not far from our new home.

I'd cycled into work on Judy's Moulton, covering the three miles in about twenty minutes. It was another sunny July morning and I'd tied my velvet-soft Irish sack across my chest as I'd always done when cycling to Barnes. I already knew that the Slough delivery postmen carried their mail in a brown pouch with a broad shoulder strap, but I was still at my non-conformist stage.

A postman was to train me for a week. His name was Mr Khan (which was how he introduced himself to me) and he represented something else that was different about Slough: its diversity. Migrants had long been drawn to the town by the promise of jobs. In the 1930s the Welsh travelled down the Great West Road to find work there; when growth resumed after the Second World War they were joined by hundreds of Poles who had served in the British armed forces. Londoners migrated up the Great West Road to be rehoused in the new council homes, along with new arrivals from the Commonwealth – from the Indian subcontinent and the Caribbean – encouraged to come to the mother country by a British government facing a severe shortage of labour.

By 1968, there were 13,000 Asian people living in Slough, of whom Mr Khan was one. He was from what was then called East Pakistan (now Bangladesh). He'd been a teacher there and was determined to return to his profession once he'd retrained in England. He told me how he'd come to work as a postman temporarily to earn some money before taking up his studies. It was a tale I was to hear often at the Post Office: teachers, lawyers, university lecturers, even doctors and dentists, biding their time, trying to save up enough money to fund the courses they needed to obtain UK qualifications. It was a struggle, especially for those with relatives in their home countries who were relying on their financial support.

Some did complete the laborious process of requalifying, but the majority shelved their ambitions, stayed in the Post Office and eventually, through length of service, climbed from the lower ranks to become PHGs, then assistant inspectors, inspectors, assistant head postmasters and head postmasters – all grades that have gone now, as has the whole principle of promotion through seniority, which at least ensured some arbitrary advancement for long-term employees.

Today Mr Khan's job was to accompany me, as I mounted my red Post Office bike with its front pannier for the delivery pouch, and set off to ride the three miles back to the Britwell, where I'd just come from.

The delivery was easy enough with two of us to share the burden and not much harder the following week when I did it alone – up and down Long Readings Lane, in and out of Monksfield Way, with a few more streets spurring off the main route – all of it easily completed within the two and a half hours allotted. However, I hated having to push the bike around everywhere with me. Mr Khan had warned me not to risk leaving it anywhere and walking round. Apparently, a number of bicycles had been stolen on the Britwell.

Walking with a bike or riding it, I never seemed to be without one. I'd loved being a walking postman in Barnes. I detested being a bicycling postman in Slough. I cycled into town first thing in the morning, cycled back with the delivery, cycled round, cycled back. Cycled out with the second delivery, cycled round, cycled back. Cycled home on the Moulton. I was all cycled out.

I was never more exhausted than when I stumbled round those Britwell streets on 21 July 1969, just two weeks after we'd arrived in Slough and the day of my inaugural solo delivery. On this occasion the tiredness was self-inflicted. The USA had inconsiderately chosen the early hours of that morning to put the first man on the moon.

The previous day we had been to Tring for the christening of Linda and Mike's second daughter, Tara, travelling there and back on a green country bus (Mike had offered us a lift but we didn't want to drag him away from the celebrations). After we'd returned home and put the children to bed we took the TV up to bed with us, something we'd never done before, so as not to miss the moment when a human being first set foot on another planet. Along with 500 million others worldwide, we stayed awake long enough to see the flickering black-and-white images of Neil Armstrong's 'giant leap for mankind' just before 3am.

As I did my walk a few hours later TVs were still flickering in practically every house. Through the net curtains of Long Readings Lane I saw people gaping at the inconceivable: men cavorting on the surface of the moon. The only distraction was the rattle of their letterboxes as I reminded them about the everyday concerns of life on earth.

∼

The move to Slough was our chance to start a new life – and we took it, like fugitives adopting false identities. Nobody knew us, or had known us, despite the fact that the Britwell was full of west London families, from Ealing and Acton, Shepherd's Bush and Hammersmith, North Kensington and Paddington. The majority had come in the 1950s, when the estate had been built as part of the postwar effort to provide sufficient council housing to meet the huge demand. Neither of us had had all that many friends and acquaintances in Notting Hill. And nearly all of those we did have had, like us, been displaced by the remorseless advance of the A40 extension, most moving south-westwards, to a new estate in Roehampton.

Having been given this fresh slate, I didn't want anyone to know that I wasn't Natalie's biological father and Judy didn't want anyone to know that she had been pregnant when we married. So we moved the date of our marriage back a year and left a certain ambiguity around our association at the time of Natalie's birth in 1966. Our new back story was that I had fathered Natalie at the age of sixteen and married Judy at seventeen. In the period between these two events we'd lived together. Very cutting-edge 1960s. Not so much far out as a bit out – not so far out that we couldn't get back again.

In the big old houses and crowded streets of Notting Hill it had been easier to remain anonymous. Here the ten homes around the green were grouped in an L shape with us in the corner. Our neighbours had no alternative but to watch over our comings and goings as we watched over theirs.

Martin and Karen Saunders next door to us had two little girls of similar ages to Natalie and Emma. Our neighbours on the other side, at the end of the second row of houses – separated from us by a walkway to the concrete square of garages, which could be rented by residents for a modest sum – were Brenda and Tony Gabriel, who also had two children. Two doors down from them were Robert and Kathleen Metcalfe, who had a son and daughter, as did Mick and Susan Pearson next door to them. A settlement of nuclear families: Dad, Mum and the requisite number of kids.

Martin Saunders was posh. That is to say he spoke the Queen's English and wore a suit for work. He was a salesman for a car components manufacturer. Karen was from the Mozart estate in Paddington – like Judy, a girl from a poor background who'd done well at school. I think she and Martin had met at university.

Tony, a painter and decorator, had a chunky build that belied his high-pitched voice. He had the street style of a minor gangster. His wife, Brenda, was a stunning beauty who dressed in the glamorous clothes she helped to sell from the ladieswear shop where she worked on the Farnham Road. Tony and Brenda were the Len Fairclough and Elsie Tanner of the green. They called each other 'babe' and danced together to the Platters in their front room when the children were in bed. At least, that's what they did once they were reconciled after one of their many arguments. The pattern of their lives was roughly two months reconciling to every month of arguing.

Robert Metcalfe, a big, genial man with big, dark eyes that lent him a Mediterranean appearance, a broad smile and thinning hair, was a grafter, working mostly as a lorry driver but willing to try his hand at anything that turned a penny. Kathleen, a pretty Irishwoman, had come to England as a youngster.

Slim, attractive redhead Susan Pearson spent her days stitching and sewing at an old Singer machine in a corner of her living room, doing piecework for a variety of employers. While she worked she listened to Radio 4. As a fellow Radio 4 enthusiast, I envied her constant access to its delights: from *Today* in the morning to the *Afternoon Play*. The end of the play was her cue to go and pick up her kids from school.

Her husband Mick was what was known then as an ambulanceman. Today he'd be a paramedic. He'd had a troubled childhood: he and his brother had spent most of it in a children's home, escaping a father who was a violent drunk and a mother who found it difficult to cope. He was highly intelligent and very funny but constantly unfulfilled in his working life. The ambulance job was the one he did for the majority of the ten years in which I knew him well, but he had a whole series of them, including factory worker, labourer and baggage-handler at Heathrow airport.

We were of course also acquainted with the people living in the other five houses round the green but these were the neighbours we befriended; the ones with whom we shared our revised chronology. This kind of married couples' social circle was new to Judy and me. My sister, who had always been far more outgoing than I was, had more experience of the pitfalls as well as the pleasures of such relationships. I remember Linda and Mike coming over to see us not long after we'd moved in to Long Furlong Drive. They found the Saunders in our kitchen when they arrived and we wandered in and out of their house next door as the day progressed.

I'd told Linda about our little deceit, of which she fully approved. When we found ourselves alone in the kitchen she warned me not to be tempted by friendship into revealing the truth. She knew how important it was to me that Natalie was seen as belonging to us both. I fully intended to adopt her once she was old enough to have Judy's relationship with her biological father explained to her. Natalie could then make the decision as to whether or not she wanted me to assume legal paternity.

Linda issued a word of warning. 'People become friends and just as easily cease to be friends and turn into enemies,' she said. Judy, she pointed out, was the one who would be vulnerable to nasty comments if we ever fell out with our neighbours. She urged me never to let my guard slip.

It was good advice. Married father of two I may have been, but my sister was still looking after my interests.

Chapter 6

As my old bandmate Sham had cautioned when encouraging me to become a postman, the only way to earn a decent wage was either to get a second job (half the taxi drivers in London had apparently done 'the Knowledge' while working for the Post Office) or to take advantage of the abundance of overtime generated by the perennial shortage of staff.

So I worked the 'docket', so-called because of the piece of paper we carried with the overtime for each day itemized and authorized by the initials of a supervisor. I spent as much time as possible on the 'Davy Crockett'. That fountain of extra earnings nourished my children, but it also deprived me of seeing as much of their childhood as I wanted to. They were still sound asleep when I left for work before 5am and back in bed by the time I returned at 7.30 in the evening. I remember once asking a postman who was leaving how long he'd worked at Slough sorting office. His answer was five years, nine if you counted the overtime. It was an accurate reflection of the double shifts we were working. Every morning, Monday to Saturday, I toiled on that bloody red bike. On weekday afternoons I did overtime at the parcels depot in Oxford Avenue on the trading estate.

We were also contracted to work one Sunday in six. Often I volunteered to take somebody else's shift: all Sunday overtime was paid at double time and was pensionable (not that I was even mildly interested in pensionability at that stage of my life). During the week the first six hours of overtime were paid at time and a quarter, the next six at time and a half. From the thirteenth hour double time kicked in – a curious built-in incentive to work long hours.

I envied the men who didn't do overtime and were able to head home at lunchtime every day. Most of us had no choice but to work on. I certainly hadn't, with a wife and two children to support and a basic wage that, even with my preserved London weighting, was below the maximum for the job and well below the national average. There was even the odd occasion when I'd work a 'ghoster' (filling in for a night worker on a Friday, when there was a tendency for the night men to 'blow out'). This involved working as normal until lunchtime on Friday, then taking a few hours off to rest before going back in at about 8pm to work right through to the completion of my delivery on Saturday. I swear that I once delivered all the mail in Pipers Close in Burnham while sleepwalking.

It was Burnham, though, that offered escape from the exhausting regime of cycling back and forth as part of my fifteen-hour working day. A couple of months after my transfer, a poster appeared on the sorting-office noticeboard calling for applications for a new national experiment: delivery by moped.

The tiny, ramshackle sorting office in Burnham, Buckinghamshire, a village that was expanding into a town just along the Lower Britwell Road from where we lived, was being repatriated to Slough, its parent office. Volunteers were invited to sign up for one of its eight deliveries. The duty would be fixed and therefore outside the normal rotations (usually two earlies and one late turn). The successful candidates would do the same Burnham delivery week in, week out.

A regular walk, no shifts and, best of all, no bike: for me Burnham was a godsend. The deliveries were heavy, but I didn't care about that. Becoming a Burnham postman in October 1969 restored my pride and satisfaction in my chosen occupation. It was like going back to Barnes. We even had the old-style delivery frame, with a box for each street, rather than the new whizzy Portobello racks that had been introduced in Slough (so called because they'd been trialled in the Portobello district of Edinburgh, not the more familiar Portobello Road of my childhood) and looked more like the 45rpm disc-holders in the record shops.

There was only one problem. In anticipation of having a Post Office moped that I could use, either officially or unofficially, to get to and from work, we had jumped the gun by selling Judy's Moulton.

I discovered that until the brand-new Raleigh runabout mopeds arrived, Burnham postmen were to be taken in a van from the Slough sorting office to the little telephone exchange at the top of the High Street, where the pushbikes required to carry them onwards to their respective walks would be stored. To my joy, I managed to nab the walk that began and ended at the telephone exchange and therefore didn't need a bike. But for a while I was still going to need transport between Britwell and Slough.

The cavalry arrived in the shape of another Burnham

postman, Tommy Chessman, and his Reliant Regal. Tommy had spent over twenty years as a bandsman – a trumpeter – in the army before taking the well-trodden path from the forces to the Post Office at about the same time as I'd joined in 1968. He was a small, nippy kind of chap; eternally cheerful, with an unwavering generosity of spirit. He and his wife rented a large, ancient cottage in the rural tranquillity of Lower Britwell Road, a ten-minute walk from our house.

Tommy had been based at Burnham but had moved to Slough with the mail. Now that he had to report to work there, Long Furlong Drive was on his way and he offered to pick me up at 5.15 every morning in his three-wheeler. This fibreglass beauty was Tom's little eccentricity. On those journeys to Slough he would regale me with details of the savings he made on petrol, maintenance and road tax, merely, in essence, by sacrificing a wheel.

Some mornings Tom's kindness had to be extended to the task of waking me up – a particular problem on Saturdays if I'd been for a few pints the night before with one of my new friends and neighbours around the green. Judy and I slept in the front bedroom and Tom would throw small pebbles at our window to avoid disturbing anyone else's rest by banging on the door. He was admirably persistent, patiently throwing as many stones as it took. Once I'd signalled that I was awake and getting dressed, he'd wait in the car while I pulled on my uniform and stumbled out into the cold, black pre-dawn.

At long last the mopeds arrived, done out in gleaming red livery with the royal crest on each leg guard. I was furnished with a provisional driving licence in a small burgundy booklet. At a glance it looked exactly the same as a full driving licence.

The only difference was that the specifications of the type of vehicle it licensed me to drive were printed inside in red rather than black. As long as I had L-plates fitted front and back and a couple of hours' instruction, I had the freedom of the highway. The equipment we had was the same as that given to the telegram boys, who rode proper motorbikes to deliver the urgent messages telegraphed from afar. But while they were roaring around on 175cc BSA Bantams, we plodded along on machines only marginally more powerful than a lawnmower.

I'd leave the sorting office with two pouches strapped to the carrier at the back of the moped and one across my chest. On would go the white peaked crash helmet, the brown PVC mock-leather jerkin (over my long Post Office double-breasted coat), the enormous fluorescent gauntlets and a small pair of round goggles. In Burnham I parked the moped behind a block of sheltered accommodation at the near end of Dropmore Road, leaving two pouches full of mail on the bike while I delivered the contents of the third on foot, in a circle that brought me back to the bike. Then I'd set off down Dropmore Road with a pouch on each shoulder, finishing my figure-of-eight walk back at the moped. Though it wasn't secured, the bike was never stolen; neither was any of the mail or my motorcycling gear, which I left on the carrier while I did my two-and-a-half-hour delivery.

The second delivery later in the morning combined most of the earlier walk with Burnham High Street. Because of the volume of mail destined for the High Street, home to businesses such as A.C. Frost, the estate agent, and Buck's Die Casting at the end of an alleyway off the main road, it received its heavier first post by van.

It must have been against the rules to take my moped home and, guessing what the response was likely to be if I asked, I never sought permission to do so. There again, nobody ever issued any kind of proclamation forbidding it, either. I usually managed to make it back to Long Furlong Drive at lunchtime to watch *The Herbs*, *Trumpton* or *Mary, Mungo and Midge* with Natalie and Emma, who didn't seem to enjoy it as much as I did (I was particularly fond of the officious Constable Knapweed in *The Herbs*, who kept law and order and 'watched to see that all was well along the garden border').

At 2pm I'd report for overtime at Oxford Avenue, where parcels were sorted and dispatched entirely by hand. The parcels would arrive at one end of the building to be unloaded into wheeled wicker skips and taken on to 'roads' to be sorted, emerging at the other end for dispatch. Having been allocated a road, my job was to fetch the skips of parcels and sort them by throwing them into the appropriate sack (accuracy was important, delicacy wasn't). When a sack was full I'd tie it, attach a label indicating where it was going and secure it with a lead seal by means of an iron sealer, like a massive pair of pliers. It was very satisfying to feel the lead yielding to the crushing grip of the sealer. I kept the seals – and, later, the thin aluminium clips that replaced them – in a bag velcroed round my waist. The secured bag would be hurled into one of the wheeled conveyors at the end of the road, which would be periodically rolled away by the dispatch drivers who loaded the bags on to the 600cf vans that were, at that time, the biggest used, and whisked them away to Slough Station, Reading or the big London parcels offices.

Oxford Avenue was hard, gruelling, dirty work. The dust

from the mail sacks permeated everything and made us filthy by the end of the shift. Some of the men wore dustcoats but the emphasis was on speed, which could be hampered by extra layers of clothing. We'd stop for a cup of tea at 3pm and take an hour's break between 4.30 and 5.30 ahead of the main dispatch, handled on a 'finish and go' basis. Usually we'd get away by 7pm, an hour before our shift was due to end. The rest breaks were enlivened by card schools and darts matches. Once I'd overcome my initial shyness I was soon joining in, acquiring my own set of darts and a disturbing taste for poker and three-card brag. Fortunately, we only gambled for shillings and pence.

There were around thirty men in all working the shifts at Oxford Avenue, including the supervisor, a couple of PHGs and Jimmy Hill, whose sole occupation (as Reg's had been at Barnes) was to run the canteen. A few of them were based there permanently, men who had forsaken the fresh air of early-morning deliveries for the dusty confines of the parcels depot. It wouldn't have been my choice, but some of them preferred it to the early starts and all the cycling. Among the Oxford Avenue crew was 'Pat' Paternoster, the unofficial foreman and one of the hardest workers I'd ever seen. Pat was lean and fit, his checked shirtsleeves always rolled up to the elbow, exposing muscular forearms. Though not an unsociable character, he never joined the card schools or darts teams. He was a man in perpetual motion, gulping down his tea in a couple of minutes and constantly on the lookout for tasks to keep him busy, even if it was just tidying the skips or sweeping the floor (a largely vain pursuit at Oxford Avenue).

Pat wasn't a conversationalist but over the years I worked

with him I discovered his motivation. He was determined that his children would go to university and every spare copper he made was channelled into that ambition. It wasn't a unique aspiration but it was rare among working-class men born in an era when only a tiny elite, 3 or 4 per cent of the population, went into higher education, and almost all of them were from public schools. It was as if every parcel Pat sorted, every bag he hefted on to the back of a van, every load he dragged across the parcel-office floor would bring him closer to his goal. I've never seen a smile as broad as Pat's when he told me some years later that his eldest daughter had been accepted at Cambridge.

John Esposito was another Oxford Avenue regular, a PHG from the Britwell who'd fought at Monte Cassino and was renowned for his ability to get anything anyone wanted discounted and sold from the boot of his car. John never stopped talking in his high-pitched voice, like a garrulous castrato. Before transferring from London he'd been a CCS driver. It was Central Control Services that provided the men who drove the mail across London, between the stations and out to the provinces. Unusually for the way the Post Office operated at that time, these men did nothing but drive. They certainly didn't demean themselves by helping to unload. They enjoyed some of the best terms and conditions in the organization thanks to the industrial muscle they wielded. If the handful of men at CCS were to walk out the mail network would grind to a halt.

And there was Bill Pickley, who always wore the regulation brown dustcoat over his immaculate clothes. Bill was a short man with a small, beautifully maintained 'tache that looked as if it had been painted under his nose. I was a great admirer of

Bill's style. Every day he'd walk into the gritty environs of Oxford Avenue for all the world as if he were a stockbroker arriving in the City: dazzling white shirt, dark tie and elegant suit, his shoes so highly polished they could have been used to see the cards his opponents were holding during the tea breaks had he chosen to use them for such a purpose.

Every Friday I trudged home from Oxford Avenue with my wages, in cash, contained in a sealed brown envelope with holes in the side that provided a comforting glimpse of the earnings within. With the children in bed and *Dad's Army* playing on the black-and-white TV in the corner of our front room, we'd sit down to allocate our resources and I'd tot up the overtime docket to be handed in the next morning for payment the following week.

As the 1960s drew to a close Judy and I were settled in our new surroundings. She had quickly immersed herself in the Britwell community, helping to set up a playgroup for toddlers in Wentworth Avenue. I'd joined Slough library, where I graduated from reading up on modern history to books on political theory, interspersed with the novels I preferred and read for pleasure rather than instruction.

Christmas 1969 was, in effect, our first together as Judy had been in hospital the previous year giving birth to Emma. On Christmas Eve, as she would do every year, she went to the midnight service at St George's Church, opposite our green on Long Furlong Drive. Recently built, it boasted a metal sculpture of St George slaying the dragon above the entrance. I would never darken its doorstep. Having come to the conclusion early in my teens that I was an atheist, nothing I learned or that happened to me subsequently changed my mind. However, I always admired and respected the community activists who worked with Judy and whose prime motivation was a deep and unwavering faith.

I remained as fresh-faced at nineteen as I'd been at nine, so when Judy bought me my first razor for Christmas (along with a psychedelic folk album by the Incredible String Band, *The 5000 Spirits or the Layers of the Onion* – I confess to a short flirtation with hippydom in those Flower Power days at the tail end of the sixties) there was no real use for it. None the less I rushed into the bathroom to shave with it on Christmas morning. When I came downstairs, rubbing my chin in a manly kind of way and professing to having had a 'great shave', Judy inquired whether I'd managed to get the blade in all right. I told her there had already been a blade in the razor. She informed me rather tartly that it was a dummy made of cardboard for display purposes only. It had felt fine to me.

And so my teens petered out with that momentous decade, not with a bang, but with a whimper. Even before I turned twenty, I found myself, overnight, officially an adult when the change in the law that lowered the age of majority from twenty-one to eighteen came into force on the first day of the 1970s.

The Labour government that had been in power since 1964 had steered through a good deal of groundbreaking legislation that reflected the dramatic social shifts of the 1960s. Laws had been enacted to protect ethnic minorities from racial discrimination and the kind of abuse encouraged by Oswald Mosley as he stood on a soapbox at the corner of my street in the 1950s; homosexuality had been decriminalized, capital punishment abolished, abortion legalized. Women were beginning to assert their right to equal treatment.

Even the Post Office had been revolutionized. The Post Office Act of 1969 changed it from a government department to a statutory corporation. The powers of the postmaster general were transferred to a new Cabinet position, the minister of posts and telecommunications, and within the corporation the office was replaced by a chairman and chief executive. As part of the transformation telecommunications were split from postal services. It was one of the biggest shake-ups of the Post Office since its inception. I remember being very much aware of its historical significance when I returned to the sorting office at the end of my last shift as a civil servant.

What I can't remember is any defining moment when I became politically aware. Can anyone? Is there ever an epiphany, a single event that separates the pre-political from the post-political? Perhaps university students could pin it down to joining a political society or studying politics as part of their degree course. For most of us it is a gradual development, directed to begin with by our perceptions and experiences of our own worlds.

At my school, Sloane Grammar, Mr Pallai, who'd fled his native Hungary as the Russian tanks rolled in, had integrated a bit of politics into his history and economics lessons, talking to us about why he had left his country. He told us that he was a socialist, but not a communist, and explained the difference. He would take groups of sixth-formers to the House of Commons. As I was long gone before the sixth form I missed out on those political field trips but I do remember Mr Pallai telling us younger pupils about Harold Wilson's photographic memory and how he displayed it to good effect against Ted Heath at Prime Minister's Questions.

Mr Smith had denounced apartheid in South Africa during our religious education lessons and my favourite teacher, Mr Carlen, had managed to get over thirty boys in his English class to read *Animal Farm* while he deconstructed the subtext to reveal Orwell's critique of the Russian Revolution.

I'd lived through the Cuban missile crisis, without knowing much about it, as mankind teetered on the brink of nuclear war and, like everyone else, I saw the world as being divided between capitalism and communism. I found myself in one half and was keen to understand the other. Mr Pallai and Mr Carlen weren't around to guide me any more, though Mr Carlen had sparked an enthusiasm for the work of George Orwell that led me to read almost everything Orwell had written by the time I was in my mid-twenties. While my admiration for Mike, my brother-in-law, knew no bounds, his working-class conservatism seemed dull and stunted, part of an era that was disappearing in the 'white heat' of Harold Wilson's revolutionary new age. Neither did Mike's benign view of the benefits of capitalism chime with my brief experience of living under it. Thus my political consciousness evolved from the books I borrowed from Slough library and from society as I experienced it on the Britwell estate and at Slough sorting office.

The impact of the swinging sixties on the Britwell had been limited. The 'Keep Britwell White' graffito still screamed its ignorant defiance and the estate was indeed still an all-white enclave. But this bigoted racism would be hard to sustain in a town where the growing Asian population was introducing enterprise and aspiration. At work, while brown and white mixed happily on the sorting-office floor they never sat together in the canteen, although come to think of it, neither did the postmen and the telephone engineers, who also colonized separate bits of the enormous 'staff restaurant'. Although the Post Office and Post Office Telecommunications were now separate entities, we continued to share the canteen, as well as the sports and social club with its snooker room and table-tennis tables.

As for gender equality, there still wasn't a single woman working in the sorting office other than at Christmas, when the casuals came. There were no female telephone engineers, either. Difficult though it is to imagine this now, even telephonists were subject to strict segregation. Only women could be telephonists on the day shift and only men could work nights. This practice continued until the Equal Opportunities Act became law in the mid-1970s.

As we entered the new decade, the seeds were being sown for two very different events that would mark it indelibly for me. As Judy and I were deciding that we'd like another child, pressure was building that would explode in another, far more serious, Post Office strike.

Chapter 7

I KNEW THERE WAS trouble brewing between my employer and my union in late 1970 when we were asked by the UPW to down tools in a token stoppage supporting the chairman of the Post Office, who'd just been sacked. Lord Hall was the first chairman of the newly created public corporation, which was supposed to have been removed from government control when it took us workers out of the civil service. Yet the new minister of posts and telecommunications – as it happened, the former postmaster general John Stonehouse – still had the power to hire and fire the chairman.

I knew nothing about Lord Hall then and little more now. His dismissal in November 1970 was seen as an attempt by a newly elected Conservative government to remove a chairman considered too sympathetic to the workforce. So, at the behest of the UPW, we went to the canteen for a couple of hours on what must have been one of the few occasions when a union took industrial action in support of a corporation's boss.

The Labour government that had been in office for the best part of six years had been ousted by the Conservatives barely six months into the new decade. In the June general election I'd walked across to the church hall next to St George's to cast my vote for the first time. Half of the Britwell was in the Beaconsfield constituency, which Labour would never win, and half in Eton and Slough. With my assistance, Labour held Eton and Slough: Joan Lester, our copper-haired, highly rated Labour MP, was re-elected. Britwell's Labour allegiance helped to keep the red flag flying incongruously over Eton until a boundary change transferred the little town dominated by its famous public school to the Windsor constituency.

Labour won Slough but lost the country. With the Tories, led by Edward Heath, in office, one aspect of the swirl of events propelling us towards industrial conflict was the determination of the incoming government to tame the trade-union movement through a national industrial relations court.

The UPW put in a wage claim for a 15 per cent pay increase and a reduction in the incremental scales that were keeping me and others like me on a lower wage purely on the basis of age. The Post Office offered 7 per cent. The two sides were on a collision course.

Our UPW branch secretary in Slough was Len Rigby, a Welshman with a real talent for clear and, when necessary, fiery rhetoric. What Len lacked in height he made up for in Celtic charisma. While I heard my workmates moan about the union nationally, I rarely heard a word said against Len. He'd been the secretary of the branch for as long as anyone could remember. Despite being a PHG, and therefore able to start work at a more civilized hour than us delivery postmen, he would come in early every day and strut around the delivery frames, a cigarette held aloft to one side of his face in debonair fashion, in the manner of Noël Coward. And, yes, he did strut, chest puffed out like a courting pigeon – but his air of pomposity was easily punctured. Len could self-efface but he was perfectly willing for someone to do the effacing for him.

Nobby Deadman, a big ex-soldier from the Britwell with the deep voice of a radio presenter and the looks of a film star, performed a little ritual with Len at least once a week. As Len strutted around the rural delivery frames where Nobby worked, a mock argument would break out. Len would threaten to beat up big Nobby, whereupon Nobby would pick Len up in his arms as if he were a baby, date-stamp his forehead and place him in a skip for outward dispatch. It was a show the audience never tired of.

But everyone knew when Len was being serious. In the run-up to Christmas 1970, he sought permission from the supervisors to hold an impromptu union meeting at around 6am, just after the inward sorting had been completed. He was helped up on to a rickety table, from which he addressed the 200-odd early-shift postmen who gathered round. In his most mellifluous *Under Milk Wood* voice, he conveyed the news from union headquarters with a flourish at the end designed to stiffen our resolve for the struggle ahead. 'My advice to you is to work all the hours you can over Christmas because there is a battle approaching the like of which we've never seen in the long and noble history of the Post Office. It might be a long time before you're able to earn any money again.'

The meeting ended with Len receiving a rousing cheer. In truth we didn't expect to have to go on strike. There would be a deal, some kind of compromise. There always was.

While the possibility of a strike was, of course, a concern that Christmas, it took a back seat to a more important and joyous event: the birth of our third child. Jamie was born at home on 10 January 1971. We'd chosen the name as a male alternative when Judy was pregnant with Emma after seeing an awful sixties comedy at the Odeon in Hammersmith, *Here We Go Round the Mulberry Bush*, memorable only for its soundtrack (provided mainly by Traffic, featuring the impossibly talented teenager Stevie Winwood). The lead character, played by Barry Evans, was called Jamie. We might not have liked the film but we liked the name, and firmly insisted that our son's birth certificate recorded it as Jamie, not James.

At that time the NHS was having a drive to increase the number of home births. Judy was keen to play her part and our front bedroom became a labour ward with a midwife and a nurse/assistant in attendance. They made it clear that my presence would be unwelcome and, truth to tell, I wasn't desperate to persuade them to change their minds.

I did pop my head round the door occasionally to deliver tea and platitudes but I spent most of that long night sitting downstairs, on the little two-seater sofa we'd picked up in a second-hand furniture shop in the Portobello Road, while the drama unfolded in the room above me.

Jamie arrived into the world exactly as I had in 1950, with the umbilical cord wrapped around his neck. Judy told me later how calm and collected the midwife had been as she skilfully prevented our son from strangling himself on his first appearance. Having been told the baby was a boy I resumed my seat downstairs and wrote a song in his honour. The first verse ran:

> Welcome to your first day, my son.
> Now your journey really has begun

I really hope you like it on the train.
You'll never see that waiting room again.

The next day was Judy's twenty-fifth birthday. I stayed at home to look after the girls, who'd slept through the excitement of the previous night, wandering into our bedroom to examine the wonder of a new baby brother in the grey dawn of a winter's day.

Needless to say, paternity leave did not exist in those days. However, I was soon to be provided with seven weeks of it courtesy of the Union of Post Office Workers.

~

The industrial action of 1971 was the first all-out Post Office strike involving all grades across the country in the union's history. There hadn't been a vote on whether to strike. The union's rules gave the executive council complete discretion in such matters. Had a ballot taken place I have no doubt that there would have been an overwhelming majority for the action we were now taking.

There was a deep-seated grievance about pay and, now that we were no longer civil servants, it was felt that we had to assert ourselves in the new commercial environment we had been forced to enter. We were incensed by the Post Office's use of average earnings figures – which of course included a lot of overtime – to describe our wages, given that the real problem was basic pay. The only reason overtime was available to boost low pay was because, in London and the south-east in particular, the basic wages weren't sufficient to attract enough staff.

This issue alone convinced me of the justice of our case, even without taking into account the burning resentment I felt about the other bone of contention, the incremental scales. At that time a postman over the age of twenty-four started on around £18 a week (the union's claim was for another £3), while my wages, as a twenty-year-old with over two years' service, were only £12 10s.

On 26 January, a week after the strike began, I was to be found amid a long line of men at Crown Buildings on the corner of Farnham Road, opposite the Three Tuns. There were hundreds of us there, from Slough, Windsor, Maidenhead and elsewhere in Bucks and Berks, divided into three groups according to the initial of our surname. We were waiting our turn to have our entitlement to benefits assessed by social security. The irony of Post Office workers queuing to be served escaped me at the time.

As we shuffled slowly forward, the banter was entertaining and spirits were high. Like infantrymen in the First World War thinking it would all be over by Christmas, we were convinced that victory would be ours within a couple of weeks. The men around me talked of the arrangements they were making to see out the strike. Many of my workmates had secured part-time jobs working for cash in hand as drivers or labourers or factory hands on the trading estate. Others complained about not being allowed overdraft facilities by Girobank, the Post Office bank established a couple of years before. I learned that Sid Rockall (known as Smokey because of the cigarette lodged permanently in the corner of his mouth) had been stocking up food in something called a freezer. It was the first time I'd ever heard of such a state-of-the-art appliance. Judy and I didn't even have a fridge.

Despite the good-humoured bravado, being involved in an all-out strike with no end in prospect was terrifying. At that time striking workers could claim benefits but only for their dependants, not for themselves. Many of the men waiting at Crown Buildings knew they would receive nothing but felt it was worth hearing it from the horse's mouth just to be sure.

When I reached the front of my queue the middle-aged social security officer I encountered there took one look at the fresh-faced youth standing in front of her and waved me away. 'I'm sorry, young man,' she said, removing her glasses for emphasis. 'Benefits can only be claimed for dependants. The person on strike isn't entitled to anything.'

'I know,' I protested. 'I'm married and my wife isn't working because she's just given birth to our third child.'

A long interrogation followed during which the children's birth certificates were produced (with no access to my Post Office moped for the duration I'd had to walk to the registrar's office in Burnham on the first day of the strike to record Jamie's arrival), marital status was proven and calculations were made. It emerged that I was entitled to benefits of £12 17s 6d a week. The state had decided that for my family alone, I should be receiving 7s 6d more than my basic Post Office wage. In theory I was earning more for being on strike than I would have made at work (although of course, without overtime and various allowances, in practice we were much worse off). The clerk continued to glare at me suspiciously as I made off with the paperwork I needed to claim the cash.

The strike lasted for seven weeks, from deepest winter until early spring.

We thought that postal services were essential but we

discovered they weren't. The Post Office services that were deemed vital had been maintained by the union, so our counter clerks reported for work on Thursdays to pay out pensions, which could only be obtained across a Post Office counter, and postmen went in to deliver blood donor cards and urgent medical supplies.

Although the telephonists, who were also members of our union, were part of the pay claim and involved in the strike, a substantial minority continued to work. Younger telephonists were strong supporters of the action, older women less so. This wasn't surprising given that incremental scales were much worse for telephonists than for postmen. While I would not reach the threshold for maximum wages until I was twenty-four, their wait was seven years longer. But the need for large numbers of telephonists to route calls had been melting away rapidly since the introduction ten years earlier of subscriber trunk dialling (STD), which enabled callers to dial direct. It was said even then that if STD hadn't been developed, every working woman in Britain would have had to become a telephonist to cope with demand.

Few postmen broke the strike nationally and none did in Slough. I can't pretend to have been the most active striker. It was a formative period of my life and it left a deep impression but it didn't nourish an all-consuming passion for conflict. I did stand on our picket line at the gates of the Wellington Street site a few times. It was all very British and terribly polite. As the telephonists who were breaking the strike walked past we'd smile and wish each other good morning. The nine or ten pickets on duty would have been embarrassed to shout slogans so we exchanged pleasantries instead. Many telephonists were married to postmen. One guy used to drop his strike-breaking wife at the gate, park his car and then join us on the picket line.

Every week a union rally would be held in Hyde Park in London. These were huge affairs. We'd travel there in forty-seater coaches with music blaring out to keep us entertained. We youngsters (a minority contingent) would sing along to records like 'Ride a White Swan' by T Rex while being good-humouredly barracked by the old boys (the men in their forties) waiting to hear Jimmy Young on Radio 2. I would wear my pride and joy, a long blue overcoat with wide lapels.

In the early days there would be three coachloads of us marching behind our branch banner but the numbers dwindled as the weeks went by. The London UPW branches were always at the front of the procession down Oxford Street, which meant that by the time we reached Hyde Park we would be too far away from the stage to hear very much of what the speakers were saying.

There was a little group of us youngsters, postmen and telephonists, who hung around together, and we'd be lobbied by far-left sects like Red Mole or the International Socialists, who handed out bloodcurdling leaflets and magazines in a bid to recruit us as cannon fodder in the class war.

We were certainly being radicalized by the strike but never to the extent of being impressed by these college kids from middle-class backgrounds seeking to express their solidarity with the workers. Quite apart from their humourless hectoring, they dressed scruffy but talked posh. We dressed posh but talked scruffy. We knew that their interest in us was fleeting.

At that time there was another dispute going on involving college lecturers, who were pursuing some esoteric issue concerning their contracts. Sometimes our long column of marching Post Office workers crossed their much smaller demonstration. Whereas we had a clear objective ('What do we want? Three quid!'), theirs was more opaque. Their banners read: 'Rectify the Anomaly'. Very much an academic dispute.

Most of the news we received about the progress of the strike came from our own weekly meeting in the community centre on Farnham Road. Every Tuesday morning at 9.45 I'd be waiting, gloved and scarfed against the bitter winter weather, for Tommy Chessman to pick me up in his Reliant Regal, just as he'd done to take me to work before I'd acquired the Post Office moped.

Like many ex-servicemen, Tommy was a surprisingly strong supporter of industrial action. Loyalty to the union in a dispute was, I suppose, similar to loyalty to the nation during conflict. In common with the majority of my workmates, he had nothing but his savings and his wife's income from a part-time job to sustain him. But he maintained a cheery optimism that was infectious.

With 200,000 members involved, and subscriptions suspended, the UPW was never going to be able to afford strike pay. It had dispensed with its strike fund many years before when it had been decided that a sophisticated system of conciliation and arbitration was a better way of resolving disputes.

When the strike began the union had established a hardship fund with £100,000 from their coffers supplemented by donations from other unions who saw our dispute as critical to winning the wider arguments with Heath's new Conservative government and its plans to subdue the trade-union movement. We were often described as the thin red line hold-ing back the enemy.

With my £12 17s 6d a week from social security I had no right to money from the fund. Tommy was too proud to apply. Those who did had to give personal details of their finances (and their lives) to a small committee of local branch repre-sentatives whose decision was final. The hardship fund caused seething resentment as stories were recounted (exaggerated with each retelling) of those who 'qualified' compared with those who hadn't and the weekly meetings at the community centre spent more time dealing with vocal indignation about this money than it did on keeping us informed on how negotiations to resolve the dispute were going. Most of us thought we'd be better off as a union without this divisive national fund, which soon ran out anyway.

None of this affected the popularity of our inspirational branch secretary Len Rigby, who wisely delegated responsibility for allocating Slough's portion of the fund to our treasurer. Indeed his reputation was enhanced as he organized the weekly meetings, led the picketing and arranged the coach trips to London as well as being the face of the strike in the local media and appearing at endless fund-raising public meetings around the Thames Valley. At those community centre gatherings he assumed his richest baritone to stress the inevitability of our eventual victory. But his job became increasingly difficult as the weeks went by and various negotiating initiatives came and went with no progress made.

One freezing Tuesday, Tommy and I arrived to find a national officer of the UPW there to address us. It was none other than Dickie Lawlor, the London official who'd come to

Barnes to inform us of the one-day strike in support of the overseas telegraph officers. By now Dickie had risen to the rank of assistant general secretary, a paid employee of the UPW. With the membership's initial enthusiasm for the strike gradually ebbing away, he was touring the country with his fellow officers to bolster our resolve and lift our morale.

Dickie was a card-carrying member of the Communist Party of Great Britain, a political institution that was fading as its adherents grew older and it failed to find new recruits even among the radical younger generation of the late sixties. The debate on the left was still about reform versus revolution. Those who supported reform had consistently shunned communism, with its suppression of religion and of other political parties and its contempt for parliamentary democracy. The revolutionaries, on the other hand, saw the Communist party as either too timid (for the supporters of Trotsky) or too tarnished (for those horrified by revelations about Stalin and events in Hungary in the 1950s and Czechoslovakia more recently). Their strongest presence was in the trade-union movement but it was not significant in the UPW, a union founded by guild socialists and solid supporters of the Labour leadership. Dickie was the most notable communist figure.

After some preliminary discussions, mainly about the vexed issue of the hardship fund, Len Rigby introduced our illustrious visitor, who strode to the front of the stage. He was a sturdy, thickset man with close-cropped hair that on somebody younger would have been described as a crew cut. Cigarette smoke rose in a blue haze and hung in the cold air above the hundred or so striking postal workers who'd turned up and were waiting to be inspired.

Dickie Lawlor was unapologetic about his politics. The government minister responsible for the Post Office was now Christopher Chataway, the former athlete who'd been Roger Bannister's pacemaker when he ran the first sub-four-minute mile in 1954. Dickie began by saying that his dislike for the minister had begun when Chataway beat Vladimir Kuts over 5,000 metres. Apparently I was the only one in the audience who failed to understand the joke. Tommy Chessman whispered that Kuts was a great Russian athlete who'd been a rival of Chataway's in the 1950s.

The oration was impressive – a twenty-minute speech without notes delivered to a beguiled congregation. 'You are castigated because you've withdrawn your labour in pursuit of higher pay,' he told us in one memorable passage. 'But what does the capitalist do when he's not getting enough for his produce? He withdraws it from the market. The farmer destroys his apples, the factory owner slows production: they create a shortage so the price they receive goes up. You only have the sweat of your brow – your labour – and if you're not getting the right price for your labour, withdrawing it from the market is an entirely reasonable thing to do. You'll provide your labour again when the price is higher, exactly as the capitalist does. If it's acceptable for the bosses, why not for the workers?'

Lawlor went on to remind us of the validity of our claim and reassured us: 'Do not be concerned about the union's ability to finance this strike. This is a dispute about principles, not money. If we have to, we will sell union headquarters brick by brick until the battle is won and we return to work with our heads held high.'

In the Reliant on the way home Tommy Chessman enthused

about the speech we'd heard. I commented that I'd thought ex-servicemen, more than anyone, were fiercely anti-communist.

Tommy smiled. 'I am,' he said. 'But commies know what they're doing in a dispute. They won't give up easily and if we want to win we'll need their disciplined approach.'

Such was Tommy's cracker-barrel philosophy on the subject of communism. Dickie Lawlor's authority, though, was limited. He may have been a prominent officer in the union, but he wasn't our leader. That was Tom Jackson, a man who was to have a profound influence on my life.

Chapter 8

THE COMMENT MADE most often about the extravagantly bewhiskered general secretary of the UPW was that he was instantly recognizable. Tom Jackson's huge handlebar moustache lent him the air of a Battle of Britain pilot in the eyes of some; others remarked on his resemblance to the comedian Jimmy Edwards. He had grown it as a young man in an attempt to look older than he was in order to be taken more seriously by the managers with whom he negotiated.

Brought up by a single mother in a poor part of Leeds, Tom had left school at fourteen to become a telegram boy. After war service with the Navy he had returned to the Post Office as a postman, and then a PHG, rising simultaneously through the ranks of the union. Now, thanks to the strike, he was a national figure, featuring in the top story in the news most evenings as the nation coped with the protracted withdrawal of what was then its primary means of communication.

I knew very little about Tom or his background at the time but I remember warming to his personality – or to as much of it as was penetrable in his appearances on the little black-and-white TV, with its two channels, perched in the corner of our front room (BBC2 had been launched five years earlier but we couldn't pick it up until we could afford to buy a new set a few years later).

I liked the timbre of his voice, admired his eloquence and wondered how he could bear the strain of leading so many people through such a long dispute. There were many thousands of members with no income whatsoever, those with no dependants who couldn't find temporary work and couldn't access the by now dwindling resources of the hardship fund. Some of them also appeared on the national news, speaking of their determination to continue fighting for the £3 wage increase irrespective of whether they had to remortgage or even sell their houses.

In the early days of the strike Tom looked exuberant, eyes twinkling above the whiskers and a ready smile below. He displayed a cheerful reasonableness that must have done more for our public relations than a hundred press releases.

I recall how delighted I felt when Michael Barratt, who presented the current-affairs magazine programme *Nationwide* on the BBC every evening after the six o'clock news, told viewers that Tom Jackson was his friend; that he cooked wonderful meals for the Barratts in Brighton, where they were neighbours. Tom was not just our leader but a friend of TV stars.

That winter, *Nationwide* was followed on several evenings by a five-minute cartoon explaining 'decimalization'. On 15 February, a month after the strike began, the United Kingdom was to change its currency. Out went pounds, shillings and pence (twelve pence to a shilling, twenty shillings to a pound) and in came 'new pence', a hundred to a pound. The BBC had made a series of information films called *Decimal Five*, narrated by the newsreader Robert Dougall and leavened by songs from the Scaffold (the government also commissioned a dreadful record, 'Decimalisation', by Max Bygraves).

There were dire predictions of chaos on changeover day and, given the importance of the network of around 25,000 post offices in the planned exercise, not to mention the role of postal workers in delivering the explanatory leaflets, we strikers believed that Decimalization Day was one of our biggest weapons. Like Tom Jackson's twinkling eyes, our optimism shone brightly in the days leading up to 15 February and began to lose its sparkle as we realized that the new currency was bedding in nicely without our assistance.

The government had lifted the Post Office's statutory monopoly for the duration of the dispute and rival postal services were set up, charging 3s (now 15p) a letter at a time when a first-class stamp cost 2p. Whole sackloads of mail distributed by companies such as Randalls Postal Service were found dumped under hedges long after the dispute ended, but in spite of the lack of an effective replacement for our services, it was clear that the strike was failing.

∾

As I've mentioned, I could not have been described as an activist in the great 1971 strike. I did my bit, religiously attending the Farnham Road meetings every Tuesday, occasionally going to a Hyde Park rally; a smattering of picket duty. I can't pretend, either, that I used the time I had on my hands to toil over domestic chores in the Britwell house that was now home to two adults and three small children. Judy was coping with a newborn baby and two toddlers with minimal help from me. The changing of nappies was exclusively franchised to her without discussion or complaint. That kind of thing was (I'm embarrassed to say) considered to be the mother's responsibility. Judy prepared and cooked all the meals, cleaned the house and trudged to the row of shops on Wentworth Avenue that was already being deserted by those Britwell residents who had cars in favour of the shopping nirvana of Slough High Street or the supermarkets in Farnham Road.

We had no car and neither of us could drive. Come to think of it, as well as having no fridge, we had no washing machine, no vacuum cleaner and no phone, either. Judy washed the clothes by hand exactly as my mother had done, scrubbing the collars of my shirts against a washboard, squeezing as much water as possible out of each garment by brute force before hanging it on a clothes horse to dry in front of the fire.

It's not as if I can mitigate my appalling record of domestic inertia by claiming that I was any kind of handyman. It was Judy who changed the fuses and wired the plugs. I did once lay some awful sky-blue rubber floor tiles on the landing at the top of the stairs and I could wield a paintbrush when required. But there was no decorating done during the strike.

Our living conditions were a universe away from the slums of Southam Street where I'd spent my childhood but the memory of the tallyman and my mother's debts still haunted me. We were both terrified of debt. Judy had a similar aversion to the increasingly popular 'live now, pay later' philosophy and we elected to save up to buy what we needed. The order of the purchases we planned to make was agreed in advance, each to be saved for consecutively: a twin-tub washing machine was the priority.

In the days before disposables, nappies created a mountain of additional washing. Once the contents of the used nappy had been flushed away, both the terry towelling nappy and the muslin square placed beneath it next to the baby's skin would have to be subjected to a bleaching process involving buckets of Napisan and Milton sterilizing fluid, followed by a thorough wash to ensure that the baby's delicate skin wouldn't be burned when the clean nappy was reused.

A fridge and a Hoover were next on our wish list. We would be phoneless for another decade. In the meantime, our kitchen in 1971 was indistinguishable from how it might have looked in 1951. And as the long strike entered its sixth week, it seemed our saving regime would be suspended for some time yet.

I have two abiding memories of how I spent my time at home during those seven long weeks. The first is being around to enjoy the paternal privilege of putting Emma to bed in the evenings. She was two years old and would be settled down an hour before four-year-old Natalie in the room they shared. Working such long hours, in normal circumstances I was rarely there to play a part in her bedtime rituals but now, for almost two months, I was able to carry her upstairs at bedtime. I'd sing with Emma ('In a cottage in a wood, a little old man at the window stood') before reading her a story. Then I'd switch on Mr Moon (the cheery blue crescent-shaped night light fixed to the wall), give her a goodnight kiss and tuck her in. In the winter cold, an electric heater in the kids' room and a paraffin heater on the landing substituted for the central heating that was still years away. How I cherished those moments, lingering awhile to bask in the warmth of a father's love and absorb the scent of talcum powder, baby cream and small, clean child.

My other memory is of reading by the fire. When the washing wasn't in front of it, I was. All the living rooms on the Britwell, so far as I knew, were equipped with a Rayburn fire: a small iron stove with a slotted glass door. They were finished in a kind of spangled bronze. We had a coal shed in the back garden that would be filled up in the autumn by the coal merchant, who came with a lorry by then rather than in the horse and cart I remembered from my youth. The shed door was fitted with removable slats that could be taken out as the coal stock went down to make it easier to get at. The day's supply would be shovelled from the shed into a coal scuttle, carried inside and set down in the fireplace. Practically anything could be burned on a Rayburn. To eke out the coal supply Judy would use potato skins and other vegetable peelings as a fuel supplement, particularly overnight, when the stove just needed to be kept going. The thin walls allowed some heat to permeate the house from the fire, providing a kind of rudimentary coal-fired central heating that at least took the edge off the cold.

So when I wasn't watching *Nationwide* or *Decimal Five* on the TV, I would be sitting by the fire reading poetry and short stories, the strike having coincided with the onset of my Dylan Thomas phase. Just before we were called out I had borrowed two books from Slough library: *Collected Poems* and *Portrait of the Artist as a Young Dog*. I don't recall how I discovered Dylan. It was probably via Robert Zimmerman, who'd adopted the poet's name and whose songs had sparked my interest in poetry. It was, I concede, a poncey way to have been occupying myself but I never considered time spent reading any book to be time wasted.

In spite of the lack of assistance with her significant work-load, Judy read more voraciously than I did. She was an amazingly fast reader and no matter how tired she was she never went to sleep before propping herself up in bed for half an hour to read.

~

We were just about to board the coaches bound for another Hyde Park rally when news reached us that the strike was to be called off by the union's executive in exchange for a committee of inquiry. None the less we marched along Oxford Street loudly proclaiming our defiance: 'We ain't going back, we ain't going back, ee-aye-addio we ain't going back.'

The cry would prove to be as inaccurate as it was illiterate.

The Slough contingent was once again on the very edge of the Hyde Park crowd, with London workers at the front. We could just about make out the figure of Tom Jackson, elevated above the throng on a makeshift stage, sporting a trilby hat. He was flanked by members of his executive and officials of the London District Council, faces set like granite against the cold wind and the angry abuse being directed at them. Those of us at the back caught fragments of Tom's address as he shouted into an amplified loud-hailer, words carried to us like confetti on the currents of the freezing air.

'This . . . been . . . valiant . . . but . . . am not prepared . . . this . . . destroyed. Hardman . . . solution . . . Hardman . . . union . . . have our representative . . . committee.'

The committee of inquiry was to be led by a former senior civil servant, Henry Hardman. The union had nominated the vice-principal of Ruskin College, John Hughes, as our representative. This wasn't arbitration, a process that began with the union's claim and the Post Office's offer with the aim of reconciling them somewhere in the middle. All offers and demands were to be removed from the deliberations and Hardman would be starting from scratch, focusing on productivity as well as pay.

Our coachload of strikers grumbled about the union, Tom Jackson and the settlement all the way back to Slough. These dissenters were, in the main, the activists; not particularly politically motivated but with an allegiance to the union and the social solidarity it represented. And yet I sensed in their complaints a note of battle-weary relief that the strike was almost over.

While there had been no ballot before the strike was called, a cursory one was organized nationally before a return to work. Ours was held at Oxford Avenue: a workplace ballot. The result of each branch decision would be translated into a national vote. The result was overwhelmingly in favour of the executive council's recommendation to return to work.

I voted no. Given the anomaly that meant I was earning more than my basic pay while on strike, this may be unsurprising. Perhaps I was posturing, voting against because I knew the decision would be in favour of Hardman however I voted and it enabled me to claim some kind of moral superiority over my workmates. Maybe it was just that I was enjoying those magical evenings with Emma a little too much. Whatever my motivation, I didn't talk about the way I'd voted other than in my quiet conversations with Tommy Chessman in the Reliant or with Judy. I didn't feel betrayed by Tom Jackson and certainly harboured no animosity towards him personally. Although I believed he'd made the wrong judgement, I recognized that at least he'd had the courage to lead us back to work when he thought the failure of our action was inevitable.

The strike had lasted for forty-seven days: the highest number of working hours lost in a single dispute since the General Strike of 1926. We returned to work on 8 March to be faced with a mountain of mail and unlimited overtime (or 'open docket') to clear it. My customers seemed pleased to see me again. I'd been their regular postman for eighteen months by then and was on conversational terms with at least one family on every street.

With special arrangements in place to clear the backlog, I had two deliveries a day covering the same ground, which would only usually have happened at Christmas, and as a result I was meeting and chatting to many more customers than I would see in the early morning. I cannot recall any bad feeling over the strike – not from the posh houses in Linkswood Road, the more artisan dwellings of Hogfair Lane or the workers' cottages on Fairfield Road.

When the Hardman committee reported in May it would recommend a 9 per cent increase in pay, backdated to 1 January. Given that this was only 1 per cent more than we'd been offered in the first place and well below the £3 we'd claimed, it was seen as a crushing defeat. But for us youngsters, whose principal gripe was with the incremental scales, there was a better outcome. The scales were reduced so that a postman would now receive maximum pay at twenty-one rather than twenty-four. There were corresponding reductions for clerical staff and telephonists. As a twenty-year-old postman turning twenty-one, my own pay would therefore increase by much more than the 9 per cent norm.

The fact that Tom Jackson had made these scales such an important element of the dispute meant a lot to us juniors. Yet our older colleagues seemed to see no injustice in this blatant age discrimination. Those who'd joined young and progressed through the scales saw no reason why we shouldn't have to do the same, while those who'd come straight in on maximum pay simply thought we were daft to work for such a low wage when there were plenty of better-paid jobs available on the trading estate. But Tom Jackson was on our side regardless of the indifference of his members.

The strike had been a major national event. It was a tumultuous period in my life and in the history of the union. It would be a long time before the membership had the stomach for another national strike. If anyone had told me in 1971 that when that time came I would have the responsibility for settling it, I'd have thought they'd taken leave of their senses.

Chapter 9

THE EARLY SEVENTIES were a period of consolidation. Our house on the Britwell was the eighth address I'd lived at in nineteen years. But I was now sinking roots into the Buckinghamshire soil (though it was in fact soon to become the Berkshire soil, after Slough was redesignated to the royal county in the local government reorganization of 1974). Life there was good. Our little community round the green on Long Furlong Drive was closer than any either of us had known in our lives.

As well as being busy with her playgroup and later a youth club, Judy threw herself into organizing activities for children during the summer holidays and had a prominent role in running the Britwell Carnival, which took place every June. Within a few years Natalie, Emma and Jamie would all be at Lynch Hill, the infants' and primary school a short walk away through the garages. At the church hall they joined various Baden-Powell-inspired troops and packs appropriate to their age and gender.

For me, seven-day weeks were a regular occurrence. I'd often take on a Sunday shift for a colleague as well as doing my own, usually at Oxford Avenue, spending the early afternoon and evening alone, opening the mountain of bags and tipping the parcels into skips ready for sorting by the night staff. When I wasn't at work, my social life consisted of a Friday-night drink with my neighbours Mick, Tony and Robert, watching QPR every other Saturday and playing football on Sunday mornings, followed by a lunchtime drink with Mick and a different crowd at the British Legion in Faraday Road, just off the estate.

The Britwell was full of Queens Park Rangers supporters. This was unsurprising given that most of its residents had, like us, been exiled from QPR territory in west London. I soon found out that the PHG who ran the training school, Ron Gregory, was a devotee. He asked me if I'd like to join him and two other postmen on their fortnightly trips down the A40 to Shepherd's Bush. I was overjoyed to have this opportunity to resume a regular pilgrimage to Loftus Road to watch the team I'd revered since attending my first match at the age of nine.

Rangers had now settled back into the second division after their one awful season in the top flight. I'm sure Ron would have been predicting relegation from the moment they were promoted, because he was one of the most pessimistic people I've ever met, constantly anticipating disaster, whether for Rangers, the Post Office or the UPW. He was branch treasurer for the union and could see no way it would ever recover from the effects of the strike. Ron Gregory always erred on the side of catastrophe.

He had an unusual claim to distinction: Ron told us he was the only man ever to have played in the famously all-woman Ivy Benson Band. It had happened during the war when he served in the RAF and played drums with various bands. After

Ivy Benson's percussionist ran off with a GI, she was desperate to find a drummer for a forces concert and Ron Gregory was called upon to make musical history.

Now, twenty-five years on, he'd abandoned the drums for the organ. In his neat house in Pemberton Road on the Britwell estate, Ron would, given half a chance, play for anyone and everyone who popped in, however short the duration of the visit. If we Rangers supporters arrived at his house five minutes early on match days, he would dash over to his organ and, while we exchanged pleasantries with Mrs Gregory, reel off a melody he'd been practising. Nobody bothered to comment or took much more notice than they would have taken of the background music that used to be played in supermarkets.

Ron would then put on his coat, flat cap and leather driving gloves, utter his battle cry ('Let's go and see them get thrashed!') and lead us out to his immaculate Triumph Herald for the drive to Loftus Road. There was always plenty of space to park on the White City estate, then notorious for crime and vandalism. But Ron's car, with its little QPR talisman hanging from the rear-view mirror, was never touched.

Once inside the ground it was worth the entrance fee just to watch the great Rodney Marsh in the pre-match kick about. There was none of today's slick presentation back then. The players would emerge from the tunnel at about 2.50pm and just run around for ten minutes until kick-off. Rodney would entertain the crowd with ball-juggling tricks and generally muck around with his team-mates, nothing that could be construed as a pre-match exercise.

We all bowed down at the shrine of Rodney. I was young and prone to hero-worship but even Ron Gregory was left speechless by the dazzling skills Marsh displayed, almost none of which were captured on camera as matches weren't routinely filmed in those pre-video days. When Rodney left us for Manchester City in 1972 the programme for our next home game was edged in black. There was no resentment. We wished Rodney well on the bigger stage to which his talents were better suited.

My rather less lavish footballing skills were on show every Sunday morning playing local league football for Slough Postal FC. I helped set the club up and persuaded the Post Office to pay for our expensive red-and-black striped shirts. Our strip may have resembled that of AC Milan but that's where the comparison ended. I ended up captaining the team to our familiar mid-table position.

When the match finished at around noon I'd go straight to the British Legion where Mick Pearson, Johnny Cates (an AA patrolman), Idris and Doreen (a Welsh couple we'd befriended) and one or two others would sit together. The cast might vary if Johnny Cates was on duty, or one of the other neighbours joined us, but the play was always the same.

Act I was the greeting phase where we'd pool our resources in a whip-round, decide who was to hold the whip, get the first drink in and buy our bingo tickets ready for Act II. My tipple was a pint of mild (a drink that tastes exactly as it sounds) and I would savour those first refreshing mouthfuls after my exertions on the football pitch. Act I was the only opportunity we had for conversation so we'd chew over the week's events while helping ourselves to the cubes of cheddar cheese and silverskin onions provided free in bowls dotted around the hall.

Act II was the bingo. Books of five games could be purchased singly or in multiples. Some participants would have two or even three long strips of five books playing ten or fifteen games at once. That needed more mental dexterity than we could ever manage so we'd sit with three books apiece on the go for each game.

Bingo was a solemn pursuit. The whole of that large British Legion hall, where there would be 150 drinkers on a Sunday lunchtime, would sit like druid monks in eerie silence as the caller pronounced the sacred words 'Eyes down looking.' The prize money was £10 for the first person to get a line and £20 for a full house. We didn't pool any winnings. On the rare occasions any of us had a full house the custom was for the lucky winner to buy a round, which came to under a quid.

Act III was the card school. With the bingo finished, a gentle hum of conversation resumed, though only temporarily on our table. We'd borrow packs of cards and cribbage boards from the Legion, provided on trust for the use of patrons with no charge and no need even to pay a deposit. We'd play crib for half an hour or so, moving the small match stubs that served as pegs up and down the board. After that, the serious stuff – usually seven-card brag, occasionally poker. We played for small stakes, 5p and 10p pieces. It was rare to hear the rustle of notes from any of the card schools around us, just about visible through the thickening fog of cigarette smoke.

There was always music, usually from a trio of piano, drums and double bass belting out the old songs that my father used to play in the pubs of Notting Hill: 'Heart of My Hearts', 'On Moonlight Bay', 'Who's Sorry Now?' mingled with more recent favourites popularized by Engelbert Humperdinck, Tom Jones or Ken Dodd.

Elsewhere the working-class Sunday traditions prevalent in my youth – when men got suited up to go to the pub, as I remember my father doing, while their wives cooked the Sunday dinner – were in flux. The British Legion was more old-fashioned but here, too, times were changing. Older men still put on a suit and tie but the younger ones, including me, dressed casually. In most respects, though, Sundays remained steeped in the customs of the 1950s.

Only very rarely did Judy or Mick's wife Susan come with us. There were some female regulars. Idris's beautiful wife Doreen would play bingo but never cards. She'd sit in perfumed serenity, sipping her gin and tonic, while we covered our bets, raised the stakes or threw in our hands. Doreen was cultured and ladylike. I still have the paperback of Dylan Thomas's *Collected Poems* (the book I'd borrowed from the library during the strike) that she and Idris bought me for my twenty-fourth birthday, inscribed in her fair hand. Our shared admiration for the bard of Swansea emerged in conversation one day. I would have been reluctant to admit to a love of poetry to my other friends, not because they were in any way philistines, but for fear that I would have sounded pompous. Idris and Doreen, being Celts, were immune from such accusations.

The difference between the women who did go to the Legion then and those who stayed at home was a practical one: it boiled down to whether or not they had kids. Idris and Doreen did not have children, and those of most of the other women in attendance on Sundays had grown up. When Judy and Susan did come they were happy to play cards, although they hated brag, preferring more cerebral games like crib or Newmarket.

The British Legion, like thousands of such places around the country, provided social cohesion. Yes, there was drinking and gambling, but it wasn't excessive and it wasn't in any way immoral. Sons enjoyed a pint with fathers and grandfathers, solidifying the sense of community and continuity.

Act IV was exiting the stage. At 2.30pm (opening hours were 11.30 to 2.30 – you knew where you were with the British Legion), I would buy a bottle of light ale to take back for Judy, which she'd drink while putting the final touches to the roast dinner (never with the meal). If I was working I'd gobble down my dinner before setting off for Oxford Avenue. If I wasn't working there was *The Big Match* to watch on ITV followed by a snooze in the armchair with the Sunday papers across my lap.

I'm conscious that this creates a fair impression of Andy Capp; of a bloke with a self-centred social life that left his wife to look after the kids, cook, wash and make a comfortable home. And that was pretty much the division of labour back then. I worked as many hours as I could to bring home the bacon and Judy ran everything else. My boozing may have been confined to Friday evenings and Sunday lunchtimes and my gambling to Sunday bingo and cards, but I was none the less perpetuating the male lifestyle adopted by my father, if not the excesses to which he took it.

Judy and I did enjoy the occasional night out together. On a Saturday evening, if we could find a babysitter, we might go to the Lynchpin, one of two pubs on the estate. The other one was the less respectable Jolly Londoner where there was little jollity and plenty of 'trouble'. More often we socialized with our neighbours without venturing beyond the green. Robert Metcalfe two doors down had been born on Christmas Day and celebrated every year with a party. This began a craze for house parties and a fund was set up into which each household would pay 50p per person per week. Once there was enough in the kitty we'd take turns to host a do. There'd be huge cans of Watney's Red Barrel and Double Diamond (known as Party Sevens, because each can contained seven pints) arrayed in somebody's small kitchen, along with bottles of spirits and mixers (but rarely, in those days, wine).

Early on, the men would take up residence in the kitchen, joining their wives for dancing in the front room when they were either enticed or forced out by the women. Or, as was the case with Mick and myself, when inspired by a particular record (usually 'Brown Sugar' by the Stones) to cut ourselves a piece of the dance floor.

We were a diverse bunch united by a youthful exuberance. Our age range spanned around fifteen years. I was by some distance the youngest and Tony Gabriel the eldest. On Long Furlong Drive, as well as the beautifully spoken Martin and Karen next door, there was a couple from across the road, Glad and Del, enthusiastic party-fund contributors, who by most definitions would have been perceived as middle-class. Del, a senior manager at a film-processing company, was shy and quiet at parties while his hilarious wife, Glad, typified the 'life and soul' category. I remember her at one festive-season celebration loudly castigating her husband for buying her a book entitled *Living With Lumbago* for Christmas.

The diversity in social class might be surprising to those who think of council estates as being inhabited solely by horny-handed sons of toil like me. Perhaps this was the legacy of the elusive 1960s social mobility we hear so much about today but was scarcely mentioned then.

There again, I didn't read much sociology. After the strike, I began to broaden my consumption of poetry. Despite penning a vanity contribution to *Spring Poets '69*, I had hardly read any poetry before my immersion in Dylan Thomas. Later that year the bicentenary of the death of Thomas Gray was commemorated at the St Giles parish churchyard in Stoke Poges, where he was said to have written his famous 'Elegy Written in a Country Churchyard'.

Stoke Poges was only five minutes away from the Britwell so Judy and I went there with the kids. I bought a leather book-mark embossed with four verses from the 'Elegy' in gold lettering, including the scene-setting opening:

> The curfew tolls the knell of parting day,
> The lowing herd wind slowly o'er the lea,
> The plowman homeward plods his weary way,
> And leaves the world to darkness and to me.

My appetite whetted, I looked up the entire poem in Slough library, becoming increasingly intrigued by its theme of great-ness denied by accident of birth. I'd soon learned my favourite lines by heart:

> Full many a gem of purest ray serene,
> The dark unfathom'd caves of ocean bear:
> Full many a flow'r is born to blush unseen,
> And waste its sweetness on the desert air.

I saw those flowers all around me in Slough.

~

A year after the strike ended I resumed my quest for a proper driving licence. I'd been quite happy with my permanent moped delivery but I was still determined to take advantage of being in one of the few occupations where I could be paid to learn to drive. After the unceremonious removal from my course following the fainting fit at Barnes, I nagged the Post Office in Slough to give me another chance.

They didn't take much persuading. The shortage of drivers reflected the general shortage of staff in the Thames Valley. And driving wasn't a separate function. All postmen were expected to do every aspect of the job: sorting outward and inward letters, packets and parcels, loading and unloading mail, cycling, driving, walking – the lot.

Along with another postman I was withdrawn from normal duties, exactly as I had been in Barnes, to spend a week being taught to drive. Our tutor was Mr Clarence, a civil servant overseeing a civil-service course that would lead to a civil-service test. (The Post Office might have left the civil service but it took a long time for the civil service to leave the Post Office.) Tall and very bald, Mr Clarence spoke so softly that it was difficult to hear him, particularly above the loud rattling of our Morris Minor van.

I loved those old Morris vans, though it must be said that they had their eccentricities. For example, the driver's door locked automatically when it slammed shut. The locks were manual and were operated by the ignition key. So whenever the driver left the van, he was supposed to turn off the engine and take the key with him. For postmen and women on rural deliveries this was completely impractical. In most instances they would be out of the van for only a few seconds to deliver a letter. As a result, being locked out with the key still in the ignition and the engine running could become a regular occurrence. The solution was to leave the fly window open so that you could reach in from outside to release the door handle.

Our training model was the same as the one in which I'd had my lessons in Barnes, with dual controls and a little bench seat in the body of the van where the other learner could sit and observe while Mr Clarence instructed the postman whose turn it was to drive.

Double declutch was no longer required but I couldn't lose the habit and our instructor encouraged it, purring quietly about how useful it would be on the bigger vans where synchro-mesh gears were still rare. His quiet, steady, civil-service approach inspired confidence, like a GP's bedside manner, but there was a major problem with Mr Clarence: he was a sadist.

The slightest deviation from his orders earned a punch to the left leg just above the knee which varied in force but always hurt. This man knew how to administer a dead leg and he did it as if it were a perfectly natural part of the process of teaching somebody to drive. There was no alteration in the serene expression on his big, round face; no change to the tempo of his conversation.

'Let's turn right at the next junction. Remember: mirror, signal, manoeuvre.' *Thump.* 'Always best to switch the indicator off once you've turned.' The excruciating pain was at its worst if the driver's foot happened to be hovering anywhere near the clutch pedal when it didn't need to be.

'It's such a lovely day.' *Thump!* Muffled cry from driver pretending not to be in agony. 'Isn't it? Do try not to ride the clutch, Alan, there's a good lad.'

After a full week of being punched by Mr Clarence I was considered ready for the driving test although, I was told, it might be months before one could be arranged. In the meantime, any driver under tuition was allowed to affix his L-plates to a Post Office vehicle of his choice and press-gang its poor driver into becoming an unwilling driving instructor on his town collection or rural delivery. The fact that this could be claimed by the learner as paid overtime made it even more attractive to the novice. Grown men were known to sob quietly as they saw a learner walking purposefully towards them, L-plates in hand, across the sorting-office yard.

Actually this consensual tuition was quite a good system: it gave the learner a valuable opportunity to practise his driving skills while his workmate acquired an assistant to help with loading and unloading, opening the pillarboxes or delivering mail. I found it infinitely preferable to Mr Clarence's instruction and would invariably secure prior agreement to accompany a driver on specified afternoons or evenings.

Eventually the day of the test arrived. It was to be conducted by our civil-service examiner, Mr Brewster. There were four or five of us trainee drivers awaiting a test and we'd all heard tales of how difficult it was to pass with Mr Brewster. A small man with a stooping gait and a sunken face upon which a smile was rarely seen, he could never have been accused of carrying his authority lightly. He had two other notable characteristics: he smoked Craven 'A' cork-tipped cigarettes and he swore like a trooper.

Being tested by this man was a daunting experience. Being passed by him was a slightly less common occurrence than a full eclipse of the sun. One of my fellow learners came up with the idea of having T-shirts produced with the slogan 'I passed with Brewster' on the front. The guy who suggested this had just passed at his third attempt. It took me five.

The ignominy was even greater because by the time I took my first driving test I'd already failed my moped test twice as well – all with Mr Brewster. He was inescapable. If there was a test with an engine involved, he would be the one carrying it out. Thankfully, I was eventually able to remove the L-plates from my Raleigh Runabout RM6, but the vital licence to drive a car continued to elude me.

I knew I'd failed my first test when the van I was driving (with Mr Brewster in the passenger seat beside me) felt sluggish. Staring straight ahead in his most inscrutable manner he advised me to pull into the kerb. When I went to apply the handbrake I realized it was already on. I'd forgotten to release it when we set off.

Each test began with Mr Brewster trying to pretend he'd never set eyes on me before in his life while I, consumed by nerves and overdoing the bonhomie, would greet him like a long-lost brother. The only sign of recognition I ever got from him was 'Fuckin' Ada, not you again' at the beginning of my final ordeal. At the end of each test he would take out a Craven 'A', tap its cork tip on the box and light it up as a prelude to his interrogation on the Highway Code. As far as I recall, the cork tip on a Craven 'A' wasn't a filter, just a wrap of stronger, brown-coloured paper intended to prevent the cigarette from sticking to the smoker's top lip. Whatever its purpose, its effect was to impart a brownish hue to Mr Brewster's mouth.

By my fifth test (my eighth if you count the three I'd had on the moped) – which I'd begged the Post Office to allow me to take, pointing out that everything they had spent so far on my driving training would be wasted if they stopped short of this final hurdle – my worry wasn't whether I could drive a car, it was whether I could pass the bloody test.

Surely Mr Brewster wasn't the only civil-service examiner in the south-east region? Surely he had occasionally to take a holiday or a day off sick? But the terrible inevitability was confirmed when I saw a familiar stooped figure walking towards the van.

It was a clear, spring day as we set off from the sorting office in Reading, where the tests were held. I drove superbly, if I say so myself. On Judy's advice I had taken a herbal potion from the chemist to calm my nerves. It seemed to be working, even if it was just a placebo effect. I took every turning beautifully, reversed round a corner using my wing mirrors in textbook fashion and performed my emergency stop with such abrupt-ness that it almost sent Mr B. through the windscreen (a powerful incentive for a forceful but clean execution of that manoeuvre).

I pulled up as instructed in a quiet, tree-lined street. Mr Brewster wound down his window, tapped and then lit his Craven 'A'. 'Right,' he said, gazing straight ahead of him. 'Time for a few questions.'

The Highway Code was attached to the clipboard on his knee. By now I was an expert on that little booklet. I knew every chapter, every page, every paragraph. I felt confident enough to answer questions on its punctuation or where it had been printed, such was the scrutiny to which I'd exposed it.

Brewster asked three or four questions which I answered with panache, picturing that full driving licence, printed in black, rather than provisional red, that was on its way to me.

The examiner sucked hard on his cigarette. 'What is the most dangerous traffic light to approach?' he asked.

My serenity evaporated. 'That's not in the Highway Code!' I protested.

'Who said the questions had to be from the Highway fuckin' Code?'

I shuffled in my seat and began to flush. 'Amber,' I guessed.

'Nope.' He took a drag on his fag.

Beads of sweat were forming on my forehead. A sparrow landed on a low branch of a poplar tree and stared at me. Time stood still.

'Red,' I said eventually.

There was nowhere else to go with this question.

'It's green,' said an exasperated Mr Brewster. 'Green is the most dangerous fuckin' light to approach. You assume the cars at the fuckin' junction will stop at red, but some day some bastard won't.'

There was silence in the van, mine resentful, his reflective.

'Well, I'm not impressed,' said Mr B. after a while. 'But I'm going to give you a pass, against my better judgement, because frankly, I'm sick of the fuckin' sight of you.'

The sparrow flew off. The sun came out. At that precise moment I could have kissed Mr Brewster full on his cork-tip-stained lips.

Chapter 10

HAVING FINALLY PASSED my driving test I was lucky enough to acquire, for nothing, a 1959 Ford Anglia – the little car with the sweeping nose line and slanted rear windows – thanks to my neighbour Martin Saunders' links with the motor trade. It was perfectly serviceable and I drove it for six months before Martin offered me another Anglia, dark grey with burgundy seats, for £45.

I parked the car proudly outside the house. The Britwell had been built at a time when only a minority of its residents were expected to own cars. While there were little clusters of rented garages, with up-and-over tin doors, dotted around the estate, none of its 3,000 houses had parking spaces or lowered kerbs and most of the roads were too narrow to park on. We families round the green vandalized the environment by bumping up the kerb to park in front of our houses. As a result 'the green' would have been more accurately described as 'the brown'.

Having a car (and a licence) revolutionized family life. It made it easier for us to visit Judy's nan, living contentedly in her flat in Hanwell. Once settled there, and as she watched our family grow, her initial iciness soon thawed; in fact I think she even became quite fond of me. We could also now drive to Tring to see not only Linda and Mike but also my best friend Andrew Wiltshire who, by complete coincidence, had moved to the same town with his wife Ann. The route involved traversing Amersham Hill, down on the way there, up on the way back. With five of us in the elderly Anglia, it felt like a mountain slope. I was always so anxious coming home about whether we'd actually make the summit that Judy and I developed a little ritual of lighting cigarettes to celebrate a successful climb.

By now Linda had a third child, Dean Byron (Byron was a compromise, an alternative more acceptable to Linda than Mike's preference, Dylan), born a few months after Jamie. So we now had two daughters and a son apiece.

After hearing Shirley Williams give a speech on housing in Stevenage, my sister had joined the housing charity Shelter, for which she worked hard to raise funds.

Mike, Andrew and I would often gather in the Anchor in Tring High Street to put the world to rights. My brother-in-law and my closest friend both counselled me against spending the rest of my working life in the Post Office, a prospect that was perfectly acceptable to me. I *liked* being a postman. Whenever I was asked for my occupation I was proud to make that declaration. It had, I felt, a certain cachet. I liked the job and the camaraderie with my colleagues. Yes, the basic pay was low, but it could be supplemented and I liked the sense of security and of belonging to an historic institution.

Restless Andrew hadn't lasted long at Barnes after I'd left for Slough. He and Ann aspired to be house-owners rather than tenants and Post Office wages were hardly conducive to that ambition. They faced a long wait on the council housing list in any case. We'd been awarded our take-it-or-leave-it lifeline because we had the good fortune to be living in a house the council wanted to demolish. The local authority was under no such obligation to Ann and Andrew.

At first they rented a private flat in Tring. Having already been a butcher and a postman, by the early seventies Andrew was a salesman for McCain's frozen chips. Before long he'd become the first person I knew to work with computers. Like me he'd left school with no qualifications and longed to return to music. But he'd never replaced the drum kit that had been stolen with my amplifier from the Fourth Feathers Club off the Edgware Road and by now he, too, was immersed in the responsibilities of fatherhood. His son Toby had been born in that fertile year for me and mine of 1971 (four months after Jamie and a month after Dean) and Ann gave birth to twin sons in 1975.

In between, Andrew and Ann suffered a terrible tragedy: the cot death of their five-month-old daughter Simone, born in 1973. Ann had taken Toby and Simone to Linda's house for the day. When she left she placed the baby in the pram to sleep on the walk home. They arrived back to find Andrew assembling some flatpack furniture he'd bought. With Simone still soundly asleep in her pram, Ann took the opportunity to give him a hand. When they'd finished they tried to wake the baby for her feed. She was dead.

I can't remember now how Linda reached me. Since we had no phone, usually she would ring either the Saunders next door, who did, or the inquiry office at the Post Office, depending on the time of day. As soon as I heard the awful news I drove straight to Tring to be with our friends, who had just been questioned by the police.

They were staying with my sister. They couldn't face returning to the flat where their baby daughter had died to look again
at the flatpack furniture and relive what they'd had no way of
knowing were the last moments of their daughter's life. Not
then and not ever. They moved in with Ann's mother in
Aylesbury until their dream of owning their own house was put
on hold by the eventual allocation of a council house.

∼

'Why should I let the toad work squat on my life?' Philip Larkin
complained. In the early 1970s I had yet to discover his poetry
but the sentiment would have chimed with me.

At home I still strummed away at the battered old Spanish
guitar, its more sophisticated successors – a Vox Electric and my
much-mourned Höfner Verithin – having come and gone. I
wrote songs that were influenced by the music I listened to in
the post-Beatles 1970s: Neil Young, Cat Stevens, Joni Mitchell,
David Bowie, Crosby, Stills and Nash, Joan Armatrading,
Lindisfarne and the band probably more dogged by tragedy
than any other in rock-music history – Badfinger. But the
closest I got to being back in a band myself was harmonizing
Simon and Garfunkel songs with Martin Saunders in his living
room. Martin had a clear, almost soprano voice and, like my
songwriting, the only accompaniment our duets needed was an
acoustic guitar. I also had an old honky-tonk piano that I'd
bought for a tenner from a house sale in Colnbrook, ready for
the night classes I intended to take to learn to play it.

It was work, though, that dominated my waking hours. I
'performed' (for that is the verb that was used) my regular duty

week in, week out, rain or shine: number 229, start time 05.40, finish 13.16, Monday to Friday (10.40 on a Saturday). After nipping home for a quick sandwich it was off to Oxford Avenue for an afternoon of dust, dirt and darts. As time passed, Jamie replaced the girls on the sofa for fifteen minutes of *Trumpton* or *The Herbs* (and I was still the one who was most entertained). Before long he, too, was at school all day.

My Post Office number, 272, remained emblazoned across the black-and-gold enamel badge clipped to the breast of my smart uniform jacket. The number never changed; the uniform did, unfortunately. The navy blue serge with the red stripe down the trouser leg was replaced by a thinner, more insubstantial dark grey worsted suit that maintained the tunic jacket but never looked as smart or felt as fitting for the job. At least it ended the postman's affliction of 'blue legs', which occurred every time the old serge trousers got wet in the rain, transferring the blue dye from uniform to skin.

In summer, instead of the cotton jacket, we were forced into a light grey version of the winter uniform, in even thinner material, with the most extraordinary black trimming on the collar and cuffs. Judy said it made me look like the lead singer of Showaddywaddy.

The care I'd always taken with my clothes hadn't waned and as I spent most of my time in uniform I wanted to wear it and accessorize it in the smartest and most stylish way I could. I was among a minority of postmen to adopt the uniform waistcoat, just as old Frank Dainton had at Barnes. For cold weather I wanted a better overcoat than the regular issue and, with the assistance of the supervisor in charge, I searched through the stock in the uniform store until I found what I was looking for: a double-breasted, long, black greatcoat that fitted perfectly over my uniform, the hem reaching down to the bottom of my calves. Circa 1960, it was still in perfect condition and served me through many a winter.

I'd complain that I had the heaviest delivery in Europe and I was only half-joking. It was certainly the heaviest of any of the nine Burnham walks. I rarely left the office with fewer than three bags of mail. We Burnham men were a race apart from the Slough workforce. They were on rotation whereas we were on fixed duties; they pedalled bikes, we rode mopeds. They sorted on to the inward primary fittings while we collected the mail from the box on the frames marked 'Burnham' and did our own breakdown on separate frames in our far-flung corner of the vast sorting office.

The men I worked with were by and large a homogenous bunch. Tommy Chessman – the man who'd saved me from being sacked in my early days on the Burnham duty with his patient wake-up calls and three-wheeled taxi service – was one of three postmen who'd been centralized at Slough with the mail, leaving behind the dilapidated shed that had been the Burnham delivery office. The other two were Arthur Spearing, a sprightly cockney from Shepherd's Bush, and Ernie Norrell, one of the few genuine locals I met in my time at Slough.

Arthur delivered in the semi-rural Green Lane area, where there were long distances between clusters of housing. He soon abandoned the moped, preferring to use his yellow Volkswagen 'Jeans' Beetle with its blue denim seats. Already in his late thirties, Arthur was far too old for the car he was driving (youth was a fleeting state in the 1970s). He was forever complaining about the number of packets he had to deliver to a disc jockey nobody had heard of who lived on a road called The Fairway. They were demo discs for a bloke called Terry Wogan.

One thing that always puzzled me about Arthur was how his wallet came to be constantly full of notes even though he never worked a minute's overtime. We all took turns to pay for a round of the disgusting liquid masquerading as tea that was dispensed every morning from a wheeled urn by one of the night staff, who must have left it brewing for most of his shift. Arthur sat next to me and when it was his turn to pay he always asked me to go and fetch the required nine cups of char. Out would come the wallet and, with a flourish, he'd flick through a wad of notes, searching among the tens and twenties for a pound for our tea.

Of course he may have had a second job, as many postmen did, but if so I saw no evidence of it. He lived on the Britwell and every day from noon onwards his distinctive yellow car would be parked outside the Ex-Servicemen's Club in Wentworth Avenue. He certainly didn't work there: colleagues who used the club occasionally, such as Nobby Deadman, confirmed that Arthur was in residence every afternoon, propping up the bar until closing time. He did collect a fair number of stray golf balls on his delivery (his route circumnavigated the golf club) but I very much doubt that trading in those could have filled that substantial wallet.

Ernie Norrell, born and bred in Burnham, must have been pushing seventy. He was certainly well past the normal pension age of sixty. A jovial man with a rich country accent, he'd bought two cottages on The Gore for a few hundred pounds just after the war, which provided him with financial security. Some of our colleagues resented the fact that he was still working when he didn't need the money, taking a job that could have gone to a younger man, although that argument was somewhat illogical at the Post Office, given the number of vacancies permanently on offer. Besides, although postal workers retained the civil-service retirement age, hardly anyone actually ever left at sixty. In view of the acute shortage of staff the Post Office was reluctant to compel anyone to retire and, with no state pension payable to men until they were sixty-five, very few could afford to leave earlier.

The rest of us were new to Burnham. Ted Pedell, a rugby player a year or two older than me, was built like the proverbial outside toilet made of brick. He was another Britwellian and we played football together for Slough Postal. He convinced me to train with his rugby club, the Old Pennanians, where I was in every sense a lightweight. Week in, week out for about six months I'd go through the torture of a training regime possibly formulated by Hannibal when he was preparing to cross the Alps. To bodybuilding enthusiast Ted it was a little workout; to me it was more of a near-death experience.

Prev Patel was an Asian guy who'd come to the UK from Uganda just before the dictator Idi Amin seized power in 1971. It was a sensible decision: it wouldn't be long before 80,000 of his compatriots were expelled from the country by the murderous president. In his late twenties, tall and handsome, Prev modelled his hairstyle on that of his hero, Elvis Presley. I never knew if Prev was a nickname, an abbreviation or actually his full name. Whatever the case, it was his salutation of choice. Prev was what we used to refer to as 'flash', a characteristic that didn't always endear him to his workmates, particularly Asian guys of other religions or customs whose standards of propriety Prev failed to meet. He chain-smoked Peter Stuyvesants, which he held elegantly in his long, slim fingers. He never smoked more than half a cigarette. I think they were more of a prop than a pleasure. Like Arthur, Prev scorned his allocated moped in favour of delivering the mail from his big old gas-guzzling Peugeot. He did a lot of his overtime at Oxford Avenue and we enjoyed working together. Prev left the Post Office after a couple of years, intent on going to America to earn his fortune. I have no doubt that he succeeded.

Micky English, possibly the most decent man I've ever known, was, in spite of his surname, an Irishman with a disposition so bright it was like working alongside a sun lamp. The rest of us all had our different moods (Arthur Spearing in particular), but Micky only ever had one: happy. When he finished his delivery he'd ride around Burnham looking for any colleague who needed a hand. He'd have got the teas in every morning if we'd let him and his Embassy cigarettes would have been passed around the whole office if there'd been time.

As the two most avid consumers of overtime we'd often work together to cover Burnham deliveries whose postmen hadn't turned up that day. I have to admit that I was a provider of such work as well as a taker of it.

Every postal worker was allowed ten days' absence without a medical certificate in any twelve-month period. We called these days 'Whitleys', after the distinguished speaker of the House of Commons from 1921 to 1928, J. H. Whitley. During the First World War, as MP for Halifax, Whitley had been asked to chair an inquiry into British industrial relations. The report he produced in 1920 recommended an elaborate system of consultation between unions and management. It was intended for implementation in the coalfields but owing to a mining dispute, the Whitley Councils, as they are known to this day, came instead to the civil service. They were another legacy of the world of the GPO that no longer existed. I suspect that Speaker Whitley would have preferred to have been remembered for his contribution to reducing industrial conflict. However, at some stage the agreement to allow ten non-certified days off must have emerged from the Whitley Councils, since it still bore his name.

Our annual leave entitlement was three weeks a year and most of us supplemented it by 'taking Whitleys'. A supervisor would tour the office, clipboard in hand, solemnly advising certain miscreants of the number they'd taken that year. I was usually on the list. The supervisor would caution me that I was up to five Whitleys already. In response I'd thank him for reminding me that I had another five to take. I suppose this is one of many aspects of my time as a postman that I should feel bad about. But retrospective regret seems pretty pointless and I felt absolutely no shame at the time. Neither did my workmates, whose absence sent Micky English and me out together with sometimes three or even four deliveries to complete, breaking for lunch in the Crispin or the Garibaldi, where this most cheerful of men would confide in me about his flirtatious wife and the hard upbringing he'd had in rural Ireland. The pints having been sunk and our sandwiches consumed, Micky's smile would be reapplied as we returned to our labours.

The two other Burnham deliveries were driving 'duties' performed on rotation (along with a late turn) by Bill Higginbottom, Reg Woolley and Derek Quincy, a trio of

Britwellians who all had a cross to bear. Bill was hard of hearing, Reg was afflicted with an enormous nose, politely described as Roman, and Derek suffered from a wracking cough that frequently led to him losing his voice. Arthur Spearing dubbed them Ear, Nose and Throat.

One of the driving duties was the bulk mail delivery to the shops and businesses of Burnham High Street. The other was the only proper rural round in the office, Littleworth Common. Many deliveries were designated as rural in Slough sorting office – Datchet, Colnbrook, Hedgerley, Farnham Royal and Farnham Common, for example – but any authentic rural postman in Cornwall or Northumberland, or outside the cities of Scotland, would have laughed at the description. Littleworth Common was the only Slough delivery that would have earned their respect.

I had assisted Bill (Ear) with the Littleworth Common delivery on the late turn one afternoon while I was still on driving tuition before passing my test, his being the Morris Minor van to which I had elected to fasten my L-plates. There were only around 140 addresses on Littleworth Common compared to over 600 on my own Burnham round. Most of the time allowed for the delivery was taken up by the driving: juddering up dirt tracks, crossing farmland and cruising along sparsely populated country lanes.

One of Ear's delivery points particularly intrigued me: Dorneywood, a stately home separated from the main road by a long driveway. Halfway along the drive was a small hut which just about accommodated the substantial policeman stationed inside. 'Ah,' said Bill knowingly. 'When there's a copper on duty it means the man himself is here.' My inquiry elicited the information that the 'man himself' was the home secretary and Dorneywood his official residence.

I really want to do that job, I thought to myself later. I wasn't thinking of the role of home secretary but of the job of postman to the good folk of Littleworth Common. But Ear, Nose and Throat were well entrenched and the prospects of me achieving my objective were remote.

Chapter 11

FOUR YEARS AFTER moving to the Britwell I managed to acquire a new guitar. Henry's Radios, where Mike worked, had branched out into selling musical instruments and he assured me he could arrange a discount on any guitar I wanted. So one Saturday I took six-year-old Natalie with me on the train to Paddington.

Natalie had no memory of London and was so captivated by the Underground that, instead of travelling one stop from Paddington to Edgware Road, we went right round the Circle Line in the other direction before getting off to see her Uncle Mike in Praed Street. Henry's was packed with customers but Mike found time to show us round, whispering to me that he could knock 50 per cent off the listed price.

After much deliberation, I plumped for an Eko twelve-string acoustic model. I can't remember now how much it cost: whatever the price, it would have been unaffordable without the promised discount but must have been manageable with it. Mike invited me to join him for a lunchtime drink at his London local to celebrate my purchase but in those days, before the arrival of child-friendly gardens and family rooms, taking a child to a pub was completely impractical, not to mention frowned upon in many quarters. So Natalie and I left with the sleek, rosewood Italian guitar safely encased for the journey home. In hindsight, deciding against an electric guitar may have pointed to an acceptance that any revival in my nascent music career was now unlikely.

I was happy at the Post Office but beginning to think about some of the other opportunities it offered. I could easily have plodded round my Burnham delivery for forty years before retiring with a long-service award and the fond farewells of my customers. They were good to me, particularly at Christmas, when they were careful to give their tips to me personally rather than leaving an envelope pinned to the front door which would quite probably have landed in the hands of one of the student casuals who delivered the mail over the course of the two heavy weeks preceding Christmas Day while I stayed in the office sorting it.

There is a tale, probably apocryphal, of a less-than-diligent postman finding a note on the door of one of the houses on his walk that read: 'Postman – please call for your tip.' He knocked expectantly, to be confronted by the master of the house, who offered no money but told him forcefully: 'Here's a tip: shut the fucking gate behind you.'

I had two or three casuals who laboured for ages over their third of my walk. The exception was a bright bluestocking who one year amazed me by returning within an hour of me sending her out laden down with mail.

All the bundles were numbered in sequence and each casual would have around fifteen bundles for the third of the round for which he or she was responsible. How on earth had my helper managed to get through them so soon?

It turned out that this phenomenally clever undergraduate had simply looked at the address on the front of each bundle and then shoved the whole stack of mail through the letterbox of that house. So all the post for Dawes East Road, for example, went through the door of number one. She had then tripped merrily along to the address on the front of her next bundle, apparently without wondering why the occasional house was receiving hundreds of cards and letters while there was nothing whatsoever for all the addresses in between. Fifteen bundles, and fifteen drops, later, she was back in the office asking what she should do next.

That student must now be approaching retirement age, having perhaps pursued a life of intellectual rigour in academia or as a senior civil servant. Or possibly a brain surgeon.

My customers had no cause for complaint when I was on the job. I was meticulous about shutting gates, never walked across lawns and pocketed those wretched red elastic bands rather than discarding them on the pavement.

I had only one significant bad experience, but it was one that left me with a deep feeling of resentment which may have contributed to a general restlessness and slight dissatisfaction that began to trouble me by the mid-1970s. It happened in upmarket Linkswood Road, my favourite part of the walk – a wide avenue of beautiful houses, at the end of which was a five-bar gate. Beyond that there was nothing except rolling countryside. I would deliver up one side of the road, pause at the gate for a quiet moment of spiritual nourishment (what is life if, full of care, we have no time to stand and stare, and all that) and come down the other side. Up on the evens, down on the odds, as we said in the trade.

I had just completed my final drop in Linkswood Road one day when a car turned the corner and screeched to a halt beside me. A man jumped out and confronted me. 'OK,' he said. 'The game's up. Where's the money?'

I had no idea what he was talking about. 'What money?' I asked calmly and politely.

'The money you stole from the milk bottle outside my house.'

Twenty minutes earlier I had noticed, outside the porch of one of the houses, a milk bottle with the milkman's money pushed into the neck for him to collect with the empties. I had opened the porch door as usual, left the mail inside and carried on with my round.

I flushed with anger now as I told this gentleman that I hadn't touched his money, managing to do so with more civility than he deserved in the circumstances.

'Give me the money' – his words were spoken slowly for emphasis – 'or I'll call the police.'

What had happened, it transpired, was that on leaving for work Mr Angry had called out to his wheelchair-bound wife that he'd leave the money for the milkman on his way out. Apparently it was usually left inside the porch but on this occasion for some reason he'd put it outside. Some time later, when his wife heard me arrive with the post, she went to collect it, saw no sign of the money in the porch and phoned her husband at work to tell him I'd pinched it.

He had been on his way home when he'd accosted me. He hadn't even been back to check before accusing me of theft. Of course, when I stood my ground he returned to his house and found the money outside the porch where it had been all along.

He came to report this curtly in a surly, unapologetic manner that left me feeling even more peeved. He and his wife might well have believed that the Britwell estate was full of thieves and that if I wasn't guilty as charged on this occasion, I probably had been in the past or would be in the future.

I reported the incident when I returned to the office, hoping that the Post Office might wish to take some action to protect and defend the integrity of their staff. But the supervisor just shrugged his shoulders and said there was nothing he could do about it. He was probably right. What had happened had already been cleared up and therefore the false accusation had gone no further. The Post Office was hardly likely to sue on my behalf for defamation of character.

Still, this encounter left me with a burning sense of injustice which may have been at the root of my sense of having reached a crossroads. After five years on my Dropmore Road walk I decided to apply for promotion. I had no real enthusiasm for acquiring the gold lapel crowns of the postman higher grade but at the same time I was worried that if I didn't seek such advancement it could become a road not taken, an opportunity missed. The increase in wages would be welcome – my pay would go up by around 15 per cent – but I'd have to work inside all the time, which didn't appeal to me. While I had no ambition to become a supervisor, I wouldn't even have the option if I didn't first of all pass through this 'higher' grade.

The process required me to go on an 'acting list', which meant I remained a postman but covered PHG vacancies as and when.

In the spring of 1974 I spent two weeks at the PHG training school at Bletchley Park, the wartime headquarters of the top-secret British intelligence operation that cracked the German Enigma cipher in 1941. It was an interesting time to be there. The secrecy imposed on Bletchley staff had been maintained after the war – indeed, some of them have never discussed their work to this day – and the heroic exploits of the code-breakers were only then beginning to come to light.

The village of Bletchley was about to be engulfed by the new town of Milton Keynes, which was still under construction – a fact borne out by the vista that greeted me as my train pulled into Bletchley station: a vast, ghostly expanse of half-built houses, laid out in perfectly symmetrical grids, stretching as far as the eye could see. One evening we students went for a drink in a local pub in rural Bletchley, where we chatted to villagers who would soon become the city-dwellers of Milton Keynes without moving house.

The course taught us about 'keys and tabs', 'cash on delivery', registered letters and other services we'd be expected to handle as PHGs, the most intriguing of which was dealing with high-value packets. The HVP system had been introduced in 1930 as a means of enabling banks to transfer banknotes, cheques and other securities safely through the mail – it was HVPs that the perpetrators of the Great Train Robbery had been after when they raided the Glasgow to London mail train in 1963. Instruction on HVPs was given in hushed tones and conditions of secrecy worthy of the mansion and huts elsewhere on the site where the cryptanalysts had performed their vital work thirty years before.

In fact high-value packets were already in terminal decline as banks found more secure ways to move used notes. Having assiduously learned the esoteric procedures for dealing with them, I doubt if any of us ever actually encountered one. I certainly didn't. They were soon to become extinct as, eventually, would the postman higher grade.

$\sim$

It was one Friday night in 1974 in the Slough Supporters' Club – a social club opposite the sorting office, overlooking the greyhound track on the corner of Wexham Road and Wellington Street – that Mick Pearson and I decided to join the Labour party.

If I had any kind of political epiphany, I suppose this was it. It came in the midst of the period of personal restlessness that prompted me to apply for promotion. I was now an acting PHG; I had also been elected on to the union's postmen's committee – nominated, I think, by Ron Gregory, our glass-half-empty branch treasurer and my fellow QPR devotee – a role that had so far hardly proved arduous since no meetings of the committee ever seemed to be called.

Mick, too, was restless. Ten years my senior, and an astute and entertaining companion, he was undergoing something of an early mid-life crisis. It had nothing to do with his domestic circumstances, which were happy and stable, and he enjoyed being an ambulanceman. He just wanted more. It would be a pretentious exaggeration to say that he yearned to put his considerable intellect to good use to improve his own lot and that of his fellow man. Suffice it to say he felt unfulfilled.

We talked about politics a lot, Mick and I. Harold Wilson

was now back in Downing Street at the helm of a minority government. While we were both Labour voters neither of us was happy about what we saw as a drift away from its core principles by the party in Westminster. Mick was more focused than I was. He was keen to become a Labour councillor, or at least to do something that gave him an opportunity to have a say and make a difference.

I was all over the place politically. I had read a lot but analysed very little. I'd got hold of an Everyman edition of *Das Kapital* from somewhere and had read the first volume. I was taken by Marx's view of the struggle between labourers and capitalists as the current stage of an evolutionary process which he regarded as the final phase of humanity's march towards a classless society. I also read the novels of Upton Sinclair and John Steinbeck, as well as devouring the works of the man I would then have described as my favourite writer, George Orwell.

I understood Marx's theory of surplus value and, for a while, I would be the hopeless bore in the kitchen at parties on the Britwell. I tried to introduce a dose of Marxism into any discussion that bordered on the political. And in that tumultuous period encompassing Vietnam, the three-day week, pay and price freezes, industrial disputes, rocketing inflation, the Troubles in Ireland and the rise of the National Front, many of them did.

At the same time as all this was swimming around in my head I felt a growing affinity with the Labour movement. My political hero wasn't Wilson, Brown or Crosland, or even Benn, Castle or Foot. It wasn't anyone in the Labour party. It was the communist leader of the Upper Clyde Shipbuilders, Jimmy

Reid: a man who'd led his members to the most significant union victory against redundancies not by going on strike but by remaining at work. The nine-month work-in ended triumphantly in 1972 and Reid, a charismatic shipyard engineer who'd left school at fourteen, became a national figure.

His famous speech 'Alienation' – delivered at the University of Glasgow, where students had elected him to be their rector, and reproduced verbatim in the *New York Times*, which described it as the greatest speech since the Gettysburg address – thrilled me to the core, inspired and moved me in equal measure.

Jimmy Reid's passions – books, football, music – were my passions. He quoted Burns, Shelley and Shakespeare and was as comfortable in a pub as he was at a seminar. But for all of that, for all my adoration (which is not too strong a word) of the man, the Communist Party of Great Britain wasn't for me.

I had read somewhere that its aim was to swallow up all the forces of society for the benefit of the state. I couldn't see how a communist society could ever be a genuinely free society. Totalitarianism, repression of free speech, the burning of books: there was no doubt in my mind that allegiance to the state would eclipse freedom of the individual, which was as important to me as it was to Mike, my Conservative-voting brother-in-law.

Neither did I join the Workers' Revolutionary party, an organization of which I became aware when one of its disciples, Richard, a dishevelled schoolteacher from Kingston-upon-Thames, sold me a copy of *News Line*, the WRP newspaper, one evening in the Ponderosa, a vast, canteen-like bar on the trading estate where the parcels men sometimes went on their break.

Richard was about my age and reminded me of the Jehovah's Witnesses who regularly descended on the Britwell seeking to convert its residents in order to protect them from Armageddon. Like them he'd brave the pubs and clubs, a bundle of *News Lines* under his arm, asking for the address of anyone to whom he managed to sell a copy.

I bought one from him and even gave my real address, mainly because I felt sorry for this bedraggled figure who must have dedicated his entire leisure time to travelling round the south-east trying to recruit members. Vanessa Redgrave and her brother Corin were high-profile supporters of what was, in effect, a cult led by an ageing former communist, Gerry Healy, who reminded me, from his photograph, of Dickie Lawlor.

Richard delivered *News Line* to my door every week for about eighteen months, perpetually eager to recruit me to the cause. He was a nice, middle-class kid from Surrey who wouldn't have harmed a fly. When he told me how, if we armed the workers on the Britwell, they would throw off the yoke of capitalism and rise up in revolutionary fervour, I would patiently point out to him that in identifying a perceived enemy some of them were as likely to pick an immigrant as a capitalist oppressor.

What the WRP and *News Line* highlighted for me was the extraordinary arrogance and intolerance of the far left. When challenged on how few followers the WRP had among us working-class council-house dwellers, the very people he purported to champion, Richard attributed the lack of interest to 'false consciousness'. This was a reference to Marx's contention that 'it is not the consciousness of men that determines their being, but, on the contrary, their social being that determines their consciousness'. According to Richard, voting in parliamentary elections was 'bourgeois democracy' and needed to be replaced by street committees and a programme of mass education. Every human hope and aspiration, every object of art and beauty, had to be pickled into an all-embracing dogma that would guide our lives, no doubt with the assistance of the secret police.

The WRP's hatred of our 'bourgeois democracy' was as nothing compared to the hatred they reserved for other Marxist organizations, particularly the Communist Party of Great Britain, which was denounced as part of the establishment, with my hero Jimmy Reid condemned as a counter-revolutionary traitor.

The battle between the WRP, the International Socialists (the forerunners of the Socialist Workers' party), the Maoists and a thousand factions of Leninism and Trotskyism was what kept these elitist cliques going. Any tiny perceived deviation from the path of enlightenment, as defined by some demi-god, led to fierce censures, splits and divisions that spawned a dozen more off-shoots whose handfuls of members claimed spiritual purity.

Poor Richard: his efforts to convert me had succeeded only in determining the direction I would definitely not take.

At least communism had a solid bedrock in reality and, at the time, could boast that half the world's population lived under it. But while I wanted to live in a society that would not countenance the conditions we'd had to endure in my childhood, a society that would allow the intelligence of people like my mother to flourish rather than be suppressed, where greater equality and the eradication of poverty were fundamental objectives, I was repelled by the concept of an oligarchy.

If ever I questioned rejecting communism, a development widely reported in the press in 1975 reassured me that I had made the right decision. Jimmy Reid, whose eloquence, humour and compassion I so admired and who'd brought politics to life for me; Jimmy Reid, who'd twice almost captured a seat in Fife for the Communist party; Jimmy Reid had, not long after my conversations with Mick Pearson in the supporters' club, announced his resignation from the Communist Party of Great Britain in favour of moving to the mainstream.

And so it was that Alan Johnson, Mick Pearson and Jimmy Reid all joined the Labour party within a few months of one another.

Chapter 12

IT IS 8 FEBRUARY 1976, a Sunday morning. A weak winter light is beginning to illuminate the small back bedroom in which Judy and I now sleep. This used to be the children's room but they now occupy the bigger bedroom, partitioned by our next-door neighbour, Tony Gabriel, to create a separate space at the front for five-year-old Jamie while the girls share the larger area at the back. It means, as Jamie frequently and loudly complains, that Natalie and Emma have to walk through his room to get to theirs.

I drift away from the arms of Morpheus and into the panicked realization that I've overslept. This day could change my life for ever but only if I can get to the canteen at Slough sorting office by 10.30. Unfortunately, it's already 9.45.

It is the day of the annual general meeting of the Slough Amalgamated Branch of the Union of Post Office Workers. The first task of the fifty or sixty members present (out of the 800 in the branch) will be the election of officers for the coming year, of which the two principal posts are central secretary and branch chairman. I have been nominated and seconded for the latter.

After two years as a member of the postmen's committee

(during which time not a single meeting had been called) I'd decided to aim higher. As branch chairman I would have the opportunity to sort out its dysfunctional organization as well as having a key role in representing the members, whether in posts or telecoms, clerical or manual.

The incumbent chairman was 'Digger' Hughes. I have no idea where the nickname came from but he certainly wasn't Australian. Digger was a genial chap in his mid-fifties who'd become a postman only a couple of years previously. I didn't think he was sufficiently interested in the office and wondered how he could justify presiding over a branch whose committees never met.

Len Rigby, who had led us for so many years and been such a superb advocate of our cause during the strike five years earlier, no longer held the post of central secretary. Although, like most postmen, he continued to work past his sixtieth birthday, upon reaching pensionable age he had decided to step down as principal negotiating officer of the branch to make way for new blood.

His chosen successor was Joe Payne, one of the London diaspora, a PHG in his late thirties. Len and Joe shared the same Post Office grade and diminutive stature, but that was where the similarities between them ended. Len's eloquence and exuberance were replaced by a much more cerebral and serious approach to the role. Joe had transferred to Slough from Paddington in the 1950s when he moved to the Britwell's sister development in Langley, the Trelawney estate. He'd been a union rep in Slough for a while as assistant secretary for the PHGs and his intelligence and integrity made him an obvious candidate to replace Len.

The central secretary was given a specific duty that released him for full-time union work and a basement office next to the bike shed. Whereas Len had strutted around the sorting-office floor from 6am every day, Joe abhorred that kind of showmanship. He took the view that it was the job of the assistant secretaries for each grade to deal with any problems that arose on the sorting-office floor. He also had a fundamental aversion to overtime, on the grounds that it suppressed basic pay and prevented more people from being employed. So while Joe could have come in early on overtime he declined to do so, working his designated union release hours of 8am to 4.30pm.

On the rare occasions he did work overtime he was an unpopular workmate. At Oxford Avenue, for instance, his refusal to cut corners meant that we worked to time rather than getting away earlier on the 'finish and go' system we usually operated. 'If you go home at 7pm and get paid until 8pm, how long will it be before management proposes to cut each job by an hour?' Joe would ask. 'Then you'll expect the union to maintain the hours.'

The logic was impeccable, and few were bold enough to argue with Joe Payne. Certainly not the supervisors who allowed the scams, thereby earning Joe's contempt. He did the job properly, engaged in no scams or corner-cutting and worked hard, thus avoiding the possibility of any accusations of taking advantage of his union position.

The workforce had loved Len. His successor was respected without affection. Digger Hughes had spent his two years as chairman complaining about Joe behind his back – and he wasn't alone. Even Len, who'd nominated Joe as his replacement, moaned about Joe's aloofness, revelling in the almost universal view, expressed to him often, that things had been much better when he'd run the branch.

I decided that it would be me who'd take things in hand and run the branch. The central secretary's job was to represent the workforce; running the branch was the role of the chairman. That much I had read in the handbook circulated by UPW House in Clapham where our leader, Tom Jackson, was based. According to their *Branch Official's Guide*, the chairman was the custodian of the rules, the protector of the members' union rights and the guardian of the standing orders. So I'd put my name forward and had been duly proposed and seconded.

That was all well and good, but to stand a chance of beating Digger Hughes and actually being elected to this important position I had to get to the canteen by 10.30. The rules insisted that candidates must be there in person for their names to be entered on the ballot papers hastily produced for those attending to vote.

By 1976 the Ford Anglia had been replaced by a blue Ford Escort 1100cc saloon. Our aversion to debt had had to be suppressed temporarily if we were ever to acquire a reliable car: there was no way such an expensive purchase could be made in one hit. I was paying for the Escort in monthly instalments over three years. It was only a year old when I bought it but had already done 20,000 miles as a rep's car for Ross Fisheries in Grimsby.

It got me to the canteen at Slough sorting office at 10.29 precisely. There I found Digger Hughes laughing and joking with his supporters before opening the meeting as the incumbent chairman. Once it had been verified that candidates were present in accordance with branch rules, ballot boxes were made available at the rear of the canteen and the seventy members present, a reasonable turn-out, were invited to cast their votes, which were counted straight away.

I won by 63 votes to 7. Digger vacated the chair, I took his place and Len Rigby made a little speech about how effective I'd been on the postmen's committee (which was nonsense, seeing as there had been no meetings to attend) and praising me as 'a young man with an old head on his shoulders who will go far'.

I wasn't sure I wanted an old head on my shoulders but I appreciated Len's seal of approval. His support was still important even though he was no longer central secretary. I chaired the rest of the AGM, making competent use of a UPW gavel handed down through the years and presented to me by Len. On the dot of noon I banged it smartly on the table, thus fulfilling what I regarded as the most important function of the chair: to conclude the meeting just as the pubs opened.

~

I fell into trade-union work like an arctic explorer into a hot bath. By the end of 1976 I'd revised the branch rules, ensured that all the committees met regularly, set up more robust arrangements for the annual elections and ensured that the members were better informed about what we were doing on their behalf.

I got hold of a copy of Lord Citrine's *ABC of Chairmanship*, which is to the trade-union movement what Erskine May is to Parliament. Its author, an electrician by trade, had, as Walter Citrine, been a distinguished general secretary of the Trades Union Congress from the 1920s to the 1940s. It set out the rules of debate, the functions of the chair and quoted useful precedent. I was one of those sad individuals who found this kind of prosaic stuff satisfying but there were even more satisfying and, indeed, exciting aspects of union work. I felt I had found the answer to my restlessness: a role that offered fulfilment, that tested and stretched what abilities I had and that would perhaps provide opportunities for me to find some new ones I didn't know existed.

The trade-union movement wasn't the malevolent force increasingly being depicted by those who had an interest in its demise and no experience of, or need for, its services. At a philosophical level it was a bulwark against discrimination, a counterweight in the balance of power between employer and employee and an essential element of a mature democracy. But below the umbrella of these grand ideals was an organized body that delivered meaningful improvements to the working lives of its members. It was not merely a question of giving them a collective voice, but of involving them in the decisions that affected them. The UPW provided sick pay, legal services, medical services (established by the Post Office unions well before the creation of the NHS) and cheap life-insurance cover through our Friendly Society. There was even a death grant, which was becoming less important as working people became more prosperous but which was still crucial to families with insufficient savings to pay for a funeral.

Along with Dave Stock, the assistant secretary for postmen and women, I would visit the long-term (and sometimes terminally) sick, offering not only a financial helping hand but a familiar face that, unlike the faces of some employers, wasn't presenting an outward show of sympathy while calculating the quickest way to get them back to work or off the payroll.

Sometimes that familiarity went too far. I remember on one occasion Dave and I visiting someone who'd had a groin operation. As we sat sipping tea on the settee our host suddenly leaped up and pulled down his pyjama bottoms to show us his scar. With our cups and saucers balanced on our knees and his groin at eye level, we were a captive audience. Going to see a member took on a whole new meaning after that.

The Post Office wasn't a bad employer. On the contrary, it was among the best in the country. The sick pay arrangements were particularly generous. However, in an industry where a large chunk of take-home pay was derived from allowances and overtime, any lengthy spell of sick leave caused real financial hardship.

My first taste of the genuine excitement of trade-union work came in May 1976 when I attended the UPW's annual conference for the first time. Held at the Winter Gardens in Bournemouth, it lasted from a Sunday afternoon – opening with a rally at which the new prime minister, Jim Callaghan, spoke (he had taken over only a month before after the sudden resignation of Harold Wilson) – until the following Friday evening. Every day was a new and invigorating experience for me.

For a start, it was the first time I'd ever stayed in a hotel. I was sharing a room at the East Anglia with Dave Stock, who had been to conference before as the secretary of the Pontypridd branch. It was at a UPW conference that he'd met the Slough telecoms rep, Pam Graham, who'd been a friend of mine ever since the 1971 strike, when she and I had been part of the same group of youngsters who had banded together at the rallies and meetings we attended. Dave transferred to Slough to marry Pam and as a by-product of this union romance I benefited from the support of an experienced and loyal colleague in a position – representing postmen and postwomen (by far the most numerous grade in the branch) – that was crucial to my ambition of putting Slough on the UPW map.

The conference at its best was pure theatre, as enthralling as any stage drama. With over a thousand delegates and hundreds of visitors in attendance, the Winter Gardens was as packed as a post office on pensions day. On the stage, seated in a long row behind draped trestle tables, sat the executive council. At their centre was the familiar moustachioed figure of Tom Jackson, our general secretary.

Tom had not only survived but thrived in the aftermath of the union's comprehensive defeat in 1971. While the strike had been a disaster, it was felt that Tom had shown flair in the early stages of the dispute when presenting our case to the public, and courage at the end, when he needed to tell us what we didn't want to hear. He'd also demonstrated the advocacy skills of a leading barrister in putting the union's arguments to the Hardman commission. Even those critical of his handling of the strike accepted that, in the five years since, he'd negotiated some of the best pay deals we'd ever achieved. That year, for example, our pay was increasing monthly with inflation to protect the value of the above-inflation deal agreed in January. So if anything, he was regarded with greater affection by the union's activists than he had been before the strike.

Like almost every other member of the executive council ranged across the front of the stage and the serried ranks of headquarters staff behind them, Tom smoked almost continuously throughout the proceedings. As did a majority of us delegates, sunk into our red velvet tip-up seats. A thick fug rose into the spotlights that lit the stage, adding to the atmosphere as it reduced our life expectancy. Not for nothing was union activity characterized as taking place in smoke-filled rooms.

I was impressed by the eloquence of many of the speakers. Those from the floor (delegates like me) had their say from a rostrum positioned below the stage; raised, but not so high as to be level with the platform from which members of the executive made their speeches – invariably to oppose the propositions being put forward from the rostrum. Those who wanted to enter the debate after a proposal had been moved and seconded had to catch the chairman's eye, which meant leaping up and yelling 'Chair!' to get noticed. The executive usually had the last word before a vote was taken.

One speaker from the floor particularly caught my eye. John Taylor was a postman from the East End of London in his late thirties, skinny as a rake, sharp-suited. He stood with his shoulders pinned back as if standing to attention. John was the leader of the London District Council, the most powerful group in the union. It was the LDC that had come to Barnes to tell us about the strike in support of the overseas telegraph officers seven years previously. John Taylor had now replaced Dickie Lawlor, who had gone on to become one of the twelve national officers of the union before retiring in 1975.

John's oratory made no concessions to the Queen's English. He was an East End cockney and proud of it. The letter H was never pronounced in his everyday dialogue and therefore did not feature in his conference speeches, either, but they were no less effective for that. He wore a suit and tie throughout the proceedings, as did the men on the executive council. It was obvious that John was destined to join their ranks and the word on the street was that Tom Jackson saw John Taylor as his eventual successor.

John was staying in the East Anglia and we met in the bar one evening. To me it was like bumping into a film star at Cannes but John wasn't at all remote and was remarkably patient with me, a new delegate. Such treatment belied the advice he gave me that same evening, which was that the perfect personality trait of a union representative was arrogance tinged with compassion.

While I was thrilled by annual conference, it taught me an important lesson about conference debates, which was that decisions made solely in that rarefied atmosphere are seldom informed and often perverse. The big debate at my first conference was a proposal that Post Office staff should be compulsorily retired at the normal pension age of sixty. It was moved by John Taylor on behalf of the LDC. He spoke movingly of the need to open up job opportunities, particularly to young people. The union, having fought for a retirement age of sixty and negotiated an excellent final salary scheme, should not accept a situation where staff worked beyond pension age, thus denying somebody else the Post Office career that all of us in the conference hall had enjoyed. The union's officers were instructed to reach an agreement with the employer preventing this abuse and forcing out those who wished to carry on working.

Tom Jackson's deputy, a short, wavy-haired former telegraphist named Norman Stagg, opposed the proposition on behalf of the executive council. Norman was one of the union's finest negotiators. It was he who had formulated the excellent contributory pension scheme put in place when we left the civil service. He was also a fine debater. He pointed out the number of vacancies that existed in many parts of the country and the ramifications for the service of losing experienced staff. Those forced out in this way would have an occupational pension but not their state pension, which men couldn't draw until they were sixty-five. We would be plunging our members into financial difficulties by removing their reasonable expectation to remain in jobs around which they'd planned their future.

This splendid oration was to no avail. The platform lost and the proposal was carried. I sat transfixed throughout, itching to take to the rostrum to explain the problems such a change would create in Slough. But I lacked the courage and, I felt, the ability to hold an audience. In any case the atmosphere and rhetoric had swayed my own delegation. There were six of us there representing the various grades in Slough. A hurried consultation between us produced a majority of four to two in favour of John Taylor's argument, with Dave Stock and me in the minority. So Slough's eighty votes (one for every ten members) were cast for the proposal.

The union's national officers did as they were instructed and negotiated an agreement whereby, after a particular date (1 January 1979, I think it was), no postal or telecoms worker would be retained beyond the age of sixty. The reaction across the country was immediate. Men and women who'd planned to retire later were outraged. Those who hadn't accumulated enough service for a decent pension and needed more pensionable years were horrified. In an occupation where the average

age of the staff must have been well over forty – and, as a consequence, where pensions were closely scrutinized by a majority of the workforce – there was deep concern, manifested in a spate of resignations from the union.

In the end the Post Office and the UPW had to quietly rescind the agreement, replacing it with an arrangement that allowed staff to be retained after sixty 'subject to fitness and efficiency'. Calm prevailed. But it was a squall that should never have been whipped up in the first place. That conference debate had not been at all representative of the views of our members.

As well as being captivated by the work of conference, I enjoyed the social life that came with it. There was an event every evening – the Branch Dance, London Night, Manchester Night . . . I fell in with a bunch of Scots who insisted on taking me to the Glasgow shindig on the final evening. The leader of the pack was 'Big Joe' Menzies (pronounced, I learned, Mingus), a former railway worker from Perth. My allegiance to the Scots began that evening. I loved their humour and their sense of propriety (no man was allowed to swear within the hearing of a woman, a quaint custom I suspect may have eroded over time). Perhaps it was my Celtic blood (my mother's father was a Scot, her mother Irish) that endeared these people to me.

The evening ended in a large room at the Durley Hall Hotel where we'd gathered after Glasgow Night finished. Joe Menzies was the master of ceremonies, his huge frame dominating the centre of the room. He insisted that each one of us either sang or recited a verse. One by one, from around the room under Joe's direction, came lilting ballads, stirring folk songs, a bit of Elvis Presley and a lot of Robbie Burns. Then I was introduced by Joe as a stray Londoner and called upon to contribute to the evening's merriment. I sang a song I'd heard my father play as my sister and I sat on top of his honky-tonk piano as tiny tots in the early 1950s.

> Don't jump off the roof, Dad,
> You'll make a hole in the yard,
> Mother's just planted petunias,
> The weeding and digging was 'ard.
> If you must end it all, Dad,
> Won't you please give us a break,
> Take a walk to the park, Dad,
> And there you can jump in the lake.

It wasn't the way I'd intended to make my first contribution at conference but it was reasonably well received.

Chapter 13

IF BECOMING BRANCH chairman got me hooked on the union, going to conference reeled me in. I'd found a new world that gave me more fulfilment than promotion within the Post Office ever could. I resigned from the PHG acting list, explaining to Judy that while my union work was financially unrewarding (branch officers received an 'honorarium' of £50 a year which we always piously refused to accept), there was no reason why our finances should deteriorate as I would continue to work twenty to thirty hours of overtime every week. When I was away at conferences the union paid subsistence at civil-service rates which meant we weren't much worse off than if we were at work.

Judy was totally supportive. She knew my strengths and weaknesses better than anyone. Her view was that having joined the Post Office to work outside, unsupervised, it would be a mistake to move to indoor work, which may have been better paid but which I wouldn't enjoy and which would also prevent me from getting home during the day, as I was able to do as a delivery postman.

Among the weaknesses Judy had been forced to recognize

was my lack of ability when it came to any kind of DIY. I may have been the son of a painter and decorator but I hadn't inherited any of his practical skills. One weekend she'd taken the children to stay with Linda so that I could paint and decorate the living room. I did it so badly that Tony Gabriel from next door had to be brought in to retrieve the situation. While I was away having a good time at my first union conference, Judy completely retiled the bathroom. She claimed that my definition of DIY was Don't Involve Yourself, which was hurtful but true.

Giving up my postman higher grade role just before the fabulous summer of 1976 was unquestionably the right thing to do. It coincided with another important development in this watershed year. Bill Higginbottom (Ear of the Ear, Nose and Throat trio) took medical retirement, creating a vacancy on the coveted Littleworth Common delivery. There was also to be a complete re-sign under which, every five years or so, every duty would go up on a noticeboard to be signed for. Each postman would be allowed three choices, numbered in order of preference. The duties were then to be allocated according to seniority. In a high-turnover office, with eight years' service under my belt, I was now reasonably senior. I succeeded in my bid to become a proper rural postman.

~

Throughout that year my friendship grew with a man who was neither a union rep nor a politician but whose influence on me was significant. Ernie Sheers was another East Ender, a docker all his working life until the docks began to vanish in the early

1970s, taking with them a way of life that had existed for centuries. He'd hated leaving the docks and the tight-knit community that surrounded them. The family had come to the Britwell, moving in a few years after us, because Ernie's wife Kath was from Slough. They lived with their four beautiful children just down the hill on Wordsworth Road and Ernie had come to work at the Post Office.

Twelve years older than me, Ernie was a fascinating man. He had the dark good looks of one of those matinee idols of the silent movies. If he'd grown a 'tache he'd have looked just like Errol Flynn. His teeth were the whitest I'd ever seen and they were all his own, displayed regularly in a dazzling smile. Ernie was the only person I've ever known who spoke cockney rhyming slang completely naturally. I may have been a Londoner through and through but I was west London, not east, and the cockney lingo could be confusing, not least because it generally uses two words to represent one, and it is the second word, the one that is often not spoken, that rhymes. So those dazzling teeth were Hampsteads (Hampstead Heath), a piece of fish would be a Lillian (Lillian Gish) and chips Staffords (Stafford Cripps). The newspaper, or linen (linen draper), was paid for with coins from Ernie's sky (sky rocket – pocket). Sometimes rhyme begat rhyme so that a trail had to be followed to get to the source. Thus your backside could be either your Aris or your bottle, because the rhyming slang for arse was bottle and glass, and for bottle it was Aristotle, or Aris for short.

While Ernie wouldn't have described himself as a mathematician, he was a modest gambler on the horses and could work out winnings from odds almost instantaneously.

Calculating an each-way treble took only a little longer.

My new friend was a deep thinker; an observer of life rather than a reader of books. He took pride in never pushing himself to the front, keeping out of the spotlight. Instead he watched from life's shadows. An only son brought up with three sisters, Ernie had grown up believing he'd been a profound disappointment to his father and as our bond strengthened he began to talk to me about long-buried emotions concerning their relationship. My use of the word 'bond' to describe our friendship is no exaggeration. We became as close as brothers.

Ernie's views about unions were ambivalent. Basically he was a union man who voted Labour and, like me, wanted to see society rebalanced in favour of the disadvantaged and tilted away from the rich and powerful. He attended union meetings religiously but hardly ever spoke. Ernie hadn't joined the Post Office until after the 1971 strike but, if he'd been around at the time, he'd unquestionably have been one of those men ready to sell his house rather than give in; but his loyalty was to the collective struggle rather than to individual leaders. He had a firmly rooted distrust of demi-goddery and a built-in bullshit detector of which I (as an occasional bullshitter) had to be wary. He'd been unimpressed by Jack Dash, the radical un-official East End dockers' leader, and he was to be equally unimpressed by Arthur Scargill.

Ernie had a faith in God that had nothing to do with organized religion, which he distrusted. When I got to know him well, he told me about the force somewhere in the stratosphere that would compel him, at odd moments, to clasp his hands together with his thumbs interlinked in the sign of the cross. Whatever he was doing at the time, he felt he had to stop and pray, quietly and inwardly, and to seek forgiveness from his personal God.

Lest I paint too sombre a portrait of this handsome buccaneer I should add that he also had an engaging sense of humour, an infectious laugh and an extraordinary ability to get himself into unbelievable scrapes. Ernie's delivery was in Farnham Royal, where his customers loved him (they called him the fastest postman in the west after his milkman namesake in Benny Hill's novelty hit record). He annoyed the union puritans by coming into work before his official starting time to ensure that he got the mail to its destination as early as possible. On one occasion, delivering to a school during the holidays, he found his entry barred by the iron gates to the premises. Ernie was a one-man Wells Fargo: the mail must get through was his motto. He decided to climb over the gates but, having completed his ascent, and just as he was shifting his weight to bestride the pinnacle of these 9ft monstrosities, the gate on which he was balancing precariously slowly began to open. They hadn't been locked, as he had assumed, just shut, and now, at 6.30am, Ernie was adrift on a moving gate with no way of getting down. Eventually the caretaker came to the rescue, woken by Ernie's laughter.

Another morning, in teeming rain, Ernie's bike got a puncture and he decided to abandon it and walk the four miles back to the office. In the mêlée of the snarled traffic at Crown Point a car tooted. Ernie thought he recognized the driver as a PHG from Slough and jumped into the front passenger seat, throwing his soaking-wet delivery sack on the beautifully carpeted footwell where it sat in a puddle, oozing like a bath sponge. As Ernie, drenched and dripping over the upholstery, chatted away to the driver, en route, he assumed, to the sorting office, he noticed that his companion's responses were unusually reticent. It slowly dawned on him that, having glimpsed the man in profile, he'd jumped into the car of a complete stranger who had been tooting not at Ernie, but at another car which had cut in ahead of him. Now he was sitting there terrified, convinced that he'd been hijacked by a demented postman.

One day Ernie and I took a day off work to drive to the East End, where I met his friends and family. On the way back we stopped at St Katharine Dock, close to Tower Bridge, where Ernie stood for a long time surveying the site that, within a few years, would become the docklands development. For the moment it was eerily silent. For miles around all that could be seen was a bleak, empty landscape where once a thriving industry had sustained a community with all its history, traditions and culture. Ernie was deeply affected. As I drove us back to Slough in silence, I noticed that his hands were clasped together, thumbs intertwined in the shape of a cross.

~

There was another UPW conference at the end of 1976: a three-day rules revision conference in Brighton. I do understand how soporific that must sound but for me it was truly exciting. It was another chance to absorb the cut and thrust as people much like me, doing the same job, got together to debate important issues affecting our lives – although I admit I'd be stretching a long bow to suggest that the union's rules fell into that category.

Nevertheless, I was keen that the Slough Amalgamated Branch should be participants rather than passive observers in these debates. Lacking the courage to walk to the rostrum myself, I persuaded Joe Payne to speak against a proposed rule change that would have increased subscriptions by a substantial amount. It was designed to help the union recover from the 1971 strike, the financial consequences of which were still being felt. Joe strongly disapproved of the increase. He thought it would lose us members and we would simply end up drawing the same funds from fewer people, leaving us no better off. Eventually, over a few pints, he agreed to prepare a speech and take the rostrum on our behalf.

Joe delivered an impassioned speech in front of around 1,500 people. '. . . And if you carry this rule change, conference,' he warned as he reached the crux of his peroration, 'you will *desiccate* this union.'

There was no open mockery and Joe left the rostrum to a round of applause. I certainly wasn't going to mention his malapropism. I was enough of a smart-arse not only to know that the word should have been 'decimate', but also that it means specifically to reduce by one in ten rather than simply to destroy something, as is commonly supposed. However, it would have been impertinent of me to point this out and, besides, Joe was far wiser than I would ever be. He just hadn't read as many books.

The subscriptions duly went up but our delegation was proud to have contributed to the debate and resolved to do so again.

The showpiece debate at that conference was an attempt by John Taylor to introduce a rule change compelling the twelve national officers, including the general secretary, to stand for re-election every five years rather than to have them elected for life. This was a reform that would be forced upon unions by one of the Thatcher government's first Acts of Parliament four or five years later but for now it was an issue for unions to determine themselves. The atmosphere inside the hall was electric as John moved the proposition on behalf of the mighty London District Council. His speech and the motives behind it had nothing to do with attacking Tom Jackson in retaliation for the failure of the strike – as I've said, Tom was as secure in his position as he'd ever been and would have cruised through any re-election that was imposed upon him. There was therefore no personal animosity in the debate. It was principally about modernization, about moving with the times. There had just been a US presidential election, won by Jimmy Carter, with which more than one speaker drew parallels.

Listening to John Taylor, I felt that Ernie would have been appreciative of his East End eloquence. After setting out the argument as to why re-election would strengthen the union and the standing of its officers in their dealings with the employer, John ended with a topical flourish: 'If it's good enough for the president of the United States of America to be re-elected periodically, it should be good enough for our national officers.'

Speaker after speaker from the floor supported the rule change and when Tom Jackson rose to reply it looked as if he was facing certain defeat. But Tom's oratorical skills had been honed in this environment and he soon had command of his audience.

Re-election every five years would mean two years learning

the job, one year doing it and two years electioneering for the next contest, he pointed out. How would we convince postmen and telephonists with union ambitions to give up a secure job with the Post Office in order to stand for such a precarious position? Presidents of the United States continued to receive substantial remuneration after their period of office ended. Would the union have to provide similar arrangements for national officers? If not, there was no valid comparison. We would be imposing conditions on our officers that we would never accept for our members.

'You can get rid of me and any other officer through one simple device and you wouldn't have to wait five years to do it. It's called a motion of no-confidence. Why inflict an expensive system of re-elections on the union that would damage the ability of your officers to do a proper job and plunge us into a culture of permanent electioneering?'

It was a tour de force, and it won the day. The Oxford Union would have been proud of such a debate – although, as Tom would remind us on a regular basis, the UPW was not a debating society.

～

By the time I reached my mid-twenties I regretted leaving school at fifteen. For me the prospect of going to university had seemed about as realistic as my chances of visiting the planet Pluto and it had never remotely crossed my mind as achievable. Yet still I thirsted for knowledge. I read constantly, which served only to intensify that thirst rather than quenching it.

Becoming a trade-union official opened up a whole new

world of educational opportunity to me. As branch chairman I was eligible to attend a range of UPW training schools. But even more wonderful to me was the cornucopia of TUC correspondence courses available free of charge. The hub for this huge educational operation was Tillicoultry, a small town in Clackmannanshire, Scotland. Even though I've never managed a visit to Tillicoultry, for a couple of years in the 1970s it was the centre of my universe. I sent off essays and completed exam papers to my tutors through the post, receiving their comments, criticisms and the occasional commendation by return.

It was done for fun rather than to gain qualifications. My tutors got me thinking, studying and writing. They succeeded in inspiring and encouraging me even though they had to do so without personal contact and from a distance – so much so that I considered taking up one of the many opportunities to study full-time at Ruskin, the trade-union college in Oxford, or one of the other centres around the country offering further education for which modest grants were available, all funded by the trade-union and Labour movement. But with a family to support the finances never worked for me, so I stuck to my correspondence courses, supplemented by evening classes at Slough College, where I reached Grade 2 in piano before overtime and the increasing burden of union work took its toll.

I doubted if any correspondence course could equip me for one of my principal functions as a union official: to hold the attention of an audience through the power of oration. I wanted to develop the confidence and skills that would enable me at the very least to persuade and engage my members in

Slough on the matters affecting us most directly, but more than this I wanted to do what I'd seen John Taylor and others do: to speak convincingly to an audience of over a thousand from the rostrum at conference.

In the end it was an issue I cared about passionately that motivated me and led me to jump in at the deep end for the first time, with no training or tuition. That issue was South Africa. Ever since my schooldays, when Mr Smith had used every religious education lesson to acquaint us with the injustice and cruelty of apartheid, I'd been aware of the grievous injury inflicted on native South Africans. Mr Smith had been something of a voice in the wilderness then, but by the mid-1970s opposition to apartheid had become a cause célèbre. Following the shooting in Soweto in the summer of 1976 of hundreds of black schoolchildren demonstrating against a dictum requiring them to be taught in Afrikaans, the UPW declared that, as part of a co-ordinated international boycott, its members would refuse to handle mail or connect calls to or from South Africa during a week of protest beginning on 7 January 1977.

The boycott was elevated to the front pages of the newspapers by the activities of a shady, right-wing organization in the UK called the National Association for Freedom, which strongly supported the liberty of South African policemen to shoot black schoolchildren. They secured an injunction to stop the industrial action going ahead. During the public debate, the right of the UPW executive council to impose such a boycott was called into question.

At the time all this was going on I was away for a week at a union induction school in Bournemouth. I had already arranged a branch meeting for the Sunday following my return, but when I got back to the office that Friday, five days after the boycott had begun, I found that Joe Payne, besieged by disgruntled members, had tried to take the heat out of the situation by inviting them to record their views, either for or against the boycott, in a book made available for the purpose in the union room. A glance at the book revealed a long list of opponents and just three or four members (including Joe) in support.

I could understand how Joe had been forced into taking this action but, as I pointed out to him, it was a meaningless list and the place to decide such issues was at a properly constituted branch meeting, where the arguments could be debated.

There was a bigger attendance than usual that Sunday morning. When the contentious item on the agenda was reached I sought permission to leave the chair because I wanted to contribute to the debate (I was following the advice given by Citrine's *ABC of Chairmanship*). The canteen on the top floor of Slough sorting office hadn't been designed for public speaking. There were no microphones and the acoustics were dreadful. Words ricocheted off the big plate-glass windows and landed somewhere around the metal shutters of the serving hatch.

Nor was my audience sitting in ordered rows, lost in rapt contemplation of the profound points I was making. The members were grouped around the canteen tables, some with their backs to me. A couple of guys didn't even look up from their Sunday papers, lying open on the tables in front of them.

Cicero may well have struggled in such an environment –

and my speech was certainly not Ciceronian. To ensure that I presented my thoughts logically and that I wouldn't dry up I'd written it all out in advance, but I soon realized that reading a prepared argument wasn't going to work so I ditched it and simply spoke from the heart. I spent ten minutes describing the evils of apartheid, the repressive nature of the South African state, the need to uphold the values of the trade-union movement. I talked of my pride in a union that was showing solidarity with black South African workers. While others paid lip service to the cause, Tom Jackson had shown leadership in deciding to back words with action.

When I sat down I received a round of applause before the meeting voted narrowly to reject my arguments and censure the executive council for its actions over South Africa.

~

Engaging though I found union work, I would define it as an interest, something that added another dimension to my work, not as a passion. The passions of my life remained music, books and football. As well as writing songs, now with my new Eko guitar, I was broadening the range of the music I listened to. Judy was far more knowledgeable about classical music than I was. She helped me track down a piece that had fascinated me since I was a child, when I'd caught a snatch of it by chance while turning the Bakelite switch that controlled the trio of stations on our hired radio. It was the most majestic piece of music I'd ever heard, but I didn't know what it was called or who had composed it. This nugget turned out to be from the piano suite *Pictures at an Exhibition* by Mussorgsky. I bought a recording of it, a purchase that started a collection of classical LPs, which could be bought much more cheaply than rock albums.

My workmates in the sorting office included more lovers of literature than I've ever worked among since. There was 'Jock' Hastie (I'm afraid there were a few Jocks, Paddys and Taffs whose parents would have been mortified at how their carefully chosen Christian names had been lost to the English custom of affixing such generic labels to men of Celtic origin), who gave me an 'introduction to Shakespeare' lesson by reciting Portia's speech from *The Merchant of Venice* on the quality of mercy not being strained one afternoon over a cup of tea in the canteen. Jock was also a talented illustrator. He produced a weekly cartoon for a local paper in Windsor and was happy to sketch a workmate on request for a quid a time.

Des O'Callaghan, who worked with Ernie Sheers on the Farnham Royal deliveries, was a devoted poetry enthusiast. Judy had bought me *The Oxford Book of English Verse* one Christmas and when I mentioned this to Des as we sorted letters next to one another early in the New Year he exposed his secret passion, reeling off the first two verses of 'Naming of Parts' by Henry Reed. Des recommended Yeats and Auden and Philip Larkin, and insisted I bring my book into the office for him to flag up his favourite poems for me.

Charlie Markham, a tiny bespectacled PHG who looked like the Carry On actor Charles Hawtrey, once quoted the whole of Henry Newbolt's 'Vitaï Lampada' ('There's a breathless hush in the Close to-night . . .'), learned by rote and recited by heart as we distributed pillarbox keys together.

In fact the Slough sorting office was like a Royal Mail

university, such was the erudition of the postmen alongside whom I worked. The vice-chancellor was George Sirpal, a fresh-faced PHG from Delhi. Unlike the Scots, Welsh and Irish, whose birth names were jettisoned wholesale and replaced by national identifiers, the Asian guys were given anglicized versions of their real names, or nicknames that sounded vaguely like them but were easier to pronounce. So there was K. K. Sharma, for example, Tiger Singh, Charlie Gopal, Peter Saroan. Curiously, while the Londoners in particular seemed to find names difficult they were perfectly capable of picking up snatches of conversational Urdu and Hindi. Greetings and farewells would be exchanged in such dialects regardless of whether the speaker was from Bombay or Bermondsey.

During my acting PHG phase, George Sirpal had seen me engrossed in a book during a quiet period in the inquiry office, where members of the public called to pick up undelivered mail or to lodge complaints. George had studied English literature at university in India and his speciality was Thomas Hardy. He lent me his favourite Hardy novel, *Return of the Native*, and urged me to read Hardy's poetry.

The dark beauty of Hardy's prose had me under its spell within a couple of pages and I went on to devour nearly every novel he wrote, regretting that he hadn't written more. Poems such as 'Afterwards' and 'The Ruined Maid' became friends for life. George Sirpal never knew what a significant contribution he'd made to my happiness.

Chapter 14

As 1976 HAD DRAWN to a close we'd spent Christmas with
Linda and Mike. They had left Tring for a five-bedroom
house in Stopsley near Luton, at the end of a row of houses
down a long country lane and surrounded by fields. They
needed the space: their family of five had almost doubled in
size with the arrival of four foster children.

Linda had always possessed a protective streak, from which I
had benefited as a child, and she'd always loved kids. She was
extraordinarily patient and genuinely absorbed in their games
and their stories. Every evening, without fail, she'd read to all
seven children, separately allowing each one to choose the story
he or she wanted to hear.

They had also acquired a big van for transporting their
enlarged family and a menagerie of pets, including a white-
haired mongrel named Shandy. Walking to school every
morning with seven children and a dog, Linda sought to
impress the other mothers with the firm control she had over
the animal. As they approached the kerb to cross the road, she
would instruct the dog: 'Sit, Shandy!' in a commanding voice.
Her voice was indeed commanding, and very loud, one

morning when she fluffed her lines, shouting instead the order 'Shit, Sandy!' which suggested a level of control over her dog that must have really impressed her audience.

Mike fully supported Linda in her desire to foster. They had undergone the arduous process of becoming approved as foster parents while still living in Tring. It was their success in looking after their first two foster sons, Nicky and Eugene, that had led to their decision to buy the bigger house in Stopsley.

Nicky and Eugene, seven and six when they came to Linda and Mike, were half-brothers. They were being fostered long-term, having suffered terribly at home. Nicky had been taken into care at eighteen months after being badly beaten by his mother's boyfriend, Eugene's father. His skull had been fractured, his arm and leg broken. An attempt had been made to reunite the children with their parents a couple of years later but further violence erupted. Eugene's little body still carried the marks of the buckle of the belt with which he was beaten regularly.

After the move to Stopsley, a friend of Linda's, a social worker, rang with a problem. Two other little boys in her care had been placed with a childless couple with a view to adoption but now the wife had asked for them to be taken back as she could not muster any maternal feelings towards them. Linda's friend was desperate that they shouldn't be returned to a children's home. She asked Linda if she could take them in temporarily until a permanent placement could be found. The mere mention of a children's home was all it took. It had been Linda's biggest fear when we were children, during our mother's illness and after her death, that we would be forced into such an institution and despite her tender years she succeeded in keeping us together and out of 'the system'. Ricky and Murray, aged five and three respectively, arrived shortly afterwards.

Earlier that year the local newspaper had chosen Linda as their 'Luton Supermum', an accolade for which she had been nominated by her two eldest children, Renay and Tara, with the help of their father. With seven kids between the ages of three and nine, she was beyond question a supermum. When Judy and I arrived with our three, aged ten, eight and almost six, we spent that Christmas with ten children which, as I remarked to Linda, in some parts of rural England and on a few Scottish islands would have been a schoolful.

That year we had told Natalie about Beppe, her Italian father, who had never sought contact or even been in touch, and I had begun the process of adopting her officially. We said that it would be OK for her to look for Beppe, if she wanted to, when she was older, but reassured her that I was her father in all the ways that were important. 'I wasn't the one who planted the seed that made you,' I explained to her. 'But I'm the one who loves you and who wanted to be your daddy.'

It's a strange experience, adopting your own child. I had never thought of Natalie as anything but my eldest daughter and she'd never known any other father.

We didn't need Beppe's permission. His failure to take any responsibility for his daughter – not that we'd wanted that – was classified as abandonment. The process was rigorous all the same. After the paperwork was completed, social workers interviewed Judy and me together, then separately. Natalie was interviewed with her mother and then on her own. The school had to be involved and finally we were informed that our neighbours would be interrogated. The truth behind our ambiguous back story, in which Natalie was presented as the fruit of my sixteen-year-old loins, was to be revealed. In the event it didn't matter: none of our neighbours even mentioned it and I very much doubt that by then it would have been the subject of surreptitious gossip.

Once I became Natalie's father in the eyes of the law she acquired a new birth certificate and the chance to rectify something that had always rankled with her: she was the only one of our three children bereft of a middle name. Now, unlike Emma and Jamie or any other child at their school, Natalie would have the opportunity to choose her own. She picked Anne, Linda's middle name, but Natalie was insistent that unlike Linda Ann, her name would be spelled with an 'e'. Her wish was our command, and the Lynch Hill school register was amended to include Natalie Anne Johnson.

At Stopsley, surrounded by our ten children, I reminded Linda of the two Christmases we'd spent alone in our own childhood, especially the one when, as a ten-year-old – the same age as Natalie was now – she'd cooked my dinner, a chicken from a Christmas club hamper, with the plastic wrapping still on it. We rarely spoke of those days, mainly because Linda knew that I was bewildered by her decision to re-establish contact with our father. He'd beaten our mother, refused to contribute to our welfare and, when I was eight and Linda almost eleven, run off for good to start a new life with the barmaid from the Lads of the Village pub. It was one of the happiest days of our young lives.

Linda realized that there was no question of me following her example and having any kind of contact with Steve, our father. I hadn't laid eyes on him since he had turned up uninvited at the cemetery after our mother's funeral and I had no desire to do so now. It took me a while to understand that Linda's magnanimity was far nobler and more humane than my sulky rebelliousness. Her motivation wasn't fondness for the father who'd treated her far worse than he'd treated me. It was that streak of protectiveness. Steve and his second wife, Vera, had a daughter together. Sandra was ten years younger than me, an only child desperate to establish a relationship with her half-siblings. Sandra was the reason Linda stayed in touch and she couldn't see Sandra without seeing Steve. It was hardly a rapprochement. Linda and Mike would visit Steve, Vera and Sandra at their home in Dulwich once or twice a year. Sandra was in contact with Linda more regularly, becoming another beneficiary of Linda's endless quest to spread serenity by putting a sheltering arm around those she loved.

We had a wonderful Christmas, although Mike was quiet and withdrawn for much of the time. He was keen to get to his newly adopted pub in Stopsley during its very limited festive opening hours, yet once there he was unusually gloomy, even morose. He believed the economy was in a mess, he told me. Facing rising inflation and rising unemployment, Jim Callaghan's minority Labour government was trying to deal with the crisis by cutting public expenditure and bringing in deflationary economic policies. Mike wasn't impressed by the government throwing itself on the mercy of the International Monetary Fund. However, he was more worried about his own future. He was afraid that Henry's Radios, where he'd spent his entire working life, would go bust or be sold to new owners. Mike had a close association with the family who owned the business. They had taken him on as a Saturday boy at the age of thirteen and treated him like a son. He was concerned that, away from their benevolent regime, he would find life difficult because he had learned on the job and the skills he'd acquired over the years were unaccompanied by any certificates recording his qualifications.

As we drank our pints and smoked his Senior Service cigarettes, Mike cheered up a little when he talked about what a great thing the fostering had turned out to be. But he was so fond of the two latest additions, Ricky and Murray, that he was dreading the end of their short-term stay.

On the drive back to Slough, Judy remarked that she, too, had noticed how distracted and disengaged Mike had seemed. She put it down to overwork.

We never saw Mike again.

~

It's difficult to write this. Even now, so many years after the event, it is a struggle to form the words on the page. The tears I found it so hard to shed when my mother died have poured down my face a hundred times since for Mike and for the awful, tragic end to his short life.

It is difficult even to know where to begin, for it had all been building up over a long period but only came to a head in the space of a few short months in 1977. Perhaps the first trigger was the departure of Ricky and Murray.

They had been with Linda and Mike for a year when my sister was informed that social services had found a couple who wanted to adopt the two boys. Six-year-old Ricky pleaded with

Linda to be allowed to stay. She tried to reassure them that they'd be happy in their new home and she and Mike took the boys to visit their new parents. On the day they were due to leave for good Linda gave Ricky a book she'd compiled for him. It was the story of his life so far. She had included the handful of memories he had of his birth mother in the days before he'd been abandoned, of which he had been encouraged to speak. There were lots of photographs of his time at Stopsley and contributions from the other children. Linda felt it would provide Ricky with a sense of his own identity and value.

Linda and Mike promised to stay in touch with the two boys but it soon became clear that was going to be too difficult for Ricky, in particular, to handle. While his adoptive parents were chatting with his foster parents, he hid in the back of Mike's van and wasn't discovered until Mike and Linda were on their way home to Stopsley. Ricky had to be taken back to his new family kicking and screaming.

Mike was even more affected by this heartbreaking parting than Linda was. When his boss asked him what was wrong Mike told him he'd just lost two of his sons. When he learned that Mike was referring to his foster children he berated Mike for being too community-minded.

It was not long after this that the full extent of Mike's condition was revealed. Linda caught him unawares swigging from a bottle he'd taken out of his briefcase when he thought he was alone. It was as simple as that. She walked in to her living room and found him drinking furtively. Not thinking much of it, and assuming that what was in the bottle was wine, she suggested fetching a couple of glasses so they could sit down and have a drink together. But it wasn't wine. It was vodka.

Within minutes Mike was in tears, admitting that he'd been drinking the stuff surreptitiously for years, since before they'd met over a decade earlier. Throughout the whole of their life together – courtship, wedding, parenthood – Mike had been addicted to alcohol. He'd chosen vodka way back, in the days when he was still living at home with his parents, because it was odourless and wouldn't give rise to awkward questions. Demonstrating all the guile and cunning of the practised alcoholic, he also sucked menthol and eucalyptus sweets. Bottles of vodka were secreted all over the house in the places he was most often to be found – in his work shed, the greenhouse, the potting shed, the garage.

He had been what would today be known as a functioning alcoholic. Only now he wasn't functioning so well. As the uncertainties about his future increased his drinking had intensified. It had long ceased to offer any pleasure or even temporary relief. He drank now simply in order to feel normal.

Linda held Mike in her arms as he sobbed out his confession. She swore she'd get him through this no matter how hard it might be. Coincidentally, she'd recently read a magazine article about alcoholism that she fetched when Mike was calmer. It had one of those questionnaires alongside it – 'Ten ways to tell if you're an alcoholic'. If the answer to two or three of the questions was yes, the respondent potentially had a drink problem and was advised to seek help. Mike answered yes to eight of them. There was a contact number at the end of the article to call to find your nearest branch of Alcoholics Anonymous. Linda said she would ring the next day.

She spent the rest of the day trying to track down every

bottle of vodka in the house and tipping its noxious contents down the kitchen sink.

~

It was decided that Mike would take the rest of the week off and then, once he was back at work, attend his first AA meeting at a London branch, close to Henry's Radios and well away from where they lived.

In the meantime he would confine himself to the house and stay off the booze. They told the children Dad was sick – and he was. Very sick indeed.

Nothing prepared Linda or Mike for the horror of the withdrawal symptoms.

It was only much later that Linda told me about the terrifying hallucinations Mike endured during this drying-out period. Flesh-eating worms were entering his body, huge black insects dropped from the ceiling on to his face, enormous spiders scuttled backwards and forwards across his chest, his legs, his arms.

Their nights were sleepless as Linda clung on to her husband, who would be curled into a tight ball, shaking, crying, shivering. The demons were relentless, Mike was frail, Linda exhausted. Slowly, step by step, Mike emerged from his pit of torture and despair. He stayed off work for an extra week and then began to go to the Alcoholics Anonymous meetings, sharing his experiences with others who had passed through, or were still negotiating, the subterranean world where he'd been trapped.

Mike began to look for jobs locally, in Luton. He felt that,

Above: My mother, Lily.

Left: Linda and Mike on their wedding day.

Barnes pond, the picturesque setting for the palatial Barnes postmen's delivery office.

The night shift at Barnes, Christmas 1968. I am at the front, third from the left, in the red jumper. Behind me are, from left to right, Brian Green in the blue sweater, Peter Simonelli and Billy Fairs, in the brown coat.

even if Henry's Radios survived, the daily commute was an unnecessary pressure he could do without. Somebody from his AA group phoned Linda to offer support. She was grateful for the approach but she was confident that they were coping. She kept the caller's phone number and promised to get in touch if the situation changed.

Having said nothing of all this to anyone, they now faced the dilemma of whether to confide in Mike's parents, who had moved to Hampshire but were due to visit Linda and Mike for the weekend. Mike decided that they ought to be told. When he broke the news to his mother her reaction was one of total disbelief. 'Of course you're not an alcoholic,' she scoffed. 'Don't be so silly. I suppose this is her idea.'

This hostility towards Linda was hurtful but nothing new. It was the least of their worries.

They told nobody else and the next few weeks went well. It was now March. The dark days of winter were passing and spring was arriving. They celebrated Mother's Day. The children presented Linda with a set of sherry glasses, to which Mike added a bottle of sherry. Linda treated herself to a glass that evening. The next day she was going to London with a friend to visit the Ideal Home Exhibition. Mike dropped them off at the station after taking the children to school. He was due at a job interview in Luton later. The plan was for him to pick up Linda and her friend from the station at 6pm.

When they got off their train there was no sign of Mike. Linda eventually made her own way home, where she found the children watching television. 'Dad's upstairs asleep,' Renay told her. She found Mike comatose and she couldn't wake him. Beside him lay the empty Mother's Day sherry bottle.

He hadn't gone to the job interview. He had started drinking before collecting the children from school half cut. He had finished the bottle when he got back home.

The next day Mike was full of remorse. It was a lapse, but he'd rally and recover the lost ground. His rail season ticket had run out and now that he had resolved to find work locally he decided not to renew it and instead to hire a car and drive backwards and forwards to London (the big, thirsty van he used for ferrying the children around being deemed unsuitable for commuting). It would remove the temptations of the station bar and provide another incentive to stay off the booze and away from the breathalyser.

On the first day of this new regime Mike was deputed to pick up Renay and Tara from Girls' Brigade so that Linda could be at the local slimming club she ran one evening a week. Ann, a young girl who lived next door, would babysit the other three children until Mike got home. Linda – who never drove, even though she had passed her test at eighteen – would get a lift back from one of the people in her class.

She arrived home at 8.30pm to find Ann still there, ashen-faced. Mike hadn't picked up Renay and Tara as arranged. When he hadn't turned up, another Girls' Brigade mum had taken them home with her own daughter and phoned to let Linda know where they were.

Shortly after Ann had taken that call Mike had arrived home so drunk he'd had to crawl up the long path to the front door. While Ann kept the children in the front room away from this awful sight, Mike dragged himself up the stairs, where he'd remained ever since.

Linda called a taxi and went to collect Renay and Tara. When they got home, she thanked Ann, who had stayed on with the boys, they said their farewells and Linda ushered her out of the door. Ann had seen Mike incapable with drink; the women who ran the 'Girls' Brigade and the other mothers knew he'd failed to collect his daughters. Mike's 'problem' was beginning to become public knowledge in the small community where they lived.

Renay had run upstairs to get changed and go to the bathroom. As Linda walked back down the hall she heard her daughter cry out. She rushed upstairs to find Mike lying, fully clothed and fast asleep, in a bathful of water.

Later, when he learned that Renay had discovered him in that state, Mike burst into tears. He was a hopeless drunk, he wailed. His neighbours knew it and, worst of all, so did his eldest daughter.

It was a while before Linda suddenly remembered the hire car. Surely Mike hadn't driven home? He had. But he could remember nothing of the journey and thought he must have abandoned the car in the lane leading up to the house. It certainly wasn't outside. Linda grabbed a torch and went out to find it, check it wasn't damaged and make sure it was locked.

She discovered the car neatly parked at the side of the lane. It seemed unscathed and could be left there safely for the night. As she shone the torch across the car she noticed the number plate. The first three letters were LMJ: the initials of our mother, Lilian May Johnson.

❧

The day after the bathtub incident Mike went to see his doctor on his way to work. He came home that evening very late and very drunk and went straight to bed. Linda was desperate. Although I wasn't easy to get hold of, I think she'd taken a conscious decision not to involve me in the crisis. She knew how much I admired Mike and how upset I would have been to see him diminished (as he would have regarded it).

She had always considered it her responsibility to protect me. She had been our mother's support and confidante more or less all her life and through all our trials and tribulations, particularly when it came to my father's womanizing, their motto was 'Don't tell Alan.' In any case, I doubt she thought I could bring any wisdom to bear on the awful problems she and Mike were facing now, or shine any light into the shadows engulfing them.

Instead she confided in a close friend, who advised her to contact the person who'd rung from Alcoholics Anonymous offering help and to talk to Mike's parents. She took the plunge and called her in-laws. Ted, Mike's father, answered and they had a long conversation. Ted was sympathetic and comforting. He said he would get the train up from Fareham first thing in the morning to come and talk to his son, to help relieve the burden Linda was bearing and to ensure Mike knew that his father was not ashamed of him for what was, after all, a terrible illness and a breakdown rather than a vice.

Linda was elated. She didn't feel the need to contact AA now that she had family support. Mike and his father would be able to talk man to man and find dimensions that were beyond her understanding. It was a breakthrough.

An hour later the phone rang. It was Irene, her mother-in-law.

She asked to speak to Mike. When told he was asleep, she rounded on Linda. Ted had told her everything about the conversation he'd had with his daughter-in-law. 'Ted won't be coming to Stopsley,' she spat, 'and neither will I. Mike's your husband and you're the one who turned him into an alcoholic. It's your problem and you can just get on with it.' Then she slammed the phone down.

When Mike woke up later that night, Linda told him that his father had been extremely sympathetic but that his mother wouldn't allow him to come over. Mike was sad and remorseful. He said that he was no good to her or the kids any more. Linda reassured him that she loved him as much as ever and that they would get through this dreadful time together. She joked that if he was still like this in his forties it might be a different story. But they were young, and they had the best years of their life ahead of them once they'd confronted and overcome this obstacle. Later that year they would be celebrating their tenth wedding anniversary. She was determined to make it a new beginning with the man she loved.

Mike told her that during his visit to the doctor's that morning, a Wednesday, it had been arranged for him to be admitted to a psychiatric clinic on the Friday to 'dry out'. There was only one day to wait. Linda urged him to spend it quietly at home but he insisted on going to work to 'tie up loose ends' before going into the clinic. The doctor predicted that he would need to stay there for two or three weeks. It was only one day, he argued. In any case, he was due at an AA meeting in London on the Thursday evening. Tony, an Anglo-Chinese guy he'd befriended at AA, would call for him at Henry's Radios so that they could go together.

In the morning the van wouldn't start (the hire car had, understandably, been returned) so Mike set out to walk to the station to catch the train to London. It was a cold and windy day, and he donned a hooded, fur-lined parka that Linda said made him look like an Eskimo. She was still cross with him for not taking the day off, but she conceded that attending the AA meeting was important. And the next day a proper clinical process would commence to rid Mike of the curse that threatened to destroy their lives. She kissed him goodbye.

Mike rang home in the afternoon in a state of some distress. For a couple of weeks he'd been working alone in a vacant store that Henry's had taken over as an outlet for discounted lines. He'd been drinking at lunchtime. After re-opening the shop he had fallen asleep behind the counter with his suit jacket hanging up beside him. Somebody had come in and stolen his wallet from the inside pocket. All his money and his return rail ticket had gone. Linda told him to ring the police straight away. He said he would. She checked that Tony would be calling for him after work, which he confirmed. 'Ask him to give you a lift home after the AA meeting,' Linda suggested, certain that Mike's supportive friend would help.

Mike said he'd do that. He would see her later, he said softly. He told her that he loved her.

It was 6pm and Linda was cooking tea for the children when the phone rang. It was Tony, asking whether she knew where Mike was. He had gone to the shop as arranged but the door was locked and the shop was in darkness.

Linda was overwhelmed by a sense of dread. 'Go back! Go back! He must be waiting inside for you!' she screamed. She told Tony about the theft and implored him to call the police if he couldn't get into the shop.

But by then it was too late. Michael Whitaker, the kindest, gentlest, most decent man I'd ever know, had locked the door of the shop from the inside, drunk a bottle of vodka, descended to the basement and hanged himself with a piece of electrical cord.

~

The funeral was on Maundy Thursday. My six-year-old son Jamie was convinced that as Mike was thirty-four when he died, the same age as Jesus, he, too, would rise again on Easter Sunday.

As I took Linda's arm to lead her through the ordeal it was impossible for either of us not to feel the emotional echo of our mother's funeral thirteen years before. I was trying now to fulfil the role that Linda had assumed then. Trying but failing.

Linda was incredibly strong and determined to remain so for the sake of her five children. But she blamed herself for not having spotted the signs of alcoholism earlier; for not having done more to help her husband. Ted and Irene were adrift on the same sea of guilt that Linda was struggling to navigate. Irene's hostility towards my sister was palpable. I did my best to protect her from it.

Linda had been sent the 'Serenity Prayer' by somebody at Alcoholics Anonymous:

God, grant me the serenity to accept the things I cannot change,

> The courage to change the things I can,
> And wisdom to know the difference.

She recited it to me in a rare moment we shared on our own in her house before going out to follow the hearse. I pointed out that Irene's antipathy was something she couldn't change and that I'd be right next to her throughout the day ready to fend off any verbal aggression. But Irene was far too dazed and upset to argue and there were, thankfully, no scenes, no confrontations.

Andrew was there, no doubt reappraising, as I was, all those evenings the three of us had spent together at the Blue Anchor in Tring. Shocked and bewildered, we agreed that Mike never seemed to drink like an alcoholic. But how does an alcoholic drink? In much the same way as everybody else, we concluded. On the surface, at least.

When we cleared Mike's tools from his shed, lifted the hinged lids of bench seats, delved in the attic where he had soldered circuit boards and built speaker cabinets, we found more and more empty vodka bottles, along with a few full ones Linda had missed in her previous trawl.

The family doctor disclosed that Mike had been to see her before Christmas about his alcohol problem and told Linda how depressed he had been. Anti-depressants had been prescribed after Mike spoke of feeling an urge to jump in front of a train on his way to work. The GP, bound by patient confidentiality, couldn't have shared this information with Linda at the time, but learning it now just led her to castigate herself all the more for having been so completely unaware that Mike had sunk to this level of dependency.

'Once somebody has a strong inclination to commit suicide they usually carry it out,' the doctor explained. 'Mike's method showed how determined he was. A cry for help would have been an overdose. Mike was well beyond that stage.'

Judy and I shared Linda's feelings of guilt. Surely we should have seen the signs, been more receptive and alert to his confidences? Judy felt that Linda should have told me as soon as the truth emerged but I disagreed. I understood why Mike would pledge Linda to silence, particularly as far as I was concerned. He was well aware of how much I looked up to him. It would have increased his feelings of shame and humiliation if he'd known I was party to his secret. He had only reluctantly agreed that his parents should be informed, and in the event that had, if anything, made a bad situation worse. In any case it was more characteristic of me than of Linda to keep my own counsel. How could I blame her for reacting as I would have reacted myself?

At work I found it impossible even to touch upon what had happened to my brother-in-law. To have revealed that he'd committed suicide would have elicited well-intentioned questions, embarrassed solemnity. It was just too agonizingly personal to discuss. So I simply said that my sister had been widowed and gave as little supplementary information as I could get away with.

The only person to whom I could talk about it, apart from Judy, was Ernie Sheers. Not Mick, or my other neighbours round the Green; not Joe Payne or Dave Stock, my fellow union officials; not even Andrew. But in Ernie I sensed an empathy, a genuine awareness of Mike's vulnerability. He'd never met the man but it was in Ernie's nature to engage with the human condition on a deeper level. I did not get from him those 'Never mind, you have to be strong for your sister's sake' platitudes that perfectly decent people utter in such situations in order to move the conversation on to more comfortable terrain.

I didn't *want* comfort. I wanted discomfort. I needed someone to understand what a fine person Mike was, how tragic his descent into despair had been, how heroically he'd tried to slay his dragons and how desperately sad and lonely he must have been at the end. Ernie listened, really listened, as I tipped my misery all over him.

My sister had been orphaned in her teens and widowed in her twenties. As she entered her thirties that September, six months after Mike's death, I could see how determined she was to forge a new life. The last condition to which Linda was likely to succumb was self-pity. But it was hard for her to go on – so hard.

It was as if a planet had disappeared from our solar system, leaving an immense black void where once there had been Michael Whitaker.

Chapter 15

A S WE ALL STRUGGLED in our different ways to adjust to the permanently altered shape of our lives, I took solace in the routine of my job and my union work. Although elections were held every year there was little prospect of me being challenged, let alone defeated, as branch chairman. I was attentive to the needs of my members. They could be exasperating, troublesome, apathetic and sometimes hostile but I considered myself to be the guardian of their rights under the union's rules and I think they realized I was doing my best for them even if they never said as much. The role of a local union representative is a thankless one. Berated by the members for the employer's actions and by the employer for the actions of the members, the most he or she can hope for from either side is a rarely expressed respect.

I benefited from my members' perception of me as someone who wasn't interested in the perks of office. This stemmed from my refusal to accept any regular 'facility time', in other words to have part of my duty designated as time off for union work.

Such facilities were essential to maintaining good industrial relations. The head postmaster and his colleagues needed to talk to senior union officials on a regular basis to consult and agree on patterns of work, revised duties, promotions, disciplinary cases, the implementation of national agreements and to plan Christmas arrangements. Joe Payne, as branch secretary, had full-time release and was stationed in the union's basement office.

On the sorting-office floor, where the majority of our members worked, Dave Stock was assigned a duty with an easy first delivery and the remainder of his working hours were dedicated to union business. Thus he was on hand to resolve flashpoints, ensure that agreed arrangements were being followed and to act as a conduit between the postal executives (as the assistant inspectors were now called, having swapped their supervisors' uniforms for lounge suits) and the workforce. There were also bits and pieces of facility time given to the health and safety rep and a few others.

Despite my position as one of the two principal branch officers, I wanted none of it. I did a normal range of duties with no time off because I preferred it that way. The members appreciated what they saw as my self-sacrifice but for me it was the best of both worlds. I was regularly dragged into disputes with which Dave was dealing about delivery of advertising circulars or supposed breaches of our many local agreements. I was considered to be an articulate advocate and I prided myself on having a talent for negotiation but I also loved to be out on delivery.

I'd carry a little notebook in the inside pocket of my uniform jacket into which would go every request, complaint, comment, criticism or observation made to me by the many members who approached me during the course of my working day. I made a point of getting back to every person whose name was in my notebook with some kind of response, although sometimes by the time I did, whatever the problem was had blown over or they'd forgotten they'd even raised it with me in the first place. Once I was assailed by John Tobin, a garrulous Irish postman who worked permanently on Slough station (in those days, the vast majority of mail was transported by rail). At the station he virtually ran the show. He was better informed when it came to arrivals and departures than most of the station staff and he knew which trains had to be met for offloaded mail and which were to receive the barrowloads of sacks for outward dispatch.

The problem with John was that very few people could understand what he was saying after he'd sunk a few pints of Guinness in the station bar. On this particular day I could make no sense at all of what John was asking me to do, although it was clear he was very passionate about it. In the end I just scratched some hieroglyphics in my notebook and told him not to worry, I'd sort it out. I made a mental note to ask Dave if he knew what the problem was at Slough station but I forgot. A week later, as I was walking across the sorting-office floor, John Tobin shouted my name. I looked over, expecting to be castigated for not resolving his problem, but instead he gave me a thumbs-up, beamed a smile and shouted, 'Thank you very much, Alan.' I never found out what it had all been about but from that day on he was one of my greatest supporters.

~

Following QPR was never going to be rewarded by seasons of gold and glory. We Rangers fans had to be grateful for the few ups that struggled to balance the many downs: the odd promotion, a mid-table position here, a cup run there. The League Cup final victory in 1967 remained our proudest achievement until 1975–6, when my team finished our season at the top of the First Division. Not champions of the Third Division (South), not runners-up in Division 2 but at the very pinnacle of English football, poised to be crowned league champions.

By now I was going to Loftus Road with my friend Fred Oakham, who lived on the Britwell and worked as a scene-shifter for the BBC at White City. I'd met Fred through Judy's friendship with his wife, Barbara. During that glorious season the Rangers team was packed with internationals such as Phil Parkes, Dave Clement, Ian Gillard, Don Masson, Gerry Francis, Dave Thomas, Don Givens and, of course, Stan Bowles.

I'd first seen Bowles on a wet Saturday at the fag end of an uneventful Second Division season in a meaningless match against Carlisle United. He'd been playing for the opposition. I was at Loftus Road with another postman and we agreed as we left the ground that Rangers ought to be signing the Carlisle player who'd caused us grief throughout the afternoon – the enigmatic Stanley.

Within a couple of years he had become the toast of Shepherd's Bush, the heir to the great Rodney and, according to some (not me) a better player, having proved himself at a higher level. He was certainly a genius of grace and flair on the ball, and the essential goal-scoring component of the smooth QPR engine that was driving us towards the championship.

Since Christmas, Rangers had hit an incredible run of form

that lasted through to our final game, a 2-0 home victory over Leeds United. It left us one point ahead (in the days when it was still just two points for a win). Only Liverpool, in second place with one game to play (away at Wolves), could catch us, and they would have to win because of our superior goal average. After our last match on that glorious Saturday, Loftus Road was jubilant. The players appeared in the directors' box like the royal family at Buckingham Palace after a wedding.

The good thing about going to football with Fred was that after the match we could walk across to the BBC social club and have a drink while we waited for the crowds to clear before heading home. The BBC social club was an egalitarian place where electricians mixed with newscasters, scene-shifters with Shakespearean actors, knights of the realm with lads from the Bush. You'd travel up in the lift with Tim Brooke-Taylor and come down with Dusty Springfield.

Among Fred's gang from the props department was a quiet but very funny guy called John Sullivan. It must have been around this time that he capitalized on his proximity to this mix of artists and artisans to hand a script for a comedy programme to a television producer from light entertainment. The script was for *Citizen Smith*, whose main character, Wolfie Smith, was a would-be Marxist urban guerrilla living in a bedsit in Tooting. Within months John had stopped shifting scenery and was on his way to becoming one of the most successful comedy scriptwriters in the country. *Only Fools and Horses* will secure his place in British cultural history, but had it not been for his determination and a good pinch of luck he could so easily have been another of Thomas Gray's flowers wasting its sweetness on the desert air.

John hailed from Balham in south London so I doubt he was a Rangers supporter, but that Saturday evening at the BBC, everybody seemed to be celebrating with us.

I was on a late turn three days later, on the Tuesday evening that Wolves played Liverpool in the final match of the 1975–76 season. One of the PHGs had brought a radio into work and a little huddle of Rangers supporters gathered round it to listen to the match commentary. When I left the sorting office to do the final collection in the town centre Wolves were one up and QPR were champions. By the time I got back Liverpool had won, they were champions and we were runners-up.

I am, in all probability, destined never to see my team crowned as top-division champions. But for three days in May 1976, I got to taste what it would be like.

~

While I enjoyed union work, the rural tranquillity of Littleworth Common provided a welcome break from all the blood and thunder. I had about 140 addresses on my delivery, strung out around three square miles of lush countryside, which I covered in my red Austin van. (By this time Austins had replaced the Morris Minors. It was sad to see them go but, on the plus side, there were no more problems with postmen locking themselves out of their vans.) On my way to Burnham I'd pop into Oxford Avenue to pick up any Littleworth Common parcels. I'd then deviate from the official Post Office route to call at the newsagent's at the bottom of Burnham High Street.

The only way Littleworth Common residents could have a

newspaper delivered in the morning was via their postman. The newsagent slipped us £1.50 a week to drop off papers to sixty of his customers. In addition to those, over the years Ear, Nose and Throat had picked up about fifteen of their own private clients who didn't have an account with the newsagent.

For 'the fifteen' we had to buy the papers requested, fit them into the stack already prepared in delivery order by the newsagent and, on Saturday mornings, call at each house to recoup our money. None of this or the many other services we provided were sanctioned by the Post Office. We picked up sacks of coal from the merchant on the High Street and delivered them to the out-of-the way homes of elderly residents who'd asked for our help; we distributed potatoes from a market garden and the occasional sack of manure from farmer to gardener.

At one remote dwelling I used to feed the cat when the family who lived there were away on holiday. They would leave cat food, a tin-opener and a fork in an outside store cupboard. At 7am, in the pitch dark in winter, I'd be wielding the tin-opener and dishing up a cat's breakfast. My precise instructions were to tap the plate with the fork while calling 'Kitty, Kitty, Kitty' into the dewy morning air. Kitty would appear from the surrounding woodland or through the catflap from the comfort of the house, gazing up at me imperiously as if dismissing an over-zealous servant.

On the odd occasion we'd give a customer a lift into Burnham, seating him or her precariously in the back of the van with the parcels and the potatoes. It's said that when the writer and bon vivant Jeffrey Bernard exiled himself to the Devon countryside for a few years, he'd send a letter to himself every day so that when the postman called to deliver it he could hitch a lift to the pub. Rural transport for the price of a stamp.

When I began delivering to Littleworth Common in 1976 there was a working blacksmith's at the end of Common Lane, a short walk from the Blackwood Arms, where the thirsty smith would down a lunchtime pint. On the late turn, trailing round with just a handful of letters, I often imagined stationing myself at the Blackwood Arms or the Jolly Woodman nearby, where I could distribute mail to many of my customers and save the Post Office some petrol.

There was another pub, the Feathers, frequented mainly by tourists, on the boundary of my delivery, facing the imposing gates of Cliveden, the Italianate mansion that had once been the estate of the Astor family. This glorious piece of architecture was in Taplow, so its mail came from Maidenhead rather than Slough. The Feathers was as close as I got to the house that had had a starring role thirteen years before in the notorious Profumo affair, which I remembered my mother reading about in her *Daily Sketch* in the precious fifteen minutes she had in the mornings to put her feet up with a cup of tea and a cigarette.

By way of contrast with the echoes of the sexual shenanigans of Christine Keeler, Mandy Rice-Davies, aristocrats, politicians and spies, I also delivered to a convent and a monastery. The monastery was Nashdom Abbey, run by Anglo-Catholic Benedictine monks in a glorious Edwardian stately home built by Sir Edwin Lutyens for a Russian aristocrat. It became a monastery after the First World War. I would pull up each morning outside its magnificent porticoed entrance in my little red Austin van.

Practically every day there would be a registered letter for the monastery, which meant I had to obtain a signature. This allowed me to wander into the kitchens where the monks, in their sandals and rough, brown habits tied at the waist with a piece of rope, were busy preparing breakfast. An expensive-looking fountain pen would materialize from somewhere and the item would be signed for. There, in that sparsely equipped kitchen, ancient Benedictine order met Britwell estate. I don't remember there being much conversation between us, although this was not a silent order, unlike the community of nuns known as the Congregation of the Servants of Christ which occupied the House of Prayer in Green Lane. They, too, regularly received mail that had to be signed for, which was a complicated and sometimes disconcerting process seeing as the sisters weren't allowed any contact with the outside world.

All their post had to be taken down a stone staircase into a gloomy basement room, impervious to sunlight even on a summer's day. At the end of the room was a wooden turntable. I would place the mail on this contraption and rotate it by means of a pulley, whereupon the letters would slowly disappear to the other side (or perhaps the Other Side).

When there was something to be signed for I had to ring a little hand bell before operating the turntable and wait in silence, listening to my hair grow, until it creaked back into action and the registered letter slip or recorded delivery book slowly re-emerged bearing a signature, as if authorized by a divine hand. Funnily enough, I never felt the urge to hang around to absorb the tranquil atmosphere there.

There was another convent on the delivery. I forget its name now, but evidently it was more connected to the outside world than the House of Prayer as I had to deliver the *Daily Telegraph* to the abbess every morning, posting it, along with the mail, through a huge brass letterbox that could easily accommodate a set of telephone directories.

I have a confession to make concerning that convent which requires me to go into more detail than I want to. But I need to get this off my chest. It may sound like a tall tale but it's absolutely true. The abbess wasn't the only customer to whom I brought the *Daily Telegraph* from the newsagent in Burnham High Street. The next customer on the round was also a *Telegraph* reader. But as well as taking the newspaper he subscribed to various periodicals, among them *Playboy*, *Penthouse* and assorted other top-shelf magazines. The newsagent would tuck them inside the *Daily Telegraph*, which is how we delivered them, using the newspaper as a kind of Trojan horse. That man must have had one hell of a paper bill.

The abbess cancelled her *Telegraph* one week because she was going on holiday. I was normally pretty good at remembering which newspapers had been temporarily cancelled but if it slipped my mind it wasn't the end of the world as the pile was always in delivery order. So when I reached the address and found no paper for it on the top as usual I'd recall why (it was all about sequencing, you see). But of course, in the case of the abbess and Mr Playboy, I would normally have two consecutive *Daily Telegraphs*. On the first morning of the abbess's holiday, finding a *Telegraph* on the top of the pile, I dutifully pushed it through the big brass letterbox at the convent.

When I got to Mr Playboy's house half a mile up the road there was no *Daily Telegraph*. I knew he wasn't on holiday. And not only had his paper not been cancelled, he would have been looking forward to receiving a couple of particularly raunchy mags that I distinctly remembered the newsagent telling me were included with his paper that day.

I broke into a cold sweat as the penny dropped. I had just delivered soft porn to a convent.

I drove back as quickly as I could. All was silent. There again, it usually was. This did not necessarily indicate that nothing was going on within. I prised open the letterbox flap, crouched down and peered inside. I could see the fat wedge of papers, the *Daily Telegraph* still concealing its titillating cargo. Holding back the stiff, springed flap with my upper arm, I stretched my right hand down into the wire cage on the inside of the door, delving as far as I could. It was while I was in this position, knees bent and arm elbow-deep in the letterbox, that the door opened inwards, bringing me with it.

The woman looking down on me was so sweet. Having heard me scrabbling at the door and noticing that I'd brought the unwanted paper for her absent abbess, she thought I'd refrained from ringing the doorbell for fear of disturbing the nuns. Now I could retrieve the situation by removing the offending bundle from the convent. I carefully lifted the *Daily Telegraph* out of the wire cage as if it were a precious heirloom and disaster was averted. Nobody would ever be any the wiser.

As will have become apparent, the population of Littleworth Common was diverse. There was an air vice-marshal at Pumpkin Hill Cottage and a community of farm labourers in Chalk Pit Lane. Miss House, the head teacher, lived on the premises at the tiny village school, Dropmore Infants, and received her wages via registered letter every Friday morning, along with a magazine from the National Union of Teachers. And there was the house where a massive Irish wolfhound patrolled the front garden. So far was this beast's head from the ground that he practically looked me in the eye as I swallowed hard and unlatched the gate. Nose and Throat assured me that this was the gentlest of dogs; that all he wanted to do was escort me from the gate to the front door – a distance of about 20 yards, which can seem like a mile when you're in a state of barely controlled terror. This wasn't just an escort, it was an armed escort. The grey-and-white woolly-haired hound would seek out an elbow with its teeth and gently clasp it in its giant jaws. Off we'd go, from gate to door, as if I were an elderly gentleman being guided to my cinema seat by a kindly usherette. Thankfully I was allowed to make the return journey alone. Once back in the van I'd use a mail sack to wipe away the copious quantity of wolfhound spittle that had lodged on the elbow of my jacket.

Well-meaning colleagues would often tell me that dogs sense fear and react aggressively. I never considered that information to be at all helpful. Being scared of a dog is bad enough; thinking that the very fact that you are scared will encourage the dog to rip your throat out does nothing to quell the fear.

If the wolfhound's house was my least favourite Littleworth Common address, Hicknham Farm was the one I couldn't wait to get to – a wonderful oasis in this verdant desert. It may sound as if I've synthesized the Archers with the Larkins of *The Darling Buds of May*, but truly there could have been fewer happier places to be than in the kitchen of Mr and Mrs Rayner, who owned the farm.

Every morning at about 8.10 I'd pootle up the long drive

across open farmland, park the van and make my way through the strutting peacocks and somnolent dogs to the kitchen door. Mrs Rayner would be hovering around the Aga as Terry Wogan (now better known than seven years earlier, when Arthur Spearing had mentioned the obscure disc jockey on his round) was 'fighting the flab' from a substantial ancient radio perched high on a shelf on the facing wall. It looked as if it had been there long enough to have broadcast Edward VIII's abdication speech.

Everything was substantial about that farm kitchen, including the table where a wedge of toast made from a fresh loaf and thickly spread with butter would be placed for me alongside a steaming mug of all-milk coffee, and where one or maybe two of the Rayner sons (depending on which of the three of them wasn't out working on the farm already) would eventually come down from their bedrooms to eat. They were themselves substantial, come to think of it, big strapping lads who were not at all fazed to find the postman and, once a week, the dustmen in their kitchen as they sat, half-dressed, polishing off a substantial breakfast.

I rarely saw Mr Rayner, who had a series of voluntary and public-service roles and was gradually handing over responsibility for the farm to his sons. It was Mrs Rayner who was the absolute monarch in that kitchen; mistress of all she surveyed. She must have been in her early fifties, a handsome woman with greying hair and strong features. An old-school Tory with absolutely no sense of false superiority over the various tradesmen who trooped through her kitchen, she relished being a woman in a man's world. No workman left that farm without being treated to Mrs Rayner's hospitality or her well-developed curiosity. She had a genuine interest in people; in their lives, opinions and ambitions.

The conversation crackled and fizzed like the bacon frying on the Aga. Mrs R. soon found out that I was a union official. She was anti-union, anti-Europe and anti-state intervention (a hot topic in an era when the car manufacturer British Leyland was being nationalized). At first I was inhibited in the debates that raged in that kitchen parliament. The importance of good manners had been drilled into Linda and me by our mother, including politeness and respect for our elders. I had no experience of discussing political issues with someone from such a different background and so obviously from a different social class. But it quickly became clear to me that Mrs Rayner could take it as well as dish it out. Bert, the senior binman of the crew of three that joined me in the kitchen every Tuesday morning, shocked me with the vehemence of his albeit good-natured attacks on the farming community.

He was a small, wizened man approaching retirement (although in truth, he looked well over sixty-five). Whereas I always politely remained standing in my usual spot by the door as I consumed my coffee and toast, Bert would plonk himself down at one end of the bench seat round the kitchen table while his colleagues stood behind him.

'You fucking farmers,' I remember Bert saying to Mrs Rayner one day as she made him his piece of toast. 'You stick together like shit to a blanket.'

Mrs Rayner didn't turn a hair. Handing Bert his toast, she responded nonchalantly, 'Yes, it's called solidarity, and you bolshies could learn a lot from us.'

Bert went on to point out that while Mrs R. opposed state

intervention she was quite happy for farmers to be the biggest recipients of state largesse. Gradually I plucked up the courage to offer a view, repeating some statistics from an article I'd read in the Sunday papers about the disproportionate amount of European money paid to farmers. She countered with a detailed argument about the cost of farming and the consequences for society of ending subsidies.

Mrs Rayner gave as good as she got, enjoying the argument and never taking offence. She regarded Bert as a proper socialist and probably thought of me as too young to hold a firm opinion on anything, but she treated us all as equals – at least in that big old farm kitchen, where the problems of the universe were tackled every morning with more laughter than venom.

We became good friends, Mrs Rayner and I. When she found out how much I loved reading she lent me *Rebecca* by Daphne du Maurier, which she declared was her favourite book and insisted I read, quoting its famous opening line, 'Last night I dreamt I went to Manderley again.' (I did read it – finishing the final riveting chapter sitting on a clifftop in Cornwall, where I took the family on holiday that year.) In return I lent Mrs Rayner *Cider with Rosie*, which she'd never read.

One Christmas she stored the bicycles we'd bought for Natalie and Emma in one of the barns until Christmas Eve. She gave me a plump chicken as part of my Christmas tip. I also delivered boxes of Hicknaham Farm eggs around the common and to a few postmen at Slough who'd heard about this source of fresh farm produce.

I remember walking into the kitchen one afternoon to find Mrs Rayner in her bra and slip washing her hair at the sink. I blushed and apologized but she was completely unabashed. We townies might have been offended by such a breach of social niceties but this countrywoman couldn't give a damn.

Hicknaham Farm was a warm and welcoming place and I've never forgotten what it taught me about arguing strongly but without rancour, just as I've never forgotten the friendship of Mrs Rayner.

And of course, the Littleworth Common delivery also took in Dorneywood, the stately home I'd first seen when Bill Higginbottom took me on his round for driving tuition. Dorneywood was built in the eighteenth century. Set in 215 acres of parkland, woodland and farmland, it was donated to the National Trust in 1947 as a country home for a senior member of government. The prime minister decides which Cabinet minister should live there and a few (most recently Alec Douglas-Home) have used it themselves in preference to Chequers, the PM's official residence on the other side of Buckinghamshire. When I began delivering to Littleworth Common, Dorneywood was the country retreat of the home secretary, Merlyn Rees. I once saw him, surrounded by security guards (this was at the height of the Troubles in Northern Ireland), drinking with his family outside the Jolly Woodman, but I never saw him at the house itself.

I always knew, though, when he was in residence, thanks to the presence of that sturdy policeman in the little security hut halfway down the drive leading to the house. He never stopped and searched my Royal Mail van, simply waving me through. The mail might not have been checked going into Dorneywood but I knew that some letters and packets had already been intercepted in the sorting office. I never saw anyone handling them, but if I nipped away from my sorting frame to collect registered letters or fetch a cup of tea, I might come back to find that some of the mail I'd just sorted had disappeared. I assumed somebody from the investigation branch, who blended into the sorting-office background, had taken them to check and that they would be reintroduced into the system later. It did occur to me how easy it would be for a postman to get past the rather rudimentary security that was supposed to protect the home secretary.

I wish I could describe the interior of Dorneywood, its lavish reception rooms and its sweeping staircase, but unfortunately I never set foot inside the main house, not once in my five years on Littleworth Common. I had to take the mail to a door at the back that led to the servants' quarters. There I'd exchange a cheery word or two with a member of staff, much as I did at Nashdom Abbey, and be in and out virtually within seconds.

For me the main function of Dorneywood and its environs was as a resting place. Once the delivery was finished my next task was to collect mail from the postboxes perched on poles around the countryside and the pillarboxes in Burnham. None of these could be opened before the advertised collection times so if I finished the delivery promptly I'd have to wait somewhere. My chosen spot was the winding lane opposite the entrance to Dorneywood, where there was a handy layby with a lovely view across the fields and peace, perfect peace.

I passed the time there regularly, but when I think back to those days one summer afternoon comes to mind. I remember sitting in the van with both front windows wound down to let the breeze blow through, reading *Tess of the D'Urbervilles*. Time seemed to be suspended on the thick, balmy air. I'd just begun to contemplate standing for the executive council of the union and was glimpsing a life beyond the sorting office. But exciting as this potential expansion of my horizons was, the realization that if I took this route I might never again enjoy the serenity of Dorneywood Road on a quiet summer's afternoon gave me a pang of regret. It was one of those idyllic moments which you feel you are already experiencing as a memory, even as it occurs.

Chapter 16

HAVING TRIED MY hand at oratory in the Slough sorting-office canteen during the South Africa boycott, albeit to no avail, I was determined to hone my public-speaking skills in front of a wider audience. Apart from appealing to the show-man that lurked beneath my shy exterior, it would be essential to fulfilling my emerging ambition to become a lay member of the union's executive council. It was an ambition that at that point seemed so far beyond my reach that I was keeping it to myself. To achieve it I would need to attract the votes of branches across the country and the only way to bring myself to their attention was by speaking at conference.

Once again it would be an issue on which I had particularly strong feelings that gave me the push I needed. At my second UPW annual conference, in 1977, there was a proposition urging the executive council to seek the abolition of all remaining age-based incremental scales as part of that year's pay claim. By now I was on maximum pay and well aware that, while those plodding through these awful scales were seized, as I was, with the injustice of it all, there was a general tendency among our members to adopt a more blasé approach when the mountain had been climbed and the pinnacle reached; an attitude of 'well, we had to go through it, why shouldn't they?'

No further progress had been made in reducing these scales since the end of the 1971 strike. Now this motion sought to eradicate them completely. It was just the motivation I required, and on the day this proposal was debated I was on my feet, waving my agenda pad in the air to attract the chairman's attention. I succeeded. He pointed to me. Off I set on the long walk to the rostrum. Once there I looked out on a sea of faces waiting expectantly for my words of wisdom and sagacity.

Speakers had to start by giving their name and branch. That done, those speaking for the first time usually declared the fact, prompting a round of supportive applause. In my arrogance I'd already decided to dispense with such a pathetic effort to attract sympathy. I wanted to give the impression that I'd done this so many times it was actually becoming a bit of a bore; that those present should feel grateful I'd decided to dispense another dose of riveting rhetoric when I obviously had better things I could have been doing with my time.

Having learned that it wasn't a good idea to try to read from a prepared script, instead I'd scribbled down some notes that morning on a piece of lined paper in the hotel room I shared with Dave Stock. I hoped these would at least keep me on track. I had stopped short of attempting to rehearse what I was going to say in front of the bathroom mirror.

I had about five minutes to get my case across. Rather disconcertingly, a series of lights on the rostrum was used to indicate the time you'd used. When the red light came on it meant you needed to wind up your speech. If you ignored it, the chair would intervene and might even on occasion switch off the microphone, leaving the speaker standing there looking like a discombobulated goldfish.

It went OK. I warmed to my theme, telling the conference how, in the 1971 strike, I had got more money for my dependants from social security than I earned as a postman on incremental scales. I emphasized the nonsense of a counter clerk still having to wait until he was in his late twenties before being considered worthy of maximum pay, a telephonist until she was in her thirties.

One of the union's national officers replied, patiently explaining that while pay remained subject to the social contract – the agreement made a couple of years earlier between government and unions whereby unions agreed to abide by wage-increase limits set by the government – there was no possibility of achieving what the motion was asking for. It might be desirable but it was unattainable, and conference should reject the proposition. Which they did. Overwhelmingly.

Still, I'd taken the plunge. For the first time the conference bulletin, published each day, featured my name, the Slough Amalgamated Branch was participating in debates and, intriguingly, according to Joe and Dave, one person on the platform behind me as I spoke seemed to be taking a particular interest. That person was Tom Jackson, the general secretary.

~

Unlike me, Linda had passed her driving test at the first attempt. But at the age of eighteen she put her driving licence in a drawer and never drove again.

Now, without Mike, she was marooned at the end of that long country lane, surrounded by fields, in rural Bedfordshire. Fortunately, her neighbours in the cluster of houses around her were supportive, especially her good friend and next-door neighbour Sally, whose daughter Ann had been babysitting the children the evening Mike had arrived home roaring drunk and collapsed in the bath. They helped make life bearable in the bleak aftermath of Mike's suicide.

Often it was a case of one step forward, two steps back. Like the day Sally spent an hour digging up weeds from around Linda's house, leaving them on the doorstep on a piece of newspaper for disposal. When Linda came home and found what she took to be plants left for her as a gift, she spent an hour putting them back into the garden. Mike had always done the gardening. Like most of us city kids, Linda didn't know the difference between weeds and flowers.

I would go and stay with her at weekends, sometimes with Judy and the kids; often alone. That summer a caravan holiday in Porthcawl was arranged for Linda and her children and a friend's family. I hired a car to drive my sister, her three boys and Shandy the dog across to Wales. (Renay and Tara had gone ahead with the other family.) I can't remember why I didn't take my own car but I often lent it to Ernie Sheers, who didn't have a car of his own, when he needed to get to east London, where his mother was poorly. So perhaps he had it that day.

As we set off from Stopsley the weather was atrocious and by the time we reached the motorway it was worse – the closest Britain can get to a monsoon. As we belted along the windscreen wipers stopped in mid-wipe. I know nothing about cars, along with much else men are supposed to know about. At home on the Britwell I had a foolproof way of dealing with car trouble. I'd just lift the bonnet and lean in as if I knew what I was doing. As the car would be parked on the green in full view of my neighbours' living rooms, it would be only a matter of minutes before Martin or Tony or Robert or Mick sauntered out to ask what the problem was. Within another ten minutes I'd be standing back having a relaxing smoke, or perhaps kicking a ball around with the kids, as a couple of my neighbours bent diligently over the engine, fixing whatever was wrong. It worked every time.

But nobody was around to fix the problem now. For a while I drove very, very slowly down the inside lane but eventually the lack of visibility forced me to pull into a service station to have another go at getting the wipers to work. I was soaked to the skin, the dog was barking, the boys were restless and Linda was unhelpfully telling me that I should have joined the RAC.

Somehow, miraculously, my pulling and prodding, accompanied by profanities uttered under my breath so that the children didn't hear, succeeded in getting the windscreen wipers on this brand-new hire car working again. I dropped off my cargo at the caravan site and headed home.

My sister had something akin to a nervous breakdown on that holiday. She'd been so determined to present a brave face to the world and was so focused on the children – the two in her temporary care as much as her own three – that the grief had accumulated, like a tidal surge behind a stout harbour wall.

After our stormy journey the sun had shone over Porthcawl. Linda and her friend Jan took their combined brood of seven kids to the seaside, where they built sandcastles, ate ice-cream and lazed on the beach. But towards the end of the week two events triggered a reaction in my sister.

The first was the death of Elvis Presley. It wasn't so much grief for the King that got to Linda; more the stirring up of her own sense of loss by the huge media coverage of the demise of a young man and the ubiquitous photographs of Elvis in his coffin.

At the same time Jan's husband arrived to spend the last few days of the holiday with his wife and daughters, just as Mike would have done if he'd been alive. The double breach of her defences plunged Linda into a deep depression. She couldn't stop crying and refused to leave the caravan. Jan and her husband eventually coaxed her out and brought her home, curtailing the holiday. I was contacted and went straight to Stopsley. We talked, Linda and I, long into the night. She'd been widowed for almost five months; an attractive young woman, bright, vivacious but still reliving every day the misery of the recent past. I told her that nobody could reasonably expect her to don widow's weeds and spend the rest of her life pining for Mike. She needed to try to build a new one, for her own sake and for the sake of her children.

∽

By 1978 I'd made a firm decision to embark on the road to standing for election to the executive council. Around thirty postal workers put their names forward every year for fifteen positions – thirty out of around 180,000 postal members. The only qualification necessary was the nomination of a candidate's own branch. That might not sound like much of an obstacle but there were two major hurdles in my path. The first was my youth and significant lack of union experience. The second was myself.

My personality was steeped in the self-effacement that held back so many working-class people. The ultimate fear was of being thought too big for your boots, the ultimate humiliation the accusatory question: 'Who does he think he is?' It was why brilliant Sunday-morning footballers would play down their performance in the post-match banter. Why Len Rigby had cheerfully endured being date-stamped and dispatched every morning; why my late brother-in-law had hidden his light under a bushel and why I didn't like to be seen reading *The Times*. Perhaps this was a hangover from the era when the working classes knew their place that was supposed to have disappeared in the 1960s.

Whatever its origins, it wasn't something that could be analysed or rationalized. The simple fact was that I could never in a million years have asked Joe or Dave if the branch could nominate me for the executive council. Len Rigby had never been nominated. Joe had been around for years, and he'd never been nominated. Those who stood for the executive council were invariably holders of senior district council positions and from the big branches such as Glasgow, Manchester, Mount Pleasant or Birmingham. For me to suggest that my name should be put forward after a year or so as chairman, and at an age where some would consider me too young even to be a branch official, would have been outrageously presumptuous.

So I continued my double life as rural postman and secretly ambitious union rep. I had no interest in the many opportunities available to become a union office holder at a lower level through the Council of Post Office Unions or the regional structure of lay members. It was being at the centre of things that interested me; the sense of theatre at conference. I wanted to hold and sway an audience like the charismatic John Taylor could. I wanted to go from delivery frame to union headquarters in one jump.

Joe, who was district organizer for an area embracing the whole of Berkshire and a bit of Oxfordshire, did suggest I take the role of assistant district organizer. It was a very minor position, involving arranging district council elections and paying delegates' travel expenses at our quarterly DC meetings. In other words, a non-job at a talking shop in a tiny patch of south-east England – hardly comparable to my respected mentor suggesting I be nominated for the executive. For the moment I accepted this position and the special silver UPW badge it entitled me to pin on my lapel (we went to DC meetings in suits rather than in uniform), looking forward to the day when I would be able to wear the same badge in gold – the badge of an executive council member.

Joe and I were not entirely compatible so far as our politics were concerned. Unlike him, I was very critical of the Callaghan government. While never a Bennite, I was an opinionated fellow-traveller. Having decided that the Labour party was the appropriate vehicle for the transformation of society I wanted to see, I would often pontificate about the final scene in Orwell's *Animal Farm*, where the pigs, standing on their hind legs and wearing clothes, are no longer distinguishable to the other animals from the humans against whom they revolted. This, I'd pronounce to whoever I was talking at, was exactly how I felt when I looked at Labour and Conservative MPs.

In the British Legion with Mick and Idris on a Sunday lunchtime I'd drone on about 'my people' and declare that I wished to put whatever talents I possessed at the service of the working class. I blush now at this patronizing nonsense but I can't deny that the idealistic little prick in the tank top and flares was me.

Leaving aside the self-centred romanticism, I was and remain devoted to two causes: the eradication of poverty and greater equality. All else was a means to those ends. This put me more in tune with Tony Crosland than with Tony Benn, but the late 1970s were a tumultuous time and the dividing line between democratic socialism and dictatorship of the proletariat was sometimes difficult to discern in the battle for hearts and minds within the Labour movement.

While I wasn't particularly interested in my South-East District Council I was very interested in the London District Council which, as I've mentioned, exercised real power as the co-ordinating force in the capital. Its leader, John Taylor – who was by this time also a member of the executive council – and his assistant, Derek Walsh, had become firm friends of mine. I'd solicited their support for a couple of Slough amendments aimed at preventing the casualization of the industry and improving protection for the men and women who delivered cash to post offices. By now, with equal-opportunities legislation taking effect, there were postwomen in Slough. Brenda, a 4ft 10in dynamo, became our first full-time female delivery officer around this time. Within a year she'd entered the most macho enclave of the office: the HGV drivers. As she often said, even someone without a Yorkie Bar could drive a truck.

Derek Walsh was John's calm, more cerebral alter-ego. A small man with a well-trimmed moustache and beard, he always wore one of those tunic-style leather jackets. The sleeves were far too long, making him look as if he'd had his hands amputated. Brought up in a large south London family, he was, like so many union officials, completely self-educated. Derek was always discovering verses and quotations which he insisted on copying and sending to me. He also made up a few himself. 'He who would generalize, generally lies' is one that springs to mind.

Along with the snatches of Shakespeare he'd picked up, he could quote entire passages of the *Rubaiyat of Omar Khayyam*. I knew one verse by heart (which I'd found in a short story by the American author O. Henry). When Derek and I were alone we'd indulge in our guilty secret and savour the beauty of this verse:

> Ah, Love! Could thou and I with Fate conspire
> To grasp this sorry Scheme of Things entire!
> Would not we shatter it to bits – and then
> Re-mould it nearer to the Heart's Desire!

∼

At around this time the UPW was embroiled in a dispute that had been simmering since the glorious summer of 1976 and became a focus for trade-union rights and labour-relations law. The dispute was over union recognition and it involved 143 mainly Asian women workers in north-west London.

Grunwick in Cricklewood processed films by mail order. The

owner, George Ward, was fiercely anti-union and, in an effort to force recognition, the women had been taking industrial action. Things came to a head when the UPW decided to 'black' the firm's mail in support of the women and in an effort to force Grunwick to go to arbitration at ACAS (the Advisory, Conciliation and Arbitration Service). While George Ward had managed to continue operating through the dispute, he couldn't cope without the mail service. He agreed to attend talks at ACAS and the embargo was lifted.

Meanwhile, the court action pursued by the right-wing National Association for Freedom over the South African boycott had led to postal workers being told that they did not have the right to take industrial action because of an ancient law, aimed at highwaymen, stating that it was an offence to 'wilfully delay the Queen's mail'.

Not only did the talks at ACAS fail, George Ward tried to sue the arbitration service because it hadn't consulted his strike-breaking labour force. When the UPW executive refused to reinstate the embargo of Grunwick's mail because of the danger of fines and sequestration, John Taylor and Derek Walsh threw the weight of the London District Council behind the hundred or so postmen at Cricklewood who wanted to cease to deliver and collect from the company. This resulted in the Cricklewood men being 'locked out' (in other words, not allowed to go back to work unless they handled Grunwick's mail), a mass picket involving thousands, including coachloads of Yorkshire miners, and disciplinary action against Taylor and Walsh by their union. The two were fined what was then a record sum for a union to impose on its own officials.

I was a firm supporter of the decision taken by the LDC to

back the Cricklewood members. Indeed, I'm sure Tom Jackson himself was extremely sympathetic. But, as he said at the following year's conference, during another high-octane debate: 'One of the penalties of leadership . . . is to make difficult and hard decisions . . . decisions which have to be taken in the interests of your union.'

Neither John nor Derek bore any antipathy towards Tom Jackson. Derek told me how wounded he'd been by a comment Tom made during a private meeting held to discuss the fall-out from Grunwick. After Derek had set out the moral argument that had persuaded him to defy the executive, Tom asked him if he considered himself to be the conscience of the union. As always, it was Derek who thought deeply about such things while the more cavalier John earned the plaudits.

I spoke in defence of my London friends at the 1978 conference but it was a different debate that led to the resolution of the tricky problem of how I could get myself nominated for the executive council.

The conference that year was held in the Winter Gardens, Blackpool. As an assistant district organizer I was allowed to move or second propositions at conference on behalf of any branch within the district and I was asked by the Reading branch to move an amendment on some subject or other that I can't recollect. It was the first time I'd done this and such was my determination to put on a good show that I even wore my silver ADO's badge, despite my mod's aversion to such fripperies, pinned to the lapel of my black suit.

I was called to the rostrum for what I thought was the Reading amendment only to hear from behind me on the platform the chairman telling me, sotto voce, that I was about to speak on the wrong proposition. It was my third annual conference, my first as an ADO, and I found myself retreating from the rostrum, dazed and confused, in front of the huge audience. As I picked my way past the delegates on the long, excruciating walk back to my delegation, seated under the magnificent balcony that was a feature of this most atmospheric of conference halls, I noticed that my silver badge had slipped from my lapel and was just about clinging to my jacket, upside down by the end of its long pin. It seemed to be a metaphor for this complete disaster.

As I sat bemoaning my fate, Dave Stock nudged me: 'Look who's walking towards us.' It was none other than our revered general secretary, who had stepped down from the platform and did indeed seem to be heading in our direction, though it was difficult to be sure as his progress was constantly being halted by delegates wanting a brief word or a handshake.

'Now then, young Alan,' he said, in his refined Yorkshire accent, when he finally reached us. 'If you're going to be a conference star you'll have to learn more about procedure.'

I was too stunned to reply. I couldn't believe that he'd bothered to leave the platform in the middle of a debate just to give a humble delegate from Slough a piece of advice. Joe Payne, Dave Stock and our wonderful telephonist rep, Rose Ticket, were all within earshot, wearing expressions reminiscent of palace kitchen staff receiving a visit below stairs from the monarch.

Tom hadn't finished. 'Have you ever thought about standing for the executive council?' he asked.

'Not really,' I said nonchalantly, lying through my teeth.

'Well, you should get the branch to nominate you next year.

You won't get on straight away but you'll get your name in the frame, and in three or four years you'll be on. There are a number of retirements coming up and you need to get yourself positioned to replace them.'

I muttered my appreciation of this counsel, still overawed to be in such close proximity to the man who'd led the union since I became a postman and who'd led us through the seven-week strike; a man who was a national figure, better known to the public, thanks to his handlebar moustache and natural eloquence, than most Cabinet ministers. I noticed that above the foliage on his upper lip was a pair of twinkling eyes, looking kindly upon me. Whatever it was, Tom had seen something in me of which I wasn't particularly aware myself. He told me years later that he'd always tried to encourage young talent and that I'd caught his eye in the incremental scales debate the previous year. The injustice of those scales was what had brought him into the union as a youngster and he was struck by the fact that I was following a similar path.

There was great excitement in the Slough delegation when we broke for lunch. Joe told me that he'd already thought about nominating me for the EC. Whether or not that was true, Tom's suggestion quickly became Joe's and it was agreed that I would be a candidate at the 1979 conference (the elections were held at annual conference). I was to succeed at my third attempt, exactly as Tom had predicted.

Chapter 17

THROUGHOUT THE LATE 1970s I looked forward to the new life that awaited me when (not if, when) I was elected to the union's national executive council.

I followed Tom Jackson's sage advice and made some half-decent speeches at conference to lift my profile, although not as many as he wanted me to make. As I stood on the rostrum ready to begin one peroration on something or other I heard Tom's voice from the platform behind me saying, 'Ah, Alan – at last a speech. I thought you were dead.'

I had an aversion to making speeches for the sake of it. There were plenty of 'rostrum runners', besotted by the smell of greasepaint and the roar of the crowd, who enjoyed the thrill of addressing conference so much that they were up at the microphone every five minutes. I liked that buzz as well, I must admit. In truth I was a bit of a show-off and this was as close as I could get to recreating my rock-and-roll years. But I was sensible (and cunning) enough to realize that the audience in front of me was assessing my suitability to be a national repre-sentative of their union. There were many more candidates than there were positions to be filled. And whereas aspiring delegates from big branches such as Glasgow or Birmingham could broker deals with each other about how to allocate their block vote, I was from a small branch with only a handful of votes. I had to rely solely on my eloquence and at the same time not appear too big for my boots. I was determined never to go begging for votes in the conference bars and meeting places as I was sometimes urged to do.

I must confess that one of the attractions of election to the executive was an escape from the early-morning starts that I'd never learned to love. I was forever hearing workmates claiming they'd become so attuned to the hours that they woke up automatically at 4am or some other ungodly hour, even when they were on holiday. That never happened to me. Left to my own devices I'd happily have slept until noon.

So concerned was I about losing my job as a result of excessive late attendances that I constructed a Heath Robinson-style system to get me into work on time. One alarm clock was positioned on a chest of drawers near the bedroom door so that I had to get out of bed and cross the room to turn it off. That one was set for 4am. I'd don my uniform and stagger downstairs, where another alarm placed next to the sofa had been set for 4.35. I'd sleep there under my greatcoat to grab that all-important extra half-hour before brushing my teeth, combing my hair and dashing out to the car for the fifteen-minute drive to work. Breakfast would have to wait until I reached Hicknaham Farm.

What those years did embed in me was the ability to catnap. I usually still managed to get home for short breaks during the day, but if I couldn't lie on my sofa for a fifteen-minute refresher I'd sit in my car in the office car park and sleep sweetly during my lunch break. Even today I can fall asleep anywhere and in any position virtually to order.

Such were the long hours worked by postmen in Slough that a large room next to the canteen was designated as a sleeping room. It was littered with battered old armchairs and those civil-service chairs made of tubular metal with two bits of canvas stretched across them, which were used as footstools. The blinds were permanently drawn and the stale air would carry the sound of gentle snoring with the occasional deep, animal grunt from the heaviest sleepers. I avoided this grim place, but for the indoor sorters in particular it was the only refuge. I remember one postman who actually lived at work for a couple of months. He'd been evicted from his lodgings and would work as many hours as he could before bedding down in the sleeping room every night.

~

Linda was coping better and, along with her friends and neighbours, I encouraged her to try to find somebody else to share her life. Outgoing and with so much to give, she wasn't the kind of person who suited being single. Gradually, she began to absorb the message, at least in terms of broadening her social life, and eventually, in typical Linda style, she took the initiative.

Ann, the daughter of Sally next door, who was single herself and four or five years younger than Linda, came up with the idea of joining a singles club called Nexus which met at a bar in Luton and sent out a weekly newsletter containing members' profiles and details. Linda and Ann paid their year's subscription to the club but decided after one short visit that the bar wasn't for them. It was, according to Linda, 'full of creepy old men'.

They decided on an alternative strategy. They'd forget about the bar evenings and simply put their photographs and contact details in the newsletter. They could then just get in touch with anyone featured there who caught their eye, or respond to anyone who got in touch with them.

The parallels with my mother's efforts to find love and security were not lost on either of us. After she'd been deserted by my father at the age of thirty-six, she had been persuaded by Linda to put an ad in the lonely-hearts section of the local paper. It didn't work out for my mother but the 1970s equivalent was – eventually – successful for my sister.

I'd agreed to spend two weeks of my annual leave helping Linda redecorate. My DIY skills might have been sadly lacking but even I could manage to slap on a bit of paint. She decided to take advantage of my visit to set up a couple of dates. As well as being able to look after the children I would be a useful deterrent should any of these men try to get beyond the doorstep when they brought Linda home. Whatever the hopes of her friends and family, she made it quite clear that she was looking for companionship rather than a relationship. She certainly wasn't seeking another husband. The profile she had put in the newsletter was straightforward: 'Woman with five children, two cats, a dog, a rabbit, gerbils, hamsters and birds seeks somebody to meet socially for occasional evenings out.'

It wasn't likely to attract Robert Redford or the Prince of Wales, who was around her age and free at the time, but it did attract a creep called Dave. When he picked her up at 7pm for their evening out, all five children waved Linda goodbye from an upstairs window.

Dave told Linda that he was a film producer. If there was any truth at all in his claim, it was probably that he manufactured rolls of the stuff at Kodak. After boring his date rigid for a couple of hours in a local pub, he drove her home. When they reached the country lane leading to her house Linda heard Dave say: 'What a lovely night for a murder.'

She surreptitiously unbuckled her seat belt and grasped the door handle ready to make a run for it as soon as the car stopped. 'Thanks for a lovely evening,' she said disingenuously, for want of anything better to say, as they drove further down the lane towards her house.

'You can thank me properly in a minute,' Dave replied ominously.

I was listening out for the doorbell but I heard Linda running up the path before she got anywhere near the front door. As I opened it she fell into my arms. Dave's car had just completed its three-point turn and I could see its tail-lights heading off towards the main road.

While I was making a cup of tea for my distraught sister she announced that she'd had it with Nexus. 'I'm never going out with anyone again' was her firm statement of intent or, I suppose, dis-intent.

The next day, as I was preparing to pick up Dean from his infants' school, the phone rang. Linda answered. It was a man named Carl, another lonely heart who'd joined Nexus.

'I'm sorry, but I'm not in Nexus any more.'

'How can that be?' asked Carl. 'I only got your details this morning.'

'Well, I've only just decided that it's not for me,' replied Linda, beginning to get irritated. She was about to hang up but Carl persisted. He was a travelling salesman currently in the area. Could he at least just come round for a cup of tea? Something about his voice attracted Linda and made her change her mind. She gave him her address and said he could come round, but only for half an hour.

When I remonstrated with her, quoting the pledge she'd made the previous night, she argued that, first of all, she wasn't going out with him so technically the pledge remained unbroken. Secondly, such was her indifference to this persistent salesman that she wasn't even going to bother to get changed. Since we had been painting her bedroom and Linda was still dressed accordingly, this declaration was more dramatic than it might otherwise have been.

As I walked down the lane towards Dean's school, a car stopped. The driver wound down his window and asked me the way to Linda's house. This was how I met the man who was to become the love of Linda's life and her second husband; the man who would rescue her from the wretched grief that had consumed her since Mike died. And I met him before she did.

Oh, and his name wasn't Carl. It was Charles. Linda had misheard. By the time I returned with Dean he was leaping round the front room, startled, after one of Linda's cats jumped through the open window on to his lap with a live mouse between its teeth. Linda, who'd been making tea in the kitchen, heard him scream and rushed in, her hair scrunched into an untidy bun and, true to her word, still wearing an old smock splattered with paint. It was like a scene from a Brian Rix farce.

This relationship won't last, I mused to myself. I was wrong. It did, and it does to this day.

~

As our children moved from primary to secondary education, we became involved in the campaign to save one of the better local schools.

Slough had retained Buckinghamshire's system of selective education even after being dragged across the county line into Berkshire. The existence of grammar schools meant that in our area the comprehensive schools were comprehensive in name only. The future education of and direction taken by our children and their classmates would hinge on their performance on the day in a test at the age of eleven, just as had happened with Linda, Judy and me and our contemporaries. With the top 20 per cent or so of those pupils considered to be the brightest on the basis of the test being creamed off by the grammars, the comprehensives were, to all intents and purposes, secondary moderns.

I loathed this state of affairs but I could do nothing about it. I couldn't even convince most of my friends and neighbours of the unfairness, the waste, the cruelty of effectively labelling children successes or failures at the start of their secondary schooling. I was active in the local Labour party by now and knew our MP, Joan Lestor, very well. She told me how much she hated the system but that its popularity with voters meant that any attempt to remove it would cost her the seat. It was as simple as that.

Warrenfield Comprehensive, the secondary school on the

Britwell, had a terrible reputation. At that time schools were still closed institutions, as they had been in my schooldays. Parental interest was discouraged, performance standards were opaque and achievements were not measurable by any meaningful comparison. Schools were largely immune from outside scrutiny but by any yardstick it was impossible to classify Warrenfield as anything other than a poor school. In its defence, it suffered from a lack of resources, since the lion's share followed the kids designated as the brightest to the grammar schools where, by and large, the best teachers wanted to be.

Natalie failed the test, as would Emma; Jamie went on to pass it. Natalie detested the thought of going to Warrenfield almost as much as I'd feared ending up in the North Kensington blackboard jungle known as the Sir Isaac Newton School for Boys when I was her age. So Judy and I fought to send her to Haymill, a school in Burnham Lane that had a better reputation. She gained her place and I became a school governor there. But within a year of Natalie starting at Haymill the school was earmarked for closure.

I joined a feisty bunch of parents and teachers determined to come to its rescue. We set out to convince the council that falling school rolls (the principal reason given for the planned closure) were a temporary blip and that it was too good a school to be sacrificed to an accountancy problem that would be rectified in a few years. We raised money for our campaign by organizing carnivals and cricket matches; we marched through Slough High Street, delved into the archives of the National Federation for Educational Research (conveniently located in Slough); we presented petitions, lobbied councillors, wrote to ministers – all to no avail. Our arguments for choice and diversity in education provision were considered to be heresy by the local education authority.

Haymill closed and Natalie, along with her classmates, was forced to move to the school she dreaded in the worst circumstances, as an older pupil from a merging school. The council used the opportunity to change Warrenfield's name to Beechwood in an effort to remove the stigma and salvage its reputation. Emma joined Natalie there the following summer. She was a bright girl expected by everybody to pass that damned test but, like so many other children over the years, she flunked it on the day. It left her with a sense of failure she could never quite overcome despite all our efforts to dispel it.

~

I became more conscious of my alcohol intake after what happened to Mike. I didn't take a vow of abstinence or join a temperance society but I was anxious to understand at what stage 'enjoying a pint' became 'having a drink problem'. I'd wince whenever I heard the term 'alcoholic' used in a pejorative or lighthearted way. I now knew what a dreadful illness alcoholism was and I missed Mike and his gentle ways more than I could tell anybody – except Ernie, the great listener.

He and I would have a few pints together every Friday evening at the Crown in Farnham Common, just off the Britwell. I'd also have a drink with my union colleagues Joe Payne and Dave Stock at least one evening a week after work. And the Sunday lunchtime ritual at the British Legion continued. Occasionally husbands and wives would go to the Legion together on a Saturday night. The women drank Bacardi and Coke or gin and orange while we men stuck to our pints of light and bitter or mild, or lager, which had become increasingly popular through the 1970s.

Nobody drank at home in those days, except at Christmas or at parties and on other special occasions. Alcohol was consumed on licensed premises, you had tea or coffee indoors and ne'er the twain shall meet. Wine with meals at home was a rarity. By the late seventies, Judy, who could turn her hand to anything, had begun distilling homemade wine as a hobby. Buckets of dandelion and burdock or turnip wine would gurgle away in plastic buckets in the cupboard under the stairs. We'd crack open a bottle of Black Tower or some other German sugar-water to accompany Christmas dinner. If we ventured out for a meal at a steakhouse or a restaurant in Windsor for a special celebration we'd demonstrate our sophistication by ordering Mateus Rosé and taking the bulbous bottle home to serve as a candle-holder. Half-empty bottles of sherry or advocaat could be found at the back of most working-class sideboards, along with the odd small bottle of Babycham or Cherry B, waiting, like the Christmas decorations, to make an annual appearance. They were hardly ever touched at other times during the year.

Almost everyone smoked. I always found the generosity of smokers touching. The way that cigarettes were offered round turned them into a small gift, presented in a spirit of friendship. Practically the only adult close to me who didn't smoke was Linda. When she was in her teens and acted as my guardian at the flat we shared on the Wilberforce Estate in Battersea, she bought twenty menthol cigarettes one Christmas. She smoked one on Christmas Day and stored the other nineteen for future Christmases. I think I might have nicked them. Whatever the case, she never smoked again.

Although I'd been puffing away from the age of twelve I rarely got through more than ten fags a day, lighting my first around lunchtime. I vowed to myself that I'd break the habit by the age of thirty. However, in 1978, two years ahead of my self-imposed deadline, while waiting to pick up Natalie, Emma and Jamie from the Post Office children's Christmas party, I stubbed out a cigarette and suddenly decided, on the spot, that it would be the last I'd ever smoke.

The money I would save was a powerful incentive. I decided I would bolster my willpower by setting aside what I would have spent on cigarettes and rewarding myself with LPs instead. Within a week or so I was able to buy a special, yellow vinyl version of Elton John's *Goodbye Yellow Brick Road*. It was followed at regular intervals by albums from Elvis Costello, Supertramp, Billy Joel and Joe Jackson.

Those records are still redolent to me of an era that was fast disappearing. The end of that decade was marked by the general election of May 1979, which brought in a Conservative government under Margaret Thatcher, the UK's first (and, to date, only) female prime minister.

Jim Callaghan, leading a Labour government without a majority in the House of Commons, had been forced to make deals with minor parties and to accept referendums on devolution in Scotland and Wales. Yet in spite of these difficulties, and the problems of trying to run the country during a time of high unemployment and rising inflation, as late as the autumn of the previous year Labour had been ahead in the opinion polls. Had Callaghan chosen to call an election then, he might just have won it. As it was, when millions of public-sector workers took strike action that winter, amid continuing pay restraints, photographs in the press of rubbish stacked high in the streets and reports of the dead remaining unburied were credited with diluting Labour's healthy lead. It was not the Winter of Discontent, though, that finally undid the government. Its demise was brought about by defeat in the House of Commons by a single vote on a motion of no-confidence over devolution, forcing Callaghan to go to the country.

I drove Joan Lestor around a few times during the election campaign and on polling day our house was used as the Labour 'committee room' for our part of the Britwell. This involved a party official basing himself in our living room with a huge map of the electoral ward balanced across our dining table. We were a hub from which information on which of our supporters had voted was sent and received. I'd always naïvely believed that political parties persuaded voters to back them on polling day by the force of their arguments, but while that is of course the aim of the national campaign, on the ground, on polling day, it all boils down to the single imperative of ensuring that your known supporters (as determined by canvass returns between elections) actually get to the polling stations.

Outside every station was a party supporter asking each voter for his or her polling-card number. These volunteers had no interest at all in how the vote might have been cast, only that it had been. The numbers would be collected by a runner, who'd bring them back to the 'committee room', where they'd be used to identify the addresses of those who had voted. The party official would then cross out the addresses on a thick duplicate pad, tear off the top copy and give it to other party workers, who'd use it to 'knock up' supporters who had yet to vote and try to shepherd them towards the polling station. The elderly and infirm would be offered lifts, although many a cunning pensioner has claimed to support a particular party, received a lift to the polling station from its volunteers and then voted for someone else. Canvass returns weren't always up to date or accurate. The motive of these more tribal voters was to ensure that Party A's car was wasted on a Party B supporter.

Our three children did stints as 'runners' (Jamie was particularly enthusiastic) while I did my share of knocking-up and giving (I hoped) honest pensioners a lift to the polling booth. Judy supervised the committee room.

Our efforts were not in vain. Joan Lestor survived in Slough in 1979 with a reduced majority. But in the country the new Conservative reign was to last for eighteen years.

Chapter 18

M Y LAST-EVER DELIVERY for the Post Office was completed on a Saturday morning in May 1981, just before my thirty-first birthday. That afternoon I left Slough in Dave Stock's car. We were off to annual conference in Brighton where, at my third attempt, I was elected to the executive council.

My life would never be the same again.

The results of the ballot for the executive, along with a swathe of other national positions such as the Standing Orders Committee and the UPW delegations to the TUC and Labour party conferences, were announced at lunchtime on the Tuesday. I was sitting in the conference hall, my heart thumping so hard I thought it would be audible in the hushed silence of that large crowd, while the chair of the Standing Orders Committee, Harry Varcoe, read out, in his rich, fruity Bristol accent, the names of the fifteen successful postal nominees in order of the number of votes they'd received. My name was the fifteenth announced. Dave Stock let out a little cheer, Joe Payne shook my hand and Rose Ticket kissed me. One of the headquarters staff immediately came to see me with an envelope of papers for my first EC meeting, which was to be held that Thursday on the conference site.

With so few full-time officers and no regional machinery worth mentioning, the twenty-two lay members of the executive council (fifteen postal and seven telecoms) covered a much wider range of activities than their counterparts in most other unions. As well as attending the various executive meetings (full EC, postal executive, organizing committee, finance committee and so on), it was EC members who supported national officers in negotiations, taught at the union's training schools and were sent to resolve disputes and as fraternal delegates to the conferences of sister unions around the world. We were the standard-bearers for the union and, as such, we were based at its headquarters in Clapham, which was to become my new place of work. The union also owned a large Regency house where EC members from 'the provinces' could lodge during the week. I was classed as 'provincial' in the sense that I was from an office outside London, but with the Britwell only an hour's drive away I never needed to take advantage of these facilities.

Becoming a member of the national executive was a big deal. I'd be a lay member, placed on permanent special leave, but only if I failed to be re-elected would I ever go back to work as a postman in Slough (although I'd remain a Post Office employee and be paid a postman's wages).

On the evening of my election, I went to hear Tony Benn speak. He'd come to conference, uninvited by the executive, to attend a fringe meeting as part of his campaign to be elected deputy leader of the Labour party. Fringe meetings were a previously unheard-of phenomenon at our conference. This one had been organized by Pete Dodd and Billy Hayes, two postmen activists a few years younger than me who were from Manchester and Liverpool respectively. These bright, articulate young men were the leading lights in a new generation who, like me, were baby-boomers. Unlike me, however, they had no memories of the strike and thus none of the inhibitions and lack of confidence that had instilled. I knew Pete well – we'd been at the same union 'induction' school. I'd never met Billy but I knew of the reputation he was building as a young dissident determined to push the union down a more radical and confrontational route.

This was a reflection of the zeitgeist in the Labour movement, where a form of collective frenzy had taken hold ever since Margaret Thatcher's victory in the 1979 election. Militant, a group built around the *Militant* newspaper and formerly known as the Revolutionary Socialist League, had initiated a serious Trotskyite insurgency, stoking a culture of betrayal against anybody connected with the previous Labour government – anybody, that is, apart from Tony Benn. Despite having been a Cabinet minister and part of that government, he not only joined in the condemnation but led the charge against the colleagues he'd worked beside. Benn's leftwards lurch made him the idol of those seeking to turn the Labour party away from democratic socialism and this all congealed into a toxic mixture of syndicalism and cynicism.

Our union had decided to support Denis Healey, the shadow foreign secretary and former chancellor of the exchequer, who was the incumbent deputy leader, against the challenge from Benn and it upheld that decision the following day.

In the meantime I went to listen to what Benn had to say. It wasn't the first time I'd heard him speak – in fact I had been with Mick Pearson to hear him at Slough College only a month or so before. Once again he was erudite, fluent and persuasive in his rhetoric and, given the Wolfie Smith phase I was in, he should have won me over. And yet there was something jarring about his attempts to claim that he was now hunting with the hounds having previously run with the hare. I distrusted the cult of personality that was being built around him and, while I admit to being attracted by his arguments for more accountable party structures and a greater role for trade unions, the venom directed by his supporters at figures such as Healey, Callaghan, Barbara Castle and all the other so-called traitors sickened me. Benn's refusal to lift a finger against this character assassination seemed to me to be the real betrayal.

My MP, Joan Lestor, was no Bennite, although she was a leading member of Tribune, the left-wing alliance formed around the newspaper of the same name. She had told me how worried she was about Tony Benn's apparent determination not to be outflanked by any grouping on the left, no matter how bizarre and eccentric their views. 'These people are nasty and intolerant,' she said, 'and Benn is placating them when he should be confronting them.' Given how close the vote was that summer for the deputy leadership, Joan's refusal, together with that of her great friend and Tribune colleague Neil Kinnock, to vote for Benn (they both abstained instead) might well have cost him the position.

On the Thursday, Dave Stock insisted I cut short my attendance at conference and go back to our bed and breakfast to rest up and prepare for my first executive council meeting later that day. But I was too excited to sleep, and arrived for the meeting twenty minutes early. It was held in the Bedford Hotel on the Brighton seafront, where the headquarters officers and staff were based. There was only one other person in the room when I arrived. It was Tom Jackson. He was standing by the window looking out to sea.

Ten years on from the strike, I was still in awe of this famous figure who, as a young postman, I'd watched remotely on a TV screen. Now here I was, not only in the same room, but one of his colleagues in the national leadership of the union.

A good deal had happened since Tom had left the platform to offer me encouragement at the 1978 conference. The name of the union had changed for a start. We were now the Union of Communication Workers (UCW), British Telecom having been separated from the Post Office.

The country had been through the Winter of Discontent, which had seen widespread strikes by public-sector unions provoked by the ongoing pay caps implemented by the government in an attempt to control inflation. That summer the TUC had rejected the government's proposed 5 per cent guideline for increases and voted for a return to free collective bargaining. The UPW had only narrowly avoided being sucked into the maelstrom thanks to some nifty footwork by the Post Office and the union that led to a pay deal at the eleventh hour.

Tom Jackson had taken a key role in the build-up to these historic events. As a member of the TUC general council he was instrumental in formulating the social contract between the Labour government and the TUC which had been in place since 1975. Tom had always supported a national pay policy. He believed that free collective bargaining was a chimera. For public-sector workers it was never free and rarely collective. The seven-week UPW strike in 1971 had caused him to think deeply about how to control inflation without the low-paid having to endure greater constraint because the more powerful unions had cut themselves the biggest slice of the pie.

By its third year the social contract was becoming increasingly difficult for the trade-union movement to deliver. The Callaghan government had declared a pay norm of 5 per cent in 1978, at a time when inflation was running at 8 per cent. Tom Jackson was president of the TUC that year, which meant that he chaired the meetings of the general council. When a helpful statement basically supporting the government's 5 per cent guideline (which, if passed, would have prevented the trauma of the Winter of Discontent) was put to the vote, an equal number of general council members voted for and against. This gave the chair the casting vote.

The reasonable expectation was that Tom, as a strong advocate of wage control, would cast his vote in favour of the supportive statement. He didn't. Instead he declared the proposition not carried. The reason was quite simple. Like any good chairman, Tom was guided by Citrine's *ABC of Chairmanship*, the little book that had been my Bible ever since I was elected as branch chairman in Slough.

Citrine said that if a proposition was tied then it self-evidently hadn't been carried. For the person in the chair to declare it carried would undermine the neutrality essential to the chair's authority and the incumbent's ability to remain in control of the gathering over which he or she presided.

I doubt that the Callaghan government appreciated the finer points of Citrine but its logic on this point was indisputable, and Tom followed it despite his disappointment at the decision he'd been forced to make.

Since the general election the EC had been wrestling with another thorny issue. One of Mrs Thatcher's first decisions as prime minister had been to order a Monopolies and Mergers Commission report into the London postal service. The fact that the Post Office had a monopoly on handling items up to a certain weight and value was crucial to its capacity to offer a universal service at a single price. There was a necessary cross-subsidy from the lucrative high-volume, easy-to-distribute city mail to the daily deliveries in remote rural areas, which were not viable in purely economic terms but which the Post Office was still expected to provide to every address, along with accessible counter services.

The Post Office and the UCW had a mutual interest in maintaining the monopoly and a shared concern about what the commission was likely to discover. Stones would be lifted and questionable practices exposed.

Slough wasn't part of London's postal empire but its problems of poor recruitment and high numbers of vacancies were, if anything, even more acute. The Thames Valley had a thriving labour market in which the Post Office couldn't compete and, unlike post offices in the capital, provincial offices couldn't offer extra pay through London weighting. Some of the deals I'd helped to negotiate, like a two-hour book-through time, a rebate delivery agreement and twelve-hour daily attendances at Christmas, mirrored the kinds of agreements that existed in the main London offices and could have been construed as old Spanish customs.

The challenge for employer and union was to find and agree

on a way to deal with this unproductive 'hourage' before the Monopolies and Mergers Commission concluded its report. Its recommendations could then be pre-empted and, it was hoped, modified so that there was a better chance of the monopoly remaining intact.

John Taylor and Derek Walsh had entered into negotiation with the new director of postal services in London, a Scotsman by the name of Bill Cockburn (or Bilco, as the London guys called him). Tom Jackson kept a close watch on the negotiations, as did the personnel director for the Post Office, an urbane diplomat named Ken Young. But this had to be a London solution.

The result was an agreement with the unimaginative title of Improved Working Methods (John and Derek insisted that the word 'productivity' must not be used, despite the fact that this was clearly a productivity scheme). Under IWM, the union would sell hours of work that weren't needed back to the Post Office. The rate for an hour's work in each office would be calculated (it varied according to the level of overtime) and the workforce would receive 70 per cent of the savings (increased to 75 per cent if certain quality-of-service targets were met) as a weekly bonus.

It was a courageous move by the union and it took all of John Taylor's charismatic leadership skills to get it accepted by the London membership. There had been a furious reaction around the rest of the country. Many union branches were understandably concerned that a policy as controversial as effectively selling jobs for local bonuses had been agreed without any reference to the membership outside London. Other branches, fearing that their slack hours might be removed with no compensation, were equally anxious, albeit for different reasons.

Slough fell into the second category. Selling jobs was hardly a concern in an office with almost a hundred vacancies. To us it was simple: either the hours would be lost with no recompense to the workforce or the union could exert some influence over which hours were extracted and negotiate extra pay for our members in return. At Christmas 1979 branches outside London had been given the chance to participate in the IWM scheme as an experiment, just for the 'pressure' period. I had convinced the branch that Slough should participate and worked with the Post Office to produce the revised hours.

The issue of worker control was important to me. I believed in what was then known as industrial democracy – the participation of the workforce in the way their business was run. The Post Office was then one of two industries (the other being British Steel) where a form of industrial democracy had been introduced as part of the reforms recommended by the Bullock report commissioned by the Callaghan government. It's fair to say that the unions (ours included) never properly engaged with that huge opportunity and the experiment was already dead before Mrs Thatcher gave it a decent burial a few years later.

The IWM trial, however, allowed me to have a significant influence on Christmas attendances across the office with the aim of declaring a saving over the previous year's 'hourage' which could be translated into something we'd never known before: a Christmas bonus to be repeated every year into the future. It worked. My members in Slough each received a bonus of around £40, which was equivalent to a week's wages back then.

At a special union conference in 1980 it had been agreed to extend this entire scheme beyond London on a non-compulsory basis. Slough volunteered for IWM and I negotiated a weekly bonus of £10, which meant that the Post Office saved money through improved productivity, the workforce earned more money and became less dependent on overtime, and being a postman or woman in Slough became a more attractive proposition in the local labour market.

As a firm advocate of IWM, I now found myself, at my first EC meeting just two days after being elected, the only member of the executive council with any experience of grappling with its intricacies at the sorting-office coalface.

As I entered that room in the Bedford Hotel in Brighton, Tom Jackson turned from the window where he'd been gazing out to sea. He welcomed me and said he had high hopes for my future; that I could rise as high as I wanted to in the UCW. It was the first time we'd spoken since my election, though he'd sent a nice handwritten note to me via one of the stewards.

I knew that Tom had come through a horrendously difficult period personally as well as industrially. At the height of the Grunwick dispute, and during a difficult set of pay negotiations (which were always handled by the general secretary), he had been diagnosed with a cancerous growth behind one of his eyes. The treatment kept him out of action for four months. It had been successful but he'd lost the eye and now had a glass one in its place.

He told me how keen he was to end the internal divisions over IWM. The key was to ensure that our branch officials understood it properly, engaged with it proactively and implemented it to the advantage of our members. 'They say that in the country of the blind the one-eyed man is king,' he said ruefully, his glass eye seeming to twinkle as much as the real one, 'but this needs a man with two eyes, and that man is you.'

He confided that he had planned to talk to me straight after the EC meeting but, since serendipity had intervened, as he put it, and we found ourselves alone, he explained now that he wanted me to write a handbook and to conduct seminars around the country explaining IWM to those branches that expressed an interest in joining the scheme. He warned me that there'd be resentment among some of my more senior colleagues on the EC, but promised that he'd use his authority to ensure that I could undertake this task properly. I might still have been a rebel but I couldn't complain any longer about not having a cause.

∼

After the excitement of that conference, back at our house on the Britwell estate, Judy and I sat down to try to gauge the effect that my elevation would have on our lives. After the upcoming bank holiday weekend I would be working from UCW House in Clapham in south London, heading to the office in a suit rather than a Post Office uniform. It was clear from what Tom had said that my job was going to involve a lot of travelling and I knew that my only reliable source of income would be a flat postman's wage. There would be none of the overtime pay that had helped us to bring up three children, now fourteen, twelve and ten. There would, though, be subsistence payments from the union for travel and time spent away from my normal place of work.

There would be no more 5am starts, which delighted me, but on the other hand there would be no more afternoons sitting in the rustic calm of Dorneywood Road reading a book while waiting to begin the evening collection.

Judy was thrilled for me, but it was hard for us both to get our heads round what all this would mean in practical terms. She suggested that we load the kids into the car and drive up to UCW House on bank holiday Monday so that I'd know the way when I started there the following day. It was a good idea: I'd never set foot in the place before.

So it was that we found ourselves in Crescent Lane, Clapham, London SW4 after an hour's drive in our Hillman Avenger, admiring the magnificent 1930s architecture of my new workplace. Judy, Natalie, Emma and Jamie and me, gazing at the bricks and mortar that represented a new phase in our lives.

Chapter 19

LINDA HAD MARRIED Charles Edwards – or Chas, as he was known – in May 1979. The wedding had clashed with the union's annual conference and I'd been unable to attend. I'm sure Linda was upset about my absence. I'm sure, too, that Judy saw it as an ominous indication of the priority the union was taking in my life.

Chas was a stocky, round-faced man with an infectious laugh and a waspish sense of humour. A grammar-school boy, like me, he'd worked in his youth at Elstree film studios. One of his claims to fame was that he'd once met Walt Disney when asked by the studios to deliver a package to the great man at a London hotel. He earned a substantial tip from Disney and an experience on which he could dine out for years. Chas went on to run his own removals business, specializing in packing and shipping the belongings of families emigrating to Canada, South Africa and Australia. By the time Linda met him the business had fallen victim to the superior financial muscle of monoliths such as Pickfords and Chas had become a jewellery salesman. He was also a singer and compère at a club in Loughton, Essex, and his other claim to fame was that he had once sung at the famous 2i's coffee bar in Soho, where British institutions such as Tommy Steele and Cliff Richard had started out.

Chas was eight years older than Linda and had three children from his first marriage. His wife of sixteen years had run off to Devon with a man she'd met at work and Chas had custody of Cindy, Ricky and Eddie, who were in their early teens when he and Linda got together.

It was these children who first endeared me to Chas. I was very protective of my sister and wary of this new man in her life. I doubted that he could provide the stability she needed after the dreadful trauma she'd been through. But those three kids were so polite, so funny and so engaging, and had such a great relationship with him, that I was won over. If he could bring up three children single-handedly to become such well-adjusted teenagers, I reasoned, he must possess the qualities necessary to take on Renay, Tara, Dean and Nicky, too (Linda's younger foster son, Eugene, had gone back to live with his mother but Nicky had remained with Linda).

Linda's children appeared to have absorbed all the shock and horror of their father's death without displaying any immediately obvious symptoms of lasting damage. But Linda worried about delayed reactions. So when she and Chas married her first priority was to move the new extended family away from what had become a house of sorrow in Stopsley. Needing somewhere big enough for two adults and seven children, they each sold their respective properties and had a five-bedroomed house built to their specification in Hockley, not far from Chas's Essex base.

I don't think Linda ever really understood what my election

to the executive council meant. She'd tell people that I worked for the TUC. She knew I wore a suit to work and travelled a lot and this convinced her that it was some kind of promotion; that I had at last got myself the sort of job that fulfilled our mother's ambitions for me. Though our mother had been determined I should become a draughtsman, I'm sure the only reason she picked that career was that draughtsmen were professionals and went to work in suits.

I thought of my mother as, fully suited up, I boarded a plane stationed on the tarmac at Heathrow airport for my first-ever flight. I chose an aisle seat because I felt it would get me through the journey better if I didn't look out of the window. Around me sat bona fide businessmen and women, flicking through newspapers, oblivious to my nervousness.

Not only was it the first time I'd ever flown, it was also my first assignment as a member of the executive council of the Union of Communication Workers. And for good measure, it would be my first trip to Scotland.

Harry Jones, the assistant secretary at UCW House responsible for IWM, had called me into his office to brief me on a dispute in Dundee. An IWM scheme had been introduced, the hours had been cut but the expected bonus had never materialized. The office was out on strike. I was to travel up to Dundee to resolve it. I asked which train I was to catch.

'That would take too long,' said Harry. 'We've worked out a quicker way. You're to travel to Manchester on the shuttle from Heathrow and from there get on a smaller plane to Dundee. If you leave now, you'll be there by tea time. The branch is organizing a meeting this evening for you to address. You're to get them back to work, hopefully by tomorrow. Good luck.'

I didn't like to mention that I'd never flown before. Even in 1981 it seemed strange for a person to have reached his thirties without ever having stepped on a plane. I'd been abroad, but only once – to Denmark with the Children's Country Holidays Fund charity when I was twelve – and we'd travelled by boat. I didn't have the kind of fear of flying that prevents some people from even attempting the experience but I can't deny that I was anxious.

At that time shuttle flights were just that. There was no pre-booking. You just turned up, piled on, found a seat and took off. It wasn't even necessary to buy a ticket before boarding. The cabin crew spent the entire journey to Manchester collecting fares, like conductors on a London bus. No tea or coffee was served.

I kept my attention focused firmly on whatever I could find to read and felt a real sense of achievement when we landed at Manchester. The second flight was on a much smaller plane, a forty-seater, a far more daunting experience for a first-time flyer. Facing the Dundee strikers that evening was a breeze compared to getting there to start with.

The next day I convinced local management to reclassify a lump of hourage as what the scheme termed 'authorized variations', in other words, hours that had arisen for reasons unassociated with fluctuating volumes of mail and un-connected to the staff's productivity. This reclassification meant that these hours were treated as if they'd never been worked, earning the bonus not just for that week but for the whole month the scheme had been running at that office.

The men went back to work, normal service was restored to the good folk of Dundee and I left the city with one of its eponymous cakes and a book of (risqué) poetry by Robbie Burns – gifts from a grateful branch. The Post Office was satisfied and Harry Jones told me there were plenty more IWM problems to be resolved, hopefully before they developed into industrial disputes.

'We must take the kettle off the gas ring before it boils over,' he said when I got back. He was one of the two national officers responsible for postmen and women and PHGs named quaintly by the union the 'indoor secretary' (Harry) and the 'outdoor secretary' (a wonderful character called Maurice Styles).

Harry had a relaxed disposition but wasn't thought to be a brilliant negotiator. Like most of the handful of national officers (elected full-time employees of the union) he disapproved of IWM and had been instructed to assume responsibility for it by Tom Jackson. To Harry this was a distraction from his main task, which was dealing with the march of what was then called 'mechanization' but would now be known as new technology.

The primary purpose of postcodes, for example, introduced in the mid-1970s, was to make 'mechanized' sorting possible. Instead of hand-sorting the mail the PHGs would sit at coding desks translating postcodes into a series of phosphorous dots that could be read by huge sorting machines and directed to the appropriate dispatch point. The skill of hand-sorting was at the start of a slow decline, although I remember thinking that the new system would never catch on because people wouldn't remember, let alone use, their postcode. By 1981 I'd already been proved wrong.

In the same way as I had when I'd first become a postman at

Barnes, I closely observed my new workmates at UCW House. Although he looked incongruously Chinese, Harry was actually of Welsh and Italian extraction. While he spoke neither language he demonstrated his devotion to his mother's country by eating spaghetti with practically everything. At any restaurant, whatever its bill of fare, Harry would ignore the menu and insist on a medium-rare steak with spaghetti piled on top.

The outdoor secretary, Maurice Styles, was a committed communist and a great friend of Dickie Lawlor, who was now retired. Both men had been expelled from the union at one stage in the early 1960s but had subsequently been rehabilitated to the extent that they'd become part of the leadership they'd spent most of their union careers attacking.

I loved Maurice. He lived a frugal life, buying all his clothes at jumble sales. As a result they were usually too small, sometimes too large, for his massive frame but he was completely unconcerned about how he looked. He once addressed conference wearing trousers that were so big his belt was somewhere around his armpits. Only we on the platform behind him could see that the seat was split right across his backside.

Maurice and Jean, his equally committed communist wife, gave away all the money they earned. They lived in Brixton and were involved in dozens of initiatives there to help the poor and repair the racial tensions that erupted into riots the year I was elected to the executive. The joke at union headquarters was that Maurice's tiny but formidable wife would call him to account every evening, standing him by the fireside as she looked up at him from her armchair and demanded to know what he'd done for 'the party' that day. But there was nothing remotely sinister in his politics. Indeed, by then the Communist Party of Great Britain had given up on revolution and was campaigning for a Labour government. Or at least, that was Maurice's position.

Fiercely intelligent, Maurice was another autodidact. He had taught himself mainly through reading and as a result he had learned a lot of words he'd never actually heard pronounced. (As an autodidact myself, I just about steered clear of the pitfalls inherent in this form of self-education by virtue of having been such an avid listener to the BBC Home Service when I was growing up.) Maurice was none the less an impressive orator. He once rose to take issue with the perpetrators of a fractious debate criticizing his actions and remarked in his south London accent that 'all I've 'eard in dis debate is clitch after clitch after clitch'.

Maurice's was the most important national officer position in the union, representing the men and women who delivered the nation's mail. He had been a postman himself – indeed, all the assistant secretaries had come from the grades they represented.

Working for the telephonists was Kim McKinley, a remarkable woman in every respect. Another eccentric dresser, Kim appeared regularly in a black leather pilot's jacket, complete with white fleece lining, and a pilot's cap. She also had a penchant for leather trousers and flowing white scarves. All she needed to complete the Biggles impersonation was a pair of flying goggles.

Many years before, Kim had been the youngest member ever elected to the EC, succeeding in her early twenties and becoming a national officer ten years later. Now she was in her fifties, a chain-smoker with a deep attractive voice who, unlike Maurice, would never have pronounced 'cliché' as 'clitch'. Indeed Kim's pronunciation was impeccable. She sounded more like a member of the royal family than an ex-telephonist from Brighton.

It was through Kim that I learned about something called the marriage bar. She was married but had kept it a secret so that her status would not hamper her advance through the union's ranks. At the time she was elected as the assistant secretary for telephonists married women weren't allowed by the union to take such a promotion. The marriage bar had been introduced into the civil service in the late nineteenth century to prevent married women taking the better-paid jobs by blocking any promotion beyond a certain grade. The rationale was to give priority in the workplace to women who had no support from a husband. The civil-service trade unions (including ours) applied the same principles to its staff and some kept them even after they'd been scrapped by employers.

Tom's deputy, Alan Tuffin, a genial West Ham supporter, was the perfect counterweight to Tom's showmanship. He had little of Tom's charisma or fluency and had become deputy general secretary through sheer hard work and application. There wasn't a devious bone in his body and I rarely heard him say a bad word about anybody, although there were plenty of colleagues who tried his patience. He had succeeded Norman Stagg, the pint-sized battler who'd been an encouraging influence on my development in the union and had retired the previous year. Alan was a meticulous negotiator, the best I've ever worked with. Along with Joe Payne at Slough, it was he who taught me the importance of attention to detail.

With the exception of Tom's, the senior positions in the union were dominated by cockneys, reflecting the fact that a third of the members, and coincidentally a third of the mail, came from London. Among them was Les Hewitt, a former communist who'd moved steadily to the political right. Olive-skinned and extremely dapper, he was a genuine epicure. He not only had a fondness for fine wines, he knew a lot about them, too. Unlike the poseurs who'd stick their noses into their wine for show after swirling it round the glass a couple of times, without knowing why they were doing it, and then take a gulp, Les could tell with one sniff if it was corked ('You don't taste corked wine,' he instructed me in his gruff, cor-blimey voice, 'you smell it.'). This nugget was one of several that came my way in his attempts to educate me properly. 'A meal without wine is like a day without sunshine' was another, along with 'water is for shaving with', his admonishment to any waiter who offered to bring a jug to the table.

～

My immersion into this new life with its fresh cast of characters away from the dust of Oxford Avenue and the sweet early-morning air of Littleworth Common came to an abrupt halt when I broke my ankle playing football.

There are two versions of what happened. The one I prefer is that I was playing the game I'd loved all my life when my involvement was ended by a harsh tackle that necessitated my retirement from the sport at the tragically early age of thirty-one.

This is true but doesn't tell the entire story. I wasn't actually playing in a match – it was a kickaround at Burnham Beeches. I was indeed tackled brutally and unfairly by Darren Speight. I could stop there with my dignity intact. Choosing to go on involves revealing that Darren Speight was ten years old and Jamie's schoolfriend at Lynch Hill.

I had taken the two of them to kick a ball about at the Beeches, a short drive away from the Britwell. After the outrageous foul I knew I had to get to hospital. I tried hard to minimize the pain I was feeling in front of the boys, dismissing the knock as a sprain and smiling manfully in a way I thought would be reassuring to the little bastard who'd inflicted this injury on me.

I dropped Jamie and Darren at home and drove on to Wexham Park hospital, where my worst fears were confirmed. I'd driven four miles in a car with manual gears, pressing down the clutch pedal with a foot on the end of a broken ankle.

I was out of circulation for over six weeks. Fortunately, by then we were on the phone. It had become essential once I was fully embroiled in my IWM mission. I wasn't just helping to resolve disputes but also assisting branches to set up schemes and beginning work on the handbook Tom Jackson had commissioned. It was eventually published as *The Step-by-Step Guide to IWM* but, like all union handbooks, had no byline on the cover, much to my disappointment.

The scheme necessitated some complex calculations and had elements like 'traffic change factors', which required working hours to be expanded or contracted in proportion to increases or decreases in the volume of mail handled (this was, after all, meant to be a productivity scheme).

I can still recall those damned factors. For every 1 per cent variation in traffic compared with the baseline, hours had to vary by 0.2 per cent on 'outdoor' hours (delivering mail, collecting from pillarboxes) and 0.7 per cent for 'indoor' (sorting for dispatch or delivery). The baseline was set using figures for traffic and hours from the year before the scheme began and mail volumes needed to be constantly measured to provide accurate information about how many letters an office was handling (something that had only previously been assessed in a one-off 'annual count'). Unfortunately, I was no mathematical genius.

When Linda, as my teenage guardian, used to go to my school on parents' evenings she'd urge poor Mr Jacobs, my maths teacher, to try harder to instil in me the skills I'd need when I left school. (While I enjoyed the subjects that interested me, I'd shown a tendency not to bother too much about those that didn't.) I could add, subtract, divide and multiply adequately. I had known all that before leaving primary school. It was equations and percentages, anything beyond the basics, really, with which I'd declined to engage at school. The arrival of the calculator was a great help to people like me but I needed to understand the formulae, not just press buttons. My salvation came from a TUC booklet I came across entitled *Working with Figures*, which gave clear explanations of how to calculate all manner of things, particularly percentages.

John Taylor and Derek Walsh had actually formulated and negotiated the introduction of the scheme but, having established the basic outline, they never went on to deal with the reams of paperwork necessary to set it up in a sorting office as I had done in Slough. And for the calculations they did make they had relied on the genius of a man named Derek Saunders, the union rep in the Notting Hill delivery office.

Derek was a fascinating if little-known part of the IWM story. A secondary-modern pupil who'd left school at fifteen to become a telegram boy, he'd been crippled by what I took to have been polio. With his shuffling gait, large frame and long, greasy hair, he looked like Ian Dury, of Blockheads fame, with undertones of Bill Sykes. Now middle-aged, his face had been etched by every painful day of his illness.

When I'd first got to know John Taylor and told him I was from Notting Hill (the place where I'd grown up had been known as North Kensington but I'd given up trying to make the distinction, for the uninitiated, between London W10 and W11), he had insisted on introducing me to Derek Saunders – 'an ugly bastard but a fuckin' genius with numbers'. Derek was indeed a brilliant mathematician who was a huge asset to the union (and indeed the Post Office, which also prized his skills) in London.

Like Ernie Sheers with his treble accumulators, Derek had become interested in mathematics as an adult, finding practical expressions for calculations that for most people were abstract. He carried no trace of his wisdom in his personality. I suspect that polite society would have been repelled by the way he looked and the difficulty he had in talking without spittle running down his badly shaved chin. But inside that battered shell was a lovely man. Ernie used to tell me that if Jesus came back to earth he wouldn't descend into the Royal Enclosure at Ascot. He'd be poor and probably infirm. I often thought about that in my dealings with Derek Saunders.

While John and Derek Walsh were the face of IWM to the

London membership and, in the main, admired for the way they'd helped defend the service from the threat of the Monopolies and Mergers Commission, Derek Saunders was unknown to all but a handful of LDC activists. He died in harness about five years after the IWM scheme was introduced, his pain ended and his contribution largely unrecognized.

So, with the help of the TUC booklet and Derek Saunders, I suppose I became the one-eyed man in the country of the blind to whom Tom had referred. Most new EC members didn't get the opportunities I had to visit the branches. It was the senior figures who'd been around for a while who were most in demand. Of course, there were those who preferred life in the comfort zone of UCW House, chairing committees or working in the backwaters of the organizing, editorial or legal and medical departments. Exposure to the membership was double-edged. Success boosted your vote and guaranteed re-election; failure could have the opposite effect. The least dangerous option was to stay out of any disputes; to march away from the sound of gunfire.

∼

During my enforced absence from UCW House, a national dispute was brewing. It had been ten years since the great strike, a period during which a repeat was never even remotely contemplated.

Yet as I sat in plastered isolation on the Britwell, a strange series of events was driving us towards just such a destination. It all seems faintly ridiculous now, but this is the gist of what happened.

One of the most important delivery offices in London was the WDO, or Western District Office, in Rathbone Place, which covered the W1 postal district – the West End. The branch secretary was an Ashanti from Ghana, Frank Osei-Tutu. The UCW was proud of Frank. He'd become a major figure in London by fighting off an attempt by the National Front to unseat him in the 1970s. The fascists were outraged that a black man could be elected to lead such a prominent branch. Frank would eventually become a colleague on the executive council, where I was able to admire his Cecil Gee suits and beautiful silk ties at closer quarters.

Frank's branch chairman and ally in the battle with the NF was Bill Willoughby. Politically well to the left of Frank, Bill was a constant critic of the leadership in general and Tom Jackson in particular. During the course of his union duties he had become embroiled in a dispute with the canteen manager at WDO for reasons I cannot recall. During the course of a heated argument Bill Willoughby swore at the manager and banged his fist aggressively on a table, as a result of which offence the Post Office gave him notice of dismissal.

The union saw this as blatant victimization of an effective union representative. Bill had been wrong to swear and act aggressively but his actions did not warrant dismissal. With no previous disciplinary offences and twenty years of unblemished service, the most severe punishment he could have expected was a written warning. It looked like the canteen manager had given as good as he got. The fact that many in the union considered Mr Willoughby to be a pain in the arse was neither here nor there: his treatment was unjust.

This was the kind of dispute that bubbled up periodically and was generally dealt with sensibly at district council level. However, the LDC had failed to make any headway with the director of postal services, Bill Cockburn ('Bilco', who'd led for the Post Office in the IWM negotiations), and to everybody's astonishment Tom Jackson ended up getting personally involved.

It was no secret that Bill Willoughby was Tom's *bête noire*. So why didn't Tom leave this to be handled by his national officers or his deputy, Alan Tuffin? I was out of the loop but it seemed that Tom regarded this action against a senior branch official as a personal affront to his authority and a serious attack on the union as a whole.

He seemed genuinely offended that, after all his attempts to establish a better climate of industrial relations, his successful if highly controversial efforts to improve productivity through IWM and his contribution to keeping the Post Office free of involvement in the Winter of Discontent, he was now being humiliated by an upstart district manager – Bill Cockburn – who was confident that the union had been rendered industrially impotent by the 1971 strike.

All this culminated in a special meeting of the executive council being called for a Wednesday evening in October. All EC members were urged to attend. By then I could get about with the assistance of a pair of crutches and a large metal support under the sole of my plastered left foot. I certainly couldn't drive, but Dave Stock offered to give me a lift to Clapham, wait for me and bring me back. Joe Payne came along for the ride. He and Dave went to the King's Head round the corner from UCW House to wait. At 8pm I hobbled into the magnificent oak-panelled boardroom at UCW House and sat in my usual position at the round, glass-topped table.

Upon arrival we were given a confidential paper setting out the strategy for a series of national strikes in support of Bill Willoughby and a transcript of the argument that our general secretary had put to Willoughby's final disciplinary hearing the previous day. A decision by the disciplinary panel was expected within the next couple of days. I have a clear memory of Tom's statement: it was the first time I'd seen the phrase 'lingua franca', which he'd employed to describe how normal it was for swearwords to be used when managers and union officials met at WDO.

The atmosphere in the boardroom was tense. We were being asked to press the union's nuclear button in the event that the appeal was lost. We'd gone on strike in far more benign circumstances, and with a better case affecting all our members, a decade earlier and been defeated. To do so now, in defiance of an anti-union government that had already presided over the separation of posts from telecoms and was champing at the bit to dilute the monopoly, seemed reckless, to say the least. Furthermore, Willoughby wasn't exactly Mr Popular with members of the executive council.

Mingled with the tension was a tingle of excitement. We were involved in an historic event for the union which could have far-reaching consequences. As Tom came into the boardroom, his assistant handed round sealed envelopes. Each had a separate number and such was their sensitivity, we were informed by the chair, they would need to be taken back after we'd had ten minutes to read the document inside.

It contained the shocking news that Tom Jackson was to take early retirement. The reason for all the secrecy was that Tom wanted the executive council to know he'd already made the decision before we embarked on an industrial dispute the outcome of which might be wrongly perceived as the reason for his retirement. If, as seemed likely, we were going to take to the battlefield, we would have to do so with our troops unaware that their commanding officer intended to leave the army.

The union's rule book insisted that all national officers retire at the age of sixty and allowed those appointed before a certain date (which included Tom) to go with a full pension at fifty-five. Tom was exhausted. The cancer that had claimed his eye had also diminished what was left of his enthusiasm for a job that was as demanding as any Cabinet minister's – and he'd been doing it for fourteen years rather than the two or three years a Cabinet minister might expect to remain in post.

In truth he was also despondent about trying to lead union activists who were increasingly reluctant to be led. He'd had one wage deal overwhelmingly rejected in 1979 and had suffered the humiliation of a vote of censure being carried against him at a subsequent conference.

To understand the shock of the announcement that night it's important to appreciate the particular regard in which this great public figure was held. I yielded to no one in my respect and affection for Tom, the man who'd singled me out to advise, encourage and cajole into standing for national office and who'd become my mentor and guide. I limped round to the pub afterwards to find Dave and Joe with a heavy heart to go with the plastered foot. I couldn't say anything to them as the executive was sworn to secrecy about Tom's announcement.

We had agreed a strategy for a national dispute that, thankfully, never took place (Bill Willoughby was eventually reinstated) and an election timetable for a general secretary vacancy that wasn't supposed to have occurred for another four years.

Chapter 20

As I was elected to the executive council, the effects of the Thatcher government's policies were starting to be felt across the country. On the Britwell the opportunity presented to council tenants to purchase their homes with the help of a government subsidy was a perfect example of a political decision having a direct and significant impact on people's lives.

Giving council tenants the right to buy their houses wasn't a new or even an exclusively Conservative policy. Local authorities had always had the ability to allow such a transfer of ownership and a national extension of that policy had been part of Labour's 1959 election manifesto. But when the Thatcher administration introduced the Housing Act 1980, the policy became mandatory nationwide, irrespective of the view or circumstances of the council to which the houses belonged.

For Judy and me and our neighbours and friends, the debate over the right-to-buy scheme wasn't some dry, academic discussion of political pros and cons. We were the council tenants government ministers were talking about when they spoke of the transfer of capital wealth from the state to the people. It was undoubtedly a political masterstroke for the Conservatives, one that resonated with people more profoundly than almost any aspect of government policy I could remember.

The effect around our small corner of the Britwell was immediate. Martin and Karen next door were the first to take advantage of the scheme. They sold their former council house very quickly after buying it, moving to a house near Swindon where Martin had acquired a car-spares business. Indeed, they sold up so speedily that I suspect they had to pay back some of the discount that was contingent on the purchasing tenants continuing to occupy the property for a certain period of time. A young couple moved in next door – first-time buyers and the very first exclusively private home-owners round the green.

They would be free from the rules stipulating that no private hedge could be higher than 3ft 6ins and that your front door had to be a certain colour. They could paint their front door any colour they liked. They could change the door altogether if they wanted. Any improvements they made to their house would not have to be ripped out when they moved on, which was what happened to the properties owned by the council, the aim being to ensure that no tenant was given an unfair advantage.

In fact, while I do remember the privet-hedge rule, I'm not sure if the colour of the paintwork was actually centrally dictated or whether it was just that when the doors were repainted on change of tenancy they were returned to their original colour. Either way, we all believed it was a rule, so all our doors had been the same. Now the mock-Georgian doors with fanlights that were popular at the time began to spring up round the estate.

I recall one passionate discussion at one of our neighbourhood parties, which had become less frequent by then and were no longer financed by subscription. My friend Mick Pearson, who'd joined the Labour party with me, argued fiercely in favour of the scheme. I can picture us now, standing in Robert and Kathleen Metcalfe's small kitchen, Mick in a vest (a brief summer fashion) with an earring in his left ear (he had been one of the first to participate in the masculinization of the earring, a physical intrusion I refused to countenance), his gin and tonic stacked with accumulated slices of lemon, wiping the floor with my carefully constructed argument that this was a bad policy that would have serious consequences for future generations.

Why should we spend the rest of our lives paying rent that would eventually exceed the value of the house, only to see the home we'd cherished through the decades handed on to someone else after we'd popped our clogs? he argued. Labour was wrong to oppose what Mrs Thatcher was doing. It would cost us votes and lose us the next election.

It was a good-natured debate and, while I lost the argument in Robert's kitchen, we all had to make our own decisions about whether or not to buy. Mick and Susan took the plunge and within three years they had gone. The Metcalfes and Gabriels had also become home-owners by the end of 1981.

For Judy and me the advantages of participating in the scheme were clear. To buy a house privately would require a hefty deposit. While we earned enough money to live reasonably comfortably with no debts, a car and a holiday every year in Cornwall or Devon, we had little in the way of savings.

As tenants for over ten years we'd qualify for a discount on the value of the house of over a third. It was a cut-price bargain that was difficult to resist. But resist it we did. I felt no piety about bucking the trend among our neighbours and our decision certainly had nothing to do with Labour party policy (which speedily changed in favour of council house sales anyway). I didn't feel in any way morally superior to the people desperate to own their own homes who saw Mrs Thatcher as a liberator.

The cost and responsibility of maintaining the house was a factor for Judy and me, particularly as I was so useless at anything calling for DIY skills and would struggle to carry out the simplest of repairs. But what convinced us in the end was remembering how lucky we felt to have been allocated a council house. When I argued with Mick that we had an obligation not to deny future generations that lifeline, it wasn't mere rhetoric. I meant it. My mother's dream of having her own front door, of whatever colour, could only have been made a reality through social housing. Hers was an ultimately futile desire; ours had been fulfilled. If our financial situation improved to the extent that we could afford a deposit we should, like many before us – including our friends Fred (the BBC scene-shifter) and Barbara – buy a house away from the Britwell and pass on what we'd been fortunate enough to acquire to another family who had no prospect of buying any kind of house. We declined to take advantage of the bargain offer and remained council tenants.

∾

In 1982, in addition to Tom Jackson, another doyen of the union was preparing to retire, albeit one whose light had shone only in our small corner of the country. Len Rigby had now reached the age of sixty-five. Since becoming branch chairman five years earlier I'd tried to discourage Len from criticizing Joe Payne, his chosen successor as branch secretary, and he'd rightly refused to take any role in the union beyond attending branch meetings, where he'd sit on the periphery, legs crossed, holding his cigarette theatrically while contemplating the ceiling. Still Nöel Coward, but now Nöel Coward watching a rehearsal for one of his plays as opposed to taking centre stage.

The only more regular attendee at our Slough branch meetings was Ernie Sheers who, like Len, observed but said nothing. Ernie would castigate anyone he heard moaning about the union if they couldn't be bothered to attend our gatherings and make their point there. He wasn't uncritical himself, warning me about what was happening in my absence on executive-council business. I was like a cricketer, he remarked, called up to represent England but still attached to his county side.

When Len took me to one side to tell me he would be retiring he offered me a final piece of advice. I should become honorary president of the branch and cease any local involvement. Otherwise I would be expected to do the chairman's job in the way I used to at the same time as having to travel up and down the country in my new capacity. I told him I'd think about it but I never did. My feeling was that branch involvement helped me to do my national job properly. I believed I needed the Slough Amalgamated Branch more than they needed me.

Len was due to be given honorary membership of the District Council and that gave me an idea. I would ask Tom Jackson to present Len with this honour as part of the round of farewells he was undertaking in the run-up to our 1982 conference, at which he would formally hand over the reins to his successor, Alan Tuffin.

Alan had been elected from five candidates for this job. These had included Kim McKinley but not John Taylor, who had focused his ambitions on replacing Maurice Styles as outdoor secretary when Maurice retired the following year. His aim was then to use that position as his launch pad for the top job. Alan Tuffin was due to retire in ten years, by which time John would be in his early fifties and perfectly placed for the succession.

My plan to bring together Tom and Len, for me the two figureheads of the 1971 strike, met with everyone's approval. The date was cleared with Tom but his attendance would be kept a closely guarded secret. Len was not to find out until Tom stepped into the hotel conference room in Ascot where the presentation was to be made.

As Tom couldn't drive it was agreed that I would take him to and from the venue. When Tom had been elected general secretary in 1967 he had inherited a union car, a Humber Snipe. Since this big, sleek, luxury motor did not come with a chauffeur it wasn't much use to Tom. One of his first acts was to get rid of it via a raffle among the union's membership. Which is how it ended up in the proud possession of a postman from Newcastle.

Dispensing with this status symbol went down well with the members in the increasingly egalitarian 1960s. Tom never went out of his way to explain that he couldn't actually drive.

Maurice Styles told me a funny story about that Humber Snipe, its previous driver and his communist ally, Dickie Lawlor. Tom's predecessor, Ron Smith, had a designated parking place for his Humber at the front of union head-quarters. It was visible from his top-floor office where, when in contemplative mood, he would often stand gazing out of the window. One morning, surveying the car park as he marshalled his thoughts, Ron saw Dickie Lawlor chugging into view on an old Velocette motorcycle. To Ron's consternation, Dickie leaned his motorbike up against the highly polished flank of the Humber Snipe.

Ron, who left the union to become the personnel director of British Steel in 1966, was an imperious man who could, I'm told, be extremely self-important. He and Dickie were sworn enemies. A tannoy message went out for Dickie Lawlor to report to the general secretary's office. When Dickie was ushered in Ron Smith was standing, hands behind his back, looking out on the offending scene of bike on car below.

'Mr Lawlor,' he said, without turning round. 'Is that your motorbike leaning against my car?'

'No,' replied Dickie.

Ron Smith whirled round, eyes blazing. 'Mr Lawlor, are you denying that Velocette is your bike?'

'No,' said Dickie cheerfully. 'It's my bike, all right. But it's not your car, it's *our* car.'

By 1982 I'd traded in my Hillman Avenger for a Mark IV Cortina, which was to be Tom's conveyance from Clapham to Ascot. The journey there and back gave us around two and a half hours to talk. Despite not being able to drive, Tom had an encyclopaedic knowledge of London's streets. He could have been a black-cab driver if he'd actually been able to drive. He showed me back streets I didn't know existed which avoided the South Circular and all the obvious routes between Clapham and the M4.

As we drove I asked him what he planned to do on his retirement. Tom told me that he'd turned down a knighthood and rejected a seat in the House of Lords. A publisher had offered a significant advance for his memoirs but it was on the understanding that he'd dish some dirt on the Labour party and trade-union movement, which he wasn't prepared to do.

With his handlebar moustache and moderate politics, Tom was a particular target for Militant and their ilk. Yet the man who was said to be lusting after grandeur as a peer of the realm was refusing all such blandishments, in marked contrast to some of his critics, who made passionate speeches against the second chamber but subsequently succumbed readily to the lure of ermine.

I also discovered on that journey that Tom had a passion for books. He was an antiquarian book collector, specializing in boys' fiction, writers like R. M. Ballantyne and G. A. Henty, and cookery books (particularly Mrs Beeton). As I'd learned from watching *Nationwide* during the 1971 strike, he was an enthusiastic cook himself and was looking forward to having more time to indulge his culinary skills.

He'd sold his terraced house in Tulse Hill (to the leader of the Greater London Council, Ken Livingstone) and intended to move with his partner, Kate, back to his native Yorkshire, where they planned to buy and sell books through mail order. He had no interest in playing any further role in public affairs.

At the union event in Ascot, Len and his wife, Elsie, were delighted when I turned up with Tom Jackson. I looked on as two men who had dedicated their working lives to the union met for the first and only time – Len, a reluctant retiree; Tom, worn down by the grinding responsibility of leadership, an enthusiastic one.

On the way back to London Tom and I talked about my future. He convinced me to aim for general secretary. I needed to become a national officer first, he said – nobody ever went from lay member of the executive to general secretary in one step. He advised me to stay in the front line because the activists respected those who took on the hardest jobs. Some EC members did as little as possible, the theory being that the less they did the fewer mistakes they'd make. Get out there, work hard and stay focused was Tom's succinct advice.

As I dropped him off he had one last message for me. 'Watch your back,' he warned. 'There are colleagues who see you as a threat. Their knives are being sharpened even as we speak.'

~

For my thirty-second birthday, which fell at my first conference as an EC member in 1982, wine buff Les Hewitt presented me with two bottles of a very nice red, telling me it was good for the libido. It was virtually the first time I'd drunk vin rouge. It tasted much better than Black Tower.

The drinking culture around work was widespread in the 1980s across many industries and businesses. The trade-union movement was no exception, though it was not an extreme example. We in the UCW were probably at the mild end of the scale. I was fortunate in that driving into the office every day (when I wasn't travelling around the country) instilled a routine and discipline that excluded excess alcohol – and an excuse not to get drawn into the boozing that usually began after working hours, when EC members from Newcastle, Glasgow, Liverpool or Penzance, for instance, had little else to do before bedding down in their sleeping quarters.

As I became involved in national talks alongside Maurice and Harry I found that the drinks cabinet was a feature of every senior manager's office, the contents considered a necessity for oiling the negotiating machine. There would be a bottle of whisky plonked on the table to seal a deal at the end of a successful negotiation; informal discussions would take place over a wine-fuelled lunch or a few pints in the pub. For most of the participants it made the process more relaxed and less arduous, but for a few, including John Taylor, it became the process itself. Through the 1980s it became clear that John's engine couldn't function without its wheels being oiled.

With my contribution to Britain's literary canon, *The Step-by-Step Guide to IWM*, in wide circulation within the union, more offices joined the scheme and the demand for my services increased. Apart from London, where Derek Saunders was resident consultant, I went everywhere.

To Newton Abbot in Devon, where a wag turned up to the meeting bedecked with boxes of Paxo and the protest message 'Stuff IWM'.

To Perth, where 'Big Joe' Menzies, my host at the Scottish cultural evening during my first conference, asked for assistance. Such was my fondness for Joe and Perth that I probably nursed the scheme more closely than was strictly necessary, visiting the office on numerous occasions.

To Glasgow, our second-biggest branch and one usually

hostile to any HQ involvement in its affairs. They were originally dead set against IWM but eventually decided to enter and sought my involvement.

To Tenby, Southend, Swindon, Milton Keynes, Peterborough, Burnley, Blackburn, Preston, Leicester, Coventry, Birmingham, Accrington, Whitby, Sheffield, Bangor, Holyhead; to all points north, south, east and west.

In Liverpool I ran a weekend seminar beginning on a Saturday lunchtime. The reps on the course had to take their calculators home with them and bring them back the next morning. One young postman, having been out on the town on Saturday night, came out of his house on Sunday with the television remote control instead of his calculator. Such was his hangover that he only became aware of his mistake after several attempts to calculate a percentage on it.

The union had purchased a hotel in Bournemouth at which I conducted a school for all postal EC members so that they could be trained up to cope themselves with the growing demand for IWM. But for some reason most of them were reluctant to engage with this work and, happily for me, like the Post Office, I retained a limited monopoly.

It was hard work but invariably I arrived in an office with more expertise than the managers and left the local membership with a pay increase and sometimes a substantial lump sum to be paid in arrears. There was no other sphere of EC work where a visit could lead to such tangible and almost universally positive results. So it is perhaps hardly surprising that within a couple of years I was topping the poll in the annual EC elections and also in the election for delegates to the TUC and Labour party conferences.

I attended my first Labour conference in 1982, when Michael Foot was leader. I was an admirer of Foot's, and particularly of his masterly biography of Nye Bevan, but he couldn't command a party that was increasingly losing touch with reality. By coincidence Jamie met Foot that year – while doing his paper round. In the run-up to a by-election in Beaconsfield, the safe Tory seat that embraced a third of the Britwell, Jamie came running home one day, breathless, to tell us that he'd seen Michael Foot in Wentworth Avenue and he'd said hello. Foot had been with the Labour candidate. Jamie couldn't remember his name but he, too, had said hello. That candidate's name would become rather better known. It was Tony Blair. Long before I did, my son met the man who would turn the Britwell back from blue to red fifteen years later.

~

My first-ever flight, to Dundee, was followed quickly by many more – to Glasgow, Edinburgh, Manchester and Belfast. It was handy that I lived only one junction on the M4 away from Heathrow. Dave Stock was a huge support, running me to the airport and back. Once, as I took off – blasé enough by then to handle a window seat – I spotted a familiar Slough landmark, traced the road that connected it with the Britwell and managed to pick out our house on the green on Long Furlong Drive. It was an incredible experience to look down on my home, and its green dot of a garden, from thousands of feet up in the air.

It was my trips to Northern Ireland that were the most memorable. With the Troubles still raging, security was such an issue that no EC member was allowed to go there without the specific permission of the general secretary. The Northern Ireland District Council covered all six counties and invited me to weekend schools and seminars across the province. I became close friends with the assistant district organizer, Tommy McCready, a sandy-haired clerical officer with bags of ability whose only ambition was to serve his members in Northern Ireland. It was, needless to say, a more difficult job than anywhere else in the country.

Tommy was a Catholic and the district organizer, Jack Hassard, a Protestant. They forged a formidable partnership. Jack was rumoured to carry a gun for self-protection, having been criticized by loyalist paramilitaries for his non-sectarian approach to union work. It was a rarely acknowledged fact that the trade-union movement was often the only non-sectarian institution capable of wielding a positive influence on events in Northern Ireland. Tommy was called into one office to resolve a dispute caused by a Catholic supervisor being appointed to a predominantly Protestant office. Somehow he found a resolution.

Jack's and Tommy's jobs were frequently dangerous and sometimes impossible. A common ploy used by terrorist factions was to hold the families of a postal worker hostage to force him or her to drive a Royal Mail van packed with explosives to a location dictated by the captors. These proxy bombings took place on a regular basis. Because they were constantly out on the streets, postal workers were particularly vulnerable. Many were killed in the course of their duties; some were specifically targeted for assassination. For a while the postal workers who transported money between post offices were declared a legitimate target by one terrorist group after thwarting a raid.

The sorting office in Derry had to be relocated six times because of explosions. And yet there was no trace of animosity or inhumanity in the wonderful people I met in Northern Ireland, least of all the union representatives who volunteered for the thankless task of trying to uphold the principles of solidarity, tolerance and compassion in that divided society.

One night I stayed with Tommy McCready, his wife Margaret and their children at their house in Belfast. As we walked to the social club that evening, one of Tommy's young sons skipped along in front of us. I saw him freeze as the sound of flutes floated towards us on the air. As the source of the music was revealed – a couple of teenagers appeared from round a corner, both playing flutes – I watched this nine-year-old-boy's expression change from cheerfulness to wariness: all within two bars of a piece of music. Tommy took his son's hand and continued his conversation with me as if nothing had happened. And it hadn't: the two lads passed by and we carried on walking. Tommy McCready never mentioned the incident and neither did I but, from the reaction of one small child to music that intimidated him, I learned more about the situation in Northern Ireland, and the realities of living within the climate of fear it created, than from any amount of media reporting.

Back at headquarters, Alan Tuffin was struggling to raise his profile to the level of his predecessor's as Mrs Thatcher's government formulated legislation to outlaw the closed shop, to make ballots before industrial action compulsory and to force trade-union general secretaries to stand for election every five years. These were measures that trade unions should have agreed with previous Labour governments but had refused to consider.

Far more important to the working lives of UCW members was the announcement in July 1982 that British Telecom would be privatized. The duopoly created by splitting British Telecom from the Post Office had already been introduced as the first phase of liberating telecommunications from state ownership. Whereas postal services were highly regarded by the public, the same could not be said for telephones. The long wait for installation and repair, plus the lack of choice of handsets and so forth, contributed to the unpopularity of the status quo.

It was clear that if the Conservatives were re-elected in 1983 nothing could stop the sell-off.

At the Post Office, a more forceful management style, geared to higher productivity and less consultation, had blown away the consensual approach to industrial relations that had existed since the war. Alan Tuffin had taken office in a climate so far removed from the one in which Tom Jackson had operated that he might have been doing a completely different job. When Tom had handed over responsibility to Alan he'd pointed to a second telephone on his desk. It was white and not the same model as the normal office phones. Tom told Alan that this was a hotline the number of which was known only to certain government ministers and senior civil servants.

'When that phone rings,' Tom said, 'it will be to consult you on matters of state. Industrial matters, certainly, but your opinion will also be gauged on wider political issues such as the economy or overseas trade.'

When Alan retired ten years later he told me wistfully that during his entire decade as general secretary the white phone had rung only once. The caller had been a woman asking if this was Sainsbury's.

Chapter 21

JUST BEFORE Mrs Thatcher swept to her second election victory, my sister and her husband decided to emigrate to Australia.

I've no idea how this decision was reached. Although Chas had been to lots of places around the world, singing in hotels and on cruise ships, Linda, now thirty-six years old, had never been abroad in her life, never mind to the other side of the globe, and it was unlike her to make such a leap in the dark.

I remembered our mother, at probably exactly the same age, staring dreamily at a poster offering 'a better life' in Australia for just £10 in the housing trust offices in Portobello Road as we queued to pay the rent. Linda and I had quickly scotched any notion she may have had of us becoming Ten Pound Poms. We were Londoners through and through and to us North Kensington was the centre of the universe.

However the decision was reached, once it had been made it was firm and Linda and Chas were soon making all the arrangements. They would sell the Hockley house with most of its contents and take practically nothing with them apart from Chas's car, which was a Mercedes and might help him find work as a salesman. With no house to go to, let alone a job, the project was a big risk as well as an adventure. Linda went to a fortune-teller about a month before they left, paying £10 (the same sum it would have cost our mother to emigrate in the mid-1950s) to hear the predictions of Gypsy Rose someone or other. She was told that she'd be moving to a house surrounded by hills. Linda replied that she was certainly moving, but to Australia which, as far as she knew, was not famous for its hills.

Linda and Chas planned to move with all six children (Nicky, Linda's foster son, had by now left care) but then Cindy got married, Ricky met a girl and Eddie said that if Cindy and Ricky weren't going, neither would he. They were in their late teens and twenties by this time and old enough to live independently.

Linda insisted that they travel by ship as she was afraid of flying. And so, on 28 May 1983, my sister, Chas, Renay, Tara and Dean sailed away on a ship bound for Perth, Australia, via Bangkok.

They came to stay with us on the Britwell the weekend before they left, full of excitement about the new life that awaited them. Given all Linda had been through, I desperately hoped that the gamble would pay off. She had been there for me my whole life and her departure was going to be a wrench. But what was certain was that the bond between us couldn't be broken by the 10,000 miles that would separate us.

When the family arrived in Perth they were met by some friends of Linda's who'd lived in Tring and emigrated some years earlier. They looked after the children for a night while Linda and Chas went to a motel. Chas was in bed, leafing through the real-estate pages of a local paper borrowed from their friends, when he came across a childcare centre for sale in Armadale, a suburb of Perth. The property consisted of three-bedroomed living accommodation above a nursery – a house and business all rolled into one. To maintain and run the nursery the successful buyer would need to have the correct childcare qualifications. That was no problem: Linda's Nursery Nurse Examination Board (NNEB) certification was universally recognized.

At ten the next morning Chas and Linda were in Armadale speaking to the owners, who had a caravan parked outside the property waiting to take them on a retirement trip round Australia. The centre had been up for sale for eighteen months with no takers. Linda was convinced that fate had a hand in holding it back for her. Chas made an offer. It was accepted on the spot.

They'd been in Australia for just thirteen and a half hours. When Linda walked out on to the balcony of what was now her new home she noticed that Armadale was surrounded by hills.

~

Just as Mick Pearson had predicted in our kitchen debate about the sell-off of council houses, Labour lost Slough in 1983. Joan Lestor's local popularity counted for little when set against the twin Conservative advantages of victory in the Falklands War and Labour's longest suicide note in history. And the right to buy council houses was undoubtedly responsible for turning both halves of the Britwell blue.

I was on the southern regional executive of the Labour party when the Thatcher government won its second term in power. In our region the SDP-Liberal Alliance had beaten us into third place. By this time, being part of the trade-union movement felt like being under siege. The government wanted free, independent trade-unionism – but only in Poland, where Solidarity was challenging the totalitarian regime. In Britain all the structures of consultation with the TUC had been abandoned. Alan Tuffin told me that when he'd gone with the general council to make representation to the Treasury, the chancellor, Nigel Lawson, had pulled a nail-clipper from the pocket of his colourful waistcoat and rocked back and forth on his chair manicuring his nails while Norman Willis, the TUC general secretary, made his presentation.

Alan was having a rough ride. At conference in 1983, for the first time in the union's history a motion of no-confidence had been carried against a national officer, poor assistant secretary Harry Jones. I had stupidly urged the postal executive to resign and walk off the platform on the basis that Harry shouldn't be left to take the rap alone. The issue upon which the motion was carried was an esoteric matter affecting a handful of members who sorted overseas mail. But it was the postal executive to which Harry reported, so the vote of no-confidence was against us collectively, despite the wording referring only to Harry.

Fortunately, calmer voices prevailed. As I stood pontificating among my colleagues, Alan Tuffin pointed out that the results of the ballot for that year's executive, due to be announced the following day, would be decisive in terms of whether the membership had any confidence in us. He was right. As things turned out, the activists carried a motion of no-confidence and re-elected us at the same time.

Harry Jones, though, was inconsolable. He'd never before experienced viciousness of the kind that was creeping into our proceedings. And our union was a model of courteous behaviour compared with some others, where factional dog fights reduced conferences to little more than five days of ritual humiliation for the leadership.

Alan Tuffin dealt with the increasingly fractious mood with calm equanimity. He knew he had none of Tom's skill at oratory but his patent decency and honesty were powerful defences and his boxer's sense of ringcraft saved the UCW from being pulled on to the punches that were landing heavily on other unions. He had a good relationship with the avuncular and shrewd chairman of the Post Office, Ron Dearing. They had a shared objective, which was to ensure that a great public institution continued to be relevant in an era of declining social mail where the fax machine – believe it or not – was seen as a serious threat to our future.

Dearing and his personnel director, Ken Young, were still keen to work with a strong union and to develop the close relationship they saw as essential in a labour-intensive sector with a long history of dedication to public service and a limited monopoly. Other senior managers, however, scented blood and were urging Dearing to take a stronger line in order to break the union's influence while he had the support of a sympathetic government.

I decided to stand in the election to replace Maurice Styles as outdoor secretary in 1983. I had no expectations of succeeding. My friend John Taylor, who'd had his sights trained on the post, was a shoo-in, and eminently qualified for it after his years of experience leading 60,000 London postmen and women. But

Maurice told me that the very act of standing for the job, the most difficult in the union apart from general secretary, would do me no harm, irrespective of how badly I fared in the election.

John Taylor saw it differently. He understood my wish to make a point, but he felt that any votes that I attracted would be at his expense. If no candidate received more than 50 per cent of the vote a second ballot would take place between the two with the highest number of votes. John was concerned that I might draw enough votes to force him into a second round.

I heard that Maurice was quietly recommending me as his successor but whether or not that was true it was irrelevant. I didn't do as badly as I'd thought I might, coming third out of five nominees and gaining a respectable number of votes. No candidate attracted over 50 per cent of the vote but John came through the second ballot as the clear victor.

Derek Walsh was also on the executive council by this time. He told me that he saw it as his mission to keep John on the straight and narrow. John, now married with two small daughters, was taking on family responsibilities for the first time in his mid-forties. It was hoped this would encourage him to put the brakes on his drinking.

≈

The backdrop to everything that was happening in the trade-union movement in the mid-1980s was the miners' strike. The defeat of the NUM encouraged Rupert Murdoch's News International to take on the print unions in the move from Fleet Street to Wapping. The entire period between

1984 and 1987 was dominated by tumultuous conflicts.

Unions in our sector had already been roundly defeated on BT privatization, with UCW members happily accepting the shares that we urged them to reject. In the Labour party, Neil Kinnock had begun the long march back to electability. At Labour party conference we working-class trade-unionists wore suits, because the culture on our side of the class divide was that you dressed smartly to represent your members. Perversely, this seemed to attract derision. We felt like aristocrats caught up in the storming of the Bastille.

We'd be surrounded by scruffs, usually well-spoken, their denim jackets weighed down with badges proclaiming opinions on every subject under the sun. To get to conference delegates had to pass through a mob of competing factions handing out flyers, most of them insultingly hostile to the leadership. Inside the hall the first hour or so of every conference day was spent dealing with points of order as a long queue of delegates snaked towards the rostrum, each one keen to shout loudly into the microphone about some awful perceived injustice being perpetrated by the leadership or, more likely, those dastardly bastards on the conference arrangements committee. The culture of betrayal seeped into every aspect of our deliberations.

Before the miners' strike, during it and for long after it had finished, when Arthur Scargill was called to the rostrum there would be a standing ovation which continued intermittently throughout his five minutes of finger-jabbing and accompanied him all the way back to his seat.

It happened at the TUC as well, and the applause seemed to get greater as the NUM delegation got smaller. In the main, we in the UCW avoided this hero-worship. I knew Mick McGahey, the former NUM vice-president, a bit, and Jack Taylor, the leader of the Yorkshire miners, whom I was asked to host when he came to address our conference during the strike. They were both incredibly loyal and while they never said anything uncomradely, their demeanour whenever the strike was discussed suggested that they were far from happy about the cult of personality that had grown up around their leader. At one conference the NUM delegation was seated in the row behind us. As Arthur fulminated at the rostrum we heard one of their senior figures exclaim to his colleagues, 'Listen to him, all "I, me, mine", never "we, us, ours".'

As for Scargill's insistence that he'd been right about the Coal Board's plans to close pits: as somebody once said, the job of the trade-union leader isn't to predict rain, it's to build the bloody ark.

The government's programme of privatization was accelerating apace, with gas, aerospace, petroleum and ferries all in the firing line and union opposition brushed aside. The Post Office appeared to be safe from this onslaught but, as a public corporation in an era when 'private sector good, public sector bad' appeared to be the mantra, we in the UCW understood that either we solved our own problems or we'd have them solved for us. Privatization had never been specifically ruled out by the government and the substantial reorganization of the Post Office into four separate businesses – mails, parcels, counters and Girobank – looked like the first phase of a move to sell off the mails business. In fact it was Girobank that would eventually be sold, so cheaply that it might as well have been on offer at a car boot sale.

The Post Office was among the few postal services around the world providing a handsome return on capital and contributing positively to the exchequer, but this public-sector success made it even more attractive to the privatization zealots in Whitehall. The resulting speculation about impending privatization was actually a helpful context in which to formulate the wide-ranging agreement Alan Tuffin and Ken Young set out to achieve. It focused the minds of our activists on the possible consequences of failing to find a way through the maze of interlocking issues that were holding the business back.

I was grateful for Alan's insistence that I accompany him not only to pay negotiations but also to the most important set of discussions with the Post Office in a generation: Safeguarding the Future of the Mails Business, as the agreement finally reached was rather grandly entitled.

Alan taught me so much about the art of negotiation: the need to earn the respect of the person on the other side of the table; to be patient, to listen carefully (a surprisingly rare talent) and to use adjournments as an alternative to making an immediate response to an important offer. He would use his glasses as a tactical prop, polishing the lenses slowly when he was playing for time, more rapidly as a prelude to a little speech about how close the negotiations were to breakdown. He would suck a temple tip thoughtfully as he ruminated on what the other side had said, or wag the spectacles up and down to emphasize a point. It was so effective it made me wish I wore glasses.

Chief among the restrictions hampering the business was the union's aversion to recruiting part-time staff. With most part-timers being women, some of this antipathy was rooted in an outdated, male-orientated view of the world in which women worked for 'pin-money'. There was a still a sense, which was by no means exclusive to the Post Office, that part-time workers were a lower form of workplace life. This was reflected in our union's rule book, where they were categorized as Class B members (full-timers, of course, were Class A).

But there was also a valid fear that our industry could easily be casualized; that the Post Office, which seemed incapable of completely resolving its recruitment problem even at times of soaring unemployment, would move towards bringing in a predominantly part-time workforce.

What the Post Office told us they wanted was a more dependable evening shift for the four hours between 5pm and 9pm when the vast majority of mail was posted, collected, sorted and dispatched. This couldn't be achieved while we relied so heavily on overtime to cover this period. The rest of the agenda included making IWM compulsory, extending machine-sorting to inward letters and experimenting with a time-and-motion study in mail processing.

The negotiations lasted for months and while they were on the brink of collapse a couple of times, those most accomplished in brinkmanship never go over the edge and Alan Tuffin never did. We concluded our negotiations with two clever innovations.

Alan came up with the idea that part-timers should be classed as associate grades, with their hourly pay pegged to that of full-time staff. Terminology is important in industrial relations and this simple change in nomenclature helped to remove concerns about casualization.

Secondly, in collaboration with a brilliant young Post Office manager called Jerry Cope, I worked up an idea to give IWM a new element whereby replacing overtime with full- or part-time jobs generated an additional bonus. I was very satisfied with this innovation. It meant that IWM now paid a bonus not only for cutting hours but also for creating jobs. It was another feather in my cap and I felt that I'd now completed my apprenticeship.

~

Through all the changes in our lives, my boyhood best friend Andrew Wiltshire and I remained in touch. Before I was elected on to the executive council, he would meet up with Ernie and me in the Crown at Farnham Royal, which was on his circuit as a salesman for McCain's frozen chips. It was a relief to me that Ernie and Andrew got on, as they were very different men. Ernie was profound and occasionally funny, while Andrew was funny and occasionally profound. But I thought so much of them both it would have been a setback if they hadn't.

After I started working at union headquarters and travelling frequently with my job, Andrew and I would talk on the phone every couple of months. By this time he and Ann and their three sons had moved to Hastings. We drove down to see them there. Our children were teenagers by now and playing together meant records and cassettes rather than toys. Andrew's son Toby and my son Jamie were already learning to play instruments, just as Andrew and I had done, in their case the saxophone and guitar respectively,

I'd bought Jamie a Westone electric guitar and a Billy Bragg songbook and instruction manual (with cassette, in that post-vinyl, pre-CD period). It was the 1980s equivalent of Bert

Weedon's *Play in a Day*, with which I'd grappled twenty-five years before.

The Wiltshires had at last fulfilled their ambition to own their own home. They loved being by the sea and intended to remain in Hastings permanently, even if Andrew had to commute to London to earn a living. I'm not sure how much my work with the UCW meant to my old friend. He was vaguely pro-union but when all was said and done I was still a postman, whereas he'd left that behind years before. I think he pitied me for having stayed in the same job for so long. Having left McCain's and dabbled in computers he was now working for a vending-machine company. Andrew always planned ahead and he set out for me his vision for the future: he wanted to get back into computers while he still had the advantage of acquiring programming skills early in their evolution.

A few months later, when I rang for a chat, Ann told me that Andrew had been taken ill. He'd been diagnosed with a brain tumour and was due to have an operation in the next few days.

We went to Hastings to see him after he came out of hospital. He was wheelchair-bound but perfectly compos mentis. I pushed my friend down to the seafront and we sat there looking at the waves, much as we had watched the Thames flow beneath us from Hammersmith Bridge when we'd been postmen together. Postmen together, at Tesco together, together in the Area, when we'd thought it would be only a matter of time before we'd be storming the charts. Together at school, when our futures lay before us like sunlit highways.

Andrew hadn't lost his sense of humour, remarking, on seeing that *The King and I* was coming to a local theatre, that his bald scalp would help him get a job as a Yul Brynner double. When I misjudged a gap while pushing his wheelchair through a narrow opening, he offered to introduce me to his specialist, telling me his tumour had only been discovered when he'd started to find it impossible to judge distances and angles. He'd apparently reversed his company car into a lamp-post when there was an acre of space to park it in.

Andrew hated me wheeling him around – I could tell. When we were fifteen we'd regularly walk from the Marquee club in Wardour Street all the way back to the flat I shared with my sister. From Soho to Battersea. But I feared we'd never walk anywhere together again. I would have pushed that wheelchair to Land's End if it would have made Andrew better.

Not long afterwards Judy and I received the news that he'd died. He was thirty-three years of age. I was desperate to put some meaningful words on the flowers that we took to the funeral. I consulted *The Oxford Book of English Verse* and, in the end, plumped for paraphrasing the lines W. H. Auden wrote for his friend W. B. Yeats:

> Earth, receive an honoured guest,
> Andrew Wiltshire is laid to rest.

All through the funeral I kept thinking of the Blue Anchor in Tring High Street, where the three of us used to meet: Andrew, Mike and me. I promised myself that one day I'd go back there, stand in our place at the corner of the bar, and drink to their memory.

I never have.

Chapter 22

BY THE MID-1980s I was spending more and more time living out of a suitcase. I would be away from home for at least eight complete weeks a year at conferences or the union residential schools where I tutored. In addition, I was travelling abroad as a fraternal delegate to the conferences of sister unions or as a delegate to the international posts and telecoms organizations, the PTTI.

Other trips were arranged by the secretary of the UCW's organizing department, Ivan Rowley – an urbane, handsome former postman from Derby who looked like a cross between Richard Harris and Bryan Ferry – who insisted that lay members of the executive undertook a kind of 'meet the members' exercise whereby one of us would visit, along with a district organizer, every Post Office establishment on his or her patch, whether they be sorting offices, parcels depots or, most frequently, small delivery offices, of which there were thousands across the country.

The first (and most memorable) such mission I undertook was to the far north of Scotland, journeying by sleeper to Inverness. The voluminous book of internal rules governing the executive council allowed lay members to travel first class only if they were with a national officer (who went first class as a matter of course) or on a sleeper, where travelling standard meant sharing a compartment with a stranger.

It was a thrilling rail trip, with the train setting off from King's Cross late at night. I settled into my little compartment with its tartan blanket and comforting depiction of a Highland scene on the wall, a brief consultation with the steward having ensured that a cup of tea would come with my wake-up call at 7am. I had no trouble at all sleeping, soothed by the rattle of the rails.

I awoke on that bright morning in 1984 to an unforgettable sight, lifting the blind after my mobile slumber to be greeted by a vista of sunlit streams falling through mountain crags and verdant hills. There was even a stag crossing a brook, as if magically transposed from the print on the wall of my compartment. I gazed in wonder at this breathtaking scenery all the rest of the way to Inverness.

The district organizer who met me off the train was a man named Simpson Barclay, who might sound like a character out of *Dr Finlay's Casebook* but was actually a postal clerk from Fort William. Simpson soon made it clear that my frenetic London ways would have to be adapted to my new environment. We would meet plenty of UCW members but in batches between long periods of travel. We didn't so much drive between venues as meander, with Simpson rarely approaching 30mph, a speed he seemed to regard as a threat to the sound barrier.

We stopped one early evening, at a deserted pub beside Loch Ness where I was served by a barmaid with an English accent who, upon inquiry, told me she came from the Britwell estate in Slough. We went by ferry to the Isle of Skye, where I passed an enchanting hour in Portree sorting office as a PHG described, in his beautiful local lilt, how integral postal services were to the Highlands and islands.

At Thurso we missed the ferry to Orkney and were forced to spend the evening in a hostelry where an elderly gentleman sang Scottish folk songs to the roaring accompaniment of everybody in the hotel bar. On Orkney I learned that there were no traffic lights on the island and that some residents had lived their entire lives without seeing a train. Simpson and I, as outsiders, were referred to as 'ferrylopers'. One of the postmen I met there told me he'd come over from Wick thirty years previously and still warranted this description.

Judy's brother Richard, who'd been brought up with her other brother, Micky, in a children's home, had settled in Thurso with his Scottish wife after leaving the army. I paid him a surprise visit after which a reunion with Judy was arranged, re-establishing a bond that had been broken in childhood.

Whether meeting the members in this way was any good for them or the union, those summer days in Scotland with Simpson were certainly an enriching experience for me. Ivan Rowley wanted me to do more of these exercises but I was heavily committed to the kind of 'front-line' activities on which Tom Jackson had advised me to concentrate, and the organiz-ing department was well to the rear of the front line.

Ivan was due to retire in 1986. The favourite to replace him was a postman named Derek Hodgson, a thick-set ball of energy from Cardiff. Although he was ten years older than me, Derek was thought of as one of the young Turks and a man with a great future in the union. He'd got on to the executive a year or two before me and made no secret of his determination to become general secretary. Married to a senior Post Office manager, he had strong links with the business and worked hard to establish a good reputation with the members. His main focus was the organizing department, where he and Ivan had become good friends.

We got on OK with one another, but it wasn't exactly a warm friendship. I certainly sensed that he saw me as a rival for the top job but at that stage not exactly a threat. His main competitor was John Taylor.

And John was struggling – not because he was unable to handle the job of outdoor secretary per se but because it was becoming increasingly obvious that he had a serious drink problem. The job was getting harder now that local managers were empowered to extract the maximum efficiency savings out of the major national agreement Alan Tuffin had secured. It may have carried the grand title of Safeguarding the Future of the Mails Business (SFMB) and earned the support of our activists at conference, but the Post Office knew that it was one thing to secure a national agreement and quite another to get it implemented in the innumerable workplaces where managers and staff interacted at all hours of day and night.

Bill Cockburn was now running the mails business with great energy and enthusiasm but also a ruthless focus on the reforms that, not unreasonably, he considered necessary and which were licensed by the agreement we'd reached. I always found Bilco to be a hard but fair negotiator. Others on the executive council, including Derek Hodgson, saw him as the Antichrist. He eventually became a hate figure for activists across the country – a pantomime villain whose very name provoked a chorus of boos at our conference. Those of us who actually dealt with him (including John Taylor and Derek Walsh, with whom he'd negotiated IWM) pointed out that the union calling for his blood served only to enhance his reputation and that if he went it was unlikely that he'd be replaced by Mother Teresa.

There were more and more spontaneous walk-outs – unballoted industrial action which by now was illegal – and John, Derek Walsh and I found ourselves firefighting across the country.

At Prestwick in Ayrshire, Derek Walsh and I had to spend three days at the office dealing with dismissal notices against a third of the staff. They'd been handed out like confetti by a young, inexperienced manager who'd been over-promoted but under-provided with sense or sensibility.

While it was true that there were some equally inexperienced union reps whose only response to a problem was to lead a walk-out – like pilots who knew how to take off but who'd never been taught to land – some of this 'spontaneous action' was unstoppable.

A particular dispute at Preston springs to mind. A PHG by the name of Bill Sprake was sorting holiday brochures on a packet frame. The brochures were in clear plastic envelopes with a press-stud fastener that could be clicked open and shut. Having noticed a brochure for a resort he and his wife were thinking of visiting, he clicked open the envelope and flicked through it, in full view of his colleagues, before slipping it back in its envelope and sending it on its way.

A few minutes later four officers from the investigation

division, who'd been observing from behind the two-way mirrors in the watching gallery, appeared and frogmarched Bill away.

Bill Sprake was a decorated war hero, now in his sixties, a palpably decent man with an unblemished record of service to the Post Office. What he did may have been a mild disciplinary offence, although most of the staff, managers included, would have done something similarly harmless during their careers. Yet it was treated not as a disciplinary case but as a criminal offence. He was taken to a police station and, for the first time in a life of service to Queen and country, placed in a prison cell.

Every postal worker in Preston walked out and no force on earth would have stopped them. I told Bill Cockburn later that if he'd been a postman at Preston that day, he'd have walked out as well.

The fact that Bill happened to be the elder brother of Gary Sprake, the Leeds United and Wales goalkeeper, brought additional attention to the case. (Since Gary was famous for some spectacular blunders on the pitch, I joked that, given his family connections, it was a wonder Bill had held on to the brochure long enough to read it.) Soon workers in other offices in the north-west, including the mighty Manchester branch, had either walked out or had been suspended for refusing to handle Preston's mail. My contact at mails HQ was Brian Thomson, a Geordie of around my own age who was one of a growing number of managers to have come to us from other industries. Brian had been in shipbuilding before joining the Post Office a couple of years earlier. John Taylor dealt with him a lot and liked him, at the same time acknowledging that Brian was one of the toughest negotiators he had to deal with.

I had to deal with him now over this dispute and, while Brian agreed that the Post Office had been heavy-handed (he had a gift for understatement), he couldn't simply reinstate Bill Sprake with a click of his fingers. It would be too much of a humiliation for local management at Preston. We agreed, though, that this was a disciplinary case and that no criminality had been involved.

In the end it was settled that Bill Sprake would be restored to normal duties immediately and that I would personally represent him at a subsequent disciplinary hearing.

While this was enough to get everyone back to work I couldn't reveal the assurance I'd sought and received from Brian: the outcome of the disciplinary appeal would be that no action would be taken against Bill Sprake. There was nothing in writing and it would have been easy for Brian to escape this commitment, but he kept his word. A bond of trust was thereby established between manager and trade-union representative, which is by far the most important element of industrial relations.

Within the union, there certainly wasn't a bond of trust between me and Derek Hodgson, particularly when I decided to stand for the position of organizing secretary after Ivan Rowley retired. It was the kind of quiet backwater job that at one time would have represented the full extent of my ambition. But that was before the car journey I'd shared with Tom Jackson in 1982. Since then I'd been aiming higher: for the very top. I was determined to become general secretary. However, as Tom had counselled, to have any chance of succeeding Alan Tuffin when he retired in 1992, I had to become a national officer first. This vacancy had come up at a time when I was flavour of the month in the union, having topped the ballots for EC, TUC and Labour party delegations. I was perfectly placed to become the next organizing secretary.

Or so I thought. Derek Hodgson inflicted upon me an even more resounding defeat than the one to which I'd been subjected in 1983 when Maurice Styles retired. It gave Derek an understandable sense of satisfaction which he found difficult to hide.

~

I was at the 1985 Labour party conference in Bournemouth when Neil Kinnock made his dramatic speech denouncing Militant. His bravery can only be fully appreciated by those in the party who'd witnessed the madness inflicted by those 'far-fetched resolutions – pickled into a rigid dogma – outdated, misplaced, irrelevant' to which Neil referred.

Slough had its Militant caucus, which soured our Labour party meetings, but we weren't as badly affected as many other local parties were. At that time any Labour party member with a Scouse accent was assumed to be Militant.

In the union, Billy Hayes, the young Liverpudlian who'd been instrumental in bringing Tony Benn to our conference, was becoming an increasingly important figure and constantly had to deal with such misconceptions. Billy wasn't, and never had been, part of this faction and to be a young union activist in Liverpool resistant to Militant didn't make for an easy life in the city in the 1980s. But the opposite of 'militant' is 'moderate', and Billy would certainly have been equally eager to repudiate any attempt to place him on the right of the political spectrum.

I wouldn't have accepted such a label either, but by this time

I saw sweet moderation not in terms of right or left but in terms of right and wrong. If anything I was a militant moderate. I saw more of the delegates to our conference on their own territory than anybody else on the executive. It was so often the case that those who postured and posed on the rostrum were the least effective in their branch. With no rostrum to shout from and no gallery to play to, when called upon to act as advocate or negotiator with the job of bringing round the person opposite to their opinion, many of them were incapable of protecting their members or advancing their cause.

It was the Billy Fairs and the Joe Paynes who I admired; the men and women who quietly got on with the difficult job of providing an eloquent, thoughtful and intelligent voice for those they represented with no concept of themselves as working-class heroes and no desire to use their members as weapons in some kind of political crusade.

I respected these people whatever their politics. Some far to the left of me met this criterion. Billy Hayes was one; so was Mike Hogan, a former Glasgow telegram boy who'd transferred to London and was by now rising through the ranks of the London District Council. Mike was totally unclubbable and could appear gruff and offhand. But he possessed a phenomenal ability to advocate and negotiate. Like so many people I met in the union, Mike's intellect could have taken him a long way in any career – medicine, the judiciary or the military. But he'd left school at fifteen and joined the Post Office, where there were no outlets for his considerable talents other than union work. He became a close ally and lifelong friend.

As trade unions struggled to ride the wave of rancour that swept towards them from Whitehall, we in the UCW tried to use our imaginations to turn government legislation to our advantage. For instance, we harnessed the much-maligned Youth Training Scheme to strike a deal with the Post Office which, in effect, reintroduced the telegram boy, albeit with no telegrams to deliver or requirement to be a boy.

The Postal Cadet Scheme would bring in sixteen-year-olds, providing them with a guaranteed job at the end of their two-year, YTS-funded apprenticeship. It was very unpopular with our members, who'd heard numerous stories of exploitation occurring elsewhere under the YTS banner. The hostile environment created by the post-miners' strike mood among trade-union activists, particularly in the north, further hindered the union's ability to get the scheme up and running.

Les Hewitt, as the officer responsible for the postal cadet agreement, wanted me to go to branch meetings around the country to help local officials to get the scheme accepted by their members. I duly obliged.

Imprinted on my memory is a brilliant, if painfully pithy speech denouncing me and the agreement delivered by an ex-miner in Wigan. It was made at an evening meeting in a room above a pub with about sixty members in attendance. I had given what I considered to be an excellent presentation on how the union had used a questionable scheme to provide an unquestionable advantage in developing proper jobs for unemployed youngsters.

The audience sat grim-faced and unconvinced. The ex-miner was called on to speak. He stood up and in a broad Lancashire accent, said: 'Tha's coom oop 'ere t'explain t'scheme and for that ah thank yee. If tha wants to fight for these kids' future I'll be there, stripped t'waist fighting wi-yer. But if tha expects us t'accept Thatcher's YTS, tha can fook off back t'London and take yer scheme wiv yer.'

I fooked off back to London and found Derek Walsh in despair over our mutual friend John Taylor, whose drinking was by now completely out of control. He'd start the day with a pint of lager and progress to his favoured whisky by mid-morning. If he was working at the office he'd be at the King's Head as soon as the pubs opened, coming back drunk in the afternoon and holding court in his office for anyone who fancied a drink. Once he returned from the pub perched next to a totter on a horse and cart he'd commandeered for £20, asking to be taken up Crescent Lane and round the driveway of UCW House, where everybody could see him, red-faced, puffing on a cigar and milking the applause.

I didn't applaud or find John's efforts to ''ave a larf' remotely humorous. What had happened to Mike had removed any levity I might once have felt about people I cared for getting drunk.

John hated being behind a desk and would use the slightest pretext to go on the road to deal with issues that should have been handled by EC members or local officials. On arriving at the trouble spot he'd establish his headquarters at a pub or club and, more often than not, end up exacerbating the dispute rather than resolving it.

Alan Tuffin had taken enormous trouble to get John's alcoholism treated, arranging for him to have time off to attend a specialist clinic to dry out. For a while it worked – and John reclaimed from alcohol was a completely different man. On a trip to Cardiff together when he was on the wagon he told me he was reading again, painting watercolours (a talent he hadn't pursued for years) and eating properly for the first time in ages. He looked clear-eyed and fit. But in the pub to which the branch officials took us that lunchtime John ordered a half of lager, telling me that it was like lemonade to him and the time to worry was if he went back on the whisky. I knew enough by then to understand that a recovering alcoholic can never touch alcohol of any description – ever. Sure enough, before long he was back to his old ways and the John Taylor I was with on the trip to Cardiff vanished again, along with the books and the watercolours.

He became obsessed with Northern Ireland. What began as a few days attending to a sensitive dispute in Belfast related to the Troubles, which John actually dealt with brilliantly, turned into a longer stay during which he spent a week or so in Derry while Derek and I held the fort back in Clapham. Not long after that, with the dispute resolved, he went back again, citing the need to address the unique set of circumstances faced by our members in the province.

In the spring of 1987 the police came to UCW House and arrested John Taylor. He was accused of involvement in a racket operated by a shirt manufacturer in Northern Ireland and its alleged attempts to secure a contract, by underhand means, to produce postmen's uniform shirts for the Post Office.

Alan Tuffin made arrangements for John to step down as a national officer before the trial and approved a compensation package that would have been impossible to deliver after any guilty verdict. His departure was thus dealt with as a medical retirement, which was perfectly reasonable. John was, after all, very ill.

I was asked to take on the job of outdoor secretary

temporarily until a ballot for the position could be organized. I saw John when he came into the office for the last time to collect some things and say goodbye to his staff. He was in a sober phase and told us that he was innocent of all charges and confident he would be cleared. Alone in what I still regarded as his office, where a portrait of a sad-looking postman by the celebrated painter Duncan Grant gazed down from the wall, John smiled and said that he was better off out of it all; that the pressure was too much for him. He predicted that I would one day take the stairway to the top floor, where the general secretary's office was situated – a stairway he would not now be ascending. We hugged, awkwardly, and John, in his well-cut suit, shoulders pushed back like a guardsman, exactly as he'd looked in 1976 when I first saw him striding to the rostrum at my first conference, walked out of UCW House and into retirement.

At his trial in Northern Ireland, Brian Thomson, the Geordie senior manager from the mails business, appeared for the defence as a character witness. John was found not guilty. The hug he'd given me was as nothing compared to the embrace he gave his barrister in the middle of the courtroom, which was so effusive it knocked off the distinguished gentleman's horsehair wig.

Derek Walsh and I both stood in the election for outdoor secretary, along with a few other candidates. This time I won. I was now an employee of the Union of Communication Workers, rather than the Post Office.

It was the end of an era for me. The business had changed more in the almost twenty years I'd worked for it than in the hundred years that went before. I'd changed with it. I'd joined as an eighteen-year-old postman and I was leaving as a thirty-seven-year-old union official. I considered myself fortunate to have worked for such a fine institution. I had been proud to wear its uniform and grateful for the security it had provided, which had enabled Judy and me to bring up our three children free from the fear of unemployment.

In the process we'd grown apart, Judy and me. Perhaps it was inevitable, especially considering how young we had been when we married. I would come back to the Britwell from wherever I'd been full of stories about the things I'd seen, the deeds I'd done, the people I'd met. Had I listened enough to her? Spent enough time talking about the changes in her life as she moved on from the playgroup to youth work? The yoga she was studying in order to become a fitness instructor? The new friends she'd made?

Ernie Sheers had warned me about being too full of what I was doing and not paying enough attention to Judy. Ernie and I still met up every so often, but not as regularly as we had done in my early days on the union's executive. Then he'd listened to all my adventures from Dundee to Derry, Newton Abbot to Newcastle. Once, when John Taylor had come to Slough for some reason and stayed with us on the Britwell, I introduced him to Ernie. They were both East Enders and had similar reference points – Kelly's pie and mash shop on Roman Road ('Kelly for jelly'), the docks, Victoria Park. But Ernie was wary of John's exuberance. He was distrustful of egos, and not only was he alert to the egotism in John but he was seeing mine developing unhealthily as well.

Perhaps Judy was, too. Once, after she'd picked me up from Slough station in her little Citroën 2CV, we were turning right into Farnham Road at the Three Tuns when she began to cry –

apropos of nothing, out of nowhere, the tears rolled down her cheeks. But of course they hadn't come from nowhere. She was deeply unhappy with the life she now led to all intents and purposes alone. Natalie was twenty-one and married. Emma, at nineteen, had a steady boyfriend. Jamie was about to sit his O-Levels (and would be among the last cohort to take them) and spent most of his spare time out with his friends.

Earlier in the year, travelling home by rail from north Wales, my train had been delayed by deep snow. I sat in the packed carriage reading the collected works of Dorothy Parker.

There was a short story set during the Second World War – about a woman who goes to great lengths to prepare for the return of her American airman husband on leave. Despite her efforts, it is not a success and she realizes that he has a completely new life while all she has is half of the old one.

It hit me like a brick. On that train, staring out at the drifting snow – that was what had happened to us, to Judy and me.

We'd done well together, the two of us. Most people who knew us hadn't expected the marriage to last anywhere near as long as it had, given all the circumstances. Now we talked things over and decided it would be best if we parted. And so we did. No longer a postman, I was also leaving the Britwell, which had been our much-loved home for nineteen years. I packed up my books, records and clothes and carried them to the car, parked on the road, the council having ended our environmental vandalism by raising the kerb to stop us parking on the green. I loaded up and drove away, keeping my eyes firmly fixed on the road ahead.

Acknowledgements

My grateful thanks to:

My sister, Linda Edwards, for her help and encouragement.

The wonderful Carolyn Burgess, for painstakingly computerizing my handwritten text and for her unceasing faith in this book.

My agent, Andrew Kidd, for his wisdom and belief.

Judy Merrit, for her help with some of the detail.

Doug Young, Patsy Irwin and all the magnificent people at Transworld.

Caroline North, now not just a brilliant editor but a good friend.

My friends Becky Milligan and Charlie Grieg for their endless enthusiasm.

Catherine Bramwell for all her assistance.

Rita Dunn and Mary McCracken for their memories of nappies.

I am also indebted to *Post Office Workers* by Alan Clinton (George Allen and Unwin, 1984) and *Masters of the Post* by Duncan Campbell-Smith (Allen Lane, 2011), which provided invaluable historical information on the Post Office.

Picture Acknowledgements

Unless otherwise credited, all photographs are from the author's collection. Every effort has been made to trace the copyright holders of photos reproduced in the book. Copyright holders not credited are invited to get in touch with the publishers.

Corner of Long Readings Lane and Long Furlong Drive, Britwell Estate: © London Metropolitan Archives, City of London (SC/PHL/02/0775)

79,242 Postmen, poster by Duncan Grant, March 1939: © Royal Mail Group 2014, courtesy of The British Postal Museum & Archive

Index

325

Alan Johnson was born in May 1950. He was General Secretary of the Communication Workers Union before entering Parliament as Labour MP for Hull West and Hessle in 1997. He served as Home Secretary from June 2009 to May 2010. Before that, he filled a wide variety of cabinet positions in both the Blair and Brown governments, including Education and Health. His first memoir, *This Boy*, was published in May 2013. It won the RSL Ondaatje Prize and the Orwell Prize.